COVERING ACCIDENT COSTS

COVERING ACCIDENT COSTS

Insurance, Liability, and Tort Reform

MARK C. RAHDERT

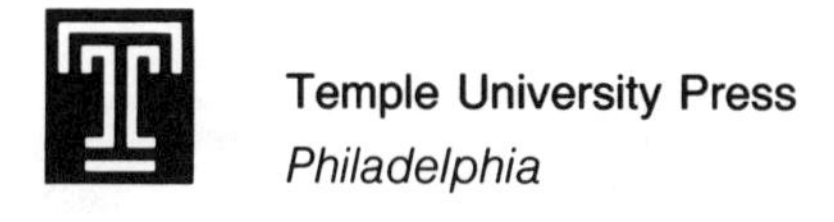

Temple University Press
Philadelphia

Temple University Press, Philadelphia 19122

Published 1995
Printed in the United States of America

The paper used in this publication meets the minimum requirements of American National Standard for Information Sciences—Permanence of paper for Printed Library Materials, ANSI Z39.48-1984. ♾

Library of Congress Cataloging-in-Publication Data
Rahdert, Mark C., 1952–
Covering accident costs : insurance, liability, and tort reform / Mark C. Rahdert.
p. cm.
Includes bibliographical references and index.
ISBN 1-56639-232-2. — ISBN 1-56639-233-0 (pbk.)
1. Torts—United States. 2. Damages—United States. 3. Law reform—United States. 4. Accident law—United States. 5. Insurance, Liability—United States. I. Title.
KF1251.R34 1994
346.7303—dc20
[347.3063] 94-830

To Ellen, Chris, and Lise,
my loving family, for all their support

Also to Judge Guido Calabresi,
who introduced me to this subject

ACKNOWLEDGMENTS

I am grateful to several colleagues who have provided me with thoughtful ideas and comments on earlier drafts of this book. In particular I would like to thank Scott Burris, Cassandra Jones Havard, Frank McClellan, Phoebe Haddon, Diane Maleson, Edward Ohlbaum, Joseph Passon, Robert Reinstein, David Skeel, Gerald Tietz, Richard Turkington, Ellen Wertheimer, and William Woodward. I am also grateful for the research assistance I received from many students at Temple University School of Law, including Marissa Boyers, Albert Brooks, Mark Dispoto, Jerry Fecher, Barbara Kahn, Terry Lohr, Rose Marie Karadsheh, Stephen McNally, Ronnie Seidel, Barbara Sicalides, Julia Vaughters, and Tami Traynor. I received help, encouragement, and sage advice from the staff at Temple University Press, particularly from Doris Braendel, senior acquisitions editor, and from my copy and production editors, Keith Monley and Deborah Stuart. Without their support, this project would never have seen the light of day. Finally, I wish to thank Temple University School of Law for financial support for the research and writing of this book.

CONTENTS

COVERING ACCIDENT COSTS

INTRODUCTION

The law of torts and the institution of insurance have enjoyed a long and complicated relationship. Scarcely anyone familiar with the American system for tort compensation would deny that it has been profoundly influenced in the twentieth century by the fact that many, if not most, defendants who wind up paying damages to plaintiffs both are able to and do routinely insure against such losses. Surely, anyone who has spent any time as a practitioner in either the plaintiffs' or defense bar is acutely aware of the many ways in which the presence of liability insurance affects the tort litigation process. At a minimum, insurance usually determines whether tort cases are brought, whom plaintiffs sue, how much they claim, who provides the defense, how the case gets litigated, the dynamics of settlement, and how much plaintiffs ultimately recover. Yet, despite a century in which torts and insurance have developed deeply intertwined legal and economic roots, the question of how liability rules should be influenced by insurance (or even whether they should be influenced by insurance at all) remains a subject of intense controversy.

There was a time in our history when most scholars, lawyers, and jurists thought that the legal rules that govern tort liability ought to be set without regard to the defendant's ability to insure or society's desire to have the costs of accidents spread through insurance.[1] But in recent decades, both in theory and in practice, that view gradually has given way to a different perspective, in which the ability of defendants to spread the costs of plaintiffs' accidents has come to be regarded as one of the great benefits of the tort system, and indeed one of the leading reasons for imposing liability. This is what I call the "insurance rationale" for tort liability—the idea that some defendants ought to be assessed with liability, in part because of their ability to insure and spread the loss. The insurance rationale has been a moving force in the development of product liability law. It has also significantly influenced the largely pro-plaintiff development of tort principles in many other areas. Indeed, it might not be too much to say that the adoption and implementation of the insurance rationale has been one of the most prominent features of tort law in the second half of the twentieth century.

Recently, however, the insurance rationale has been under siege. In the 1980s, controversy surrounding the connection between torts and insurance was rekindled by a prolonged period of steep increases in the cost of liability insurance and a concomitant call from certain circles (frequently the insurers themselves, their corporate clients, or members of various "public interest" groups funded by these institutions) for major changes in the structure of the tort liability system.[2] In the early 1990s, the controversy has been renewed in connection with the national debate over health-care reform.[3] In both instances, rising insurance costs have been blamed, in whole or in part, on the tendency of modern tort law to compensate the injured or ill by assigning liability for their injuries to those who insure.

Among the critics of the insurance rationale, those seeking the most sweeping changes often have based their arguments on the premise that pro-plaintiff trends in tort law have produced an unhealthy environment in which liability rules are deliberately set to maximize plaintiffs' access to insurance funds. This, the critics charge, has corrupted what should be a system designed to optimize safety into a system designed to maximize compensation. The result, they assert, has been an unjustified upward spiral in insurance costs that, if not contained, will cause the entire system of tort compensation to unravel. At the heart of this critique is the deeply held view that the insurance rationale for tort liability is fundamentally misguided.

Apologists for the status quo (frequently the plaintiffs' trial lawyers, whose earning power depends on expansive concepts of liability) by and large have countered these charges by questioning their underlying assumption that increased liability insurance costs have much to do with the way in which the tort liability system has developed.[4] They have advanced other explanations for the liability insurance crisis, ranging from monopolistic practices of insurers, to the insurance business cycle, to improvements in the delivery and quality of legal services rendered to tort plaintiffs. When pressed to address the relation between tort liability and insurance, defenders of the present system have differed sharply with its critics about the proper role for insurance to play. Essentially, they have maintained that spreading costs of accidents by facilitating access to liability insurance funds is a laudable and desirable goal of the tort liability system. Thus, at one level, the debate in the last decade over tort reform has been a debate about the way that tort liability rules and insurance should relate to one another.

The debate over tort reform and the insurance crisis has been a largely partisan affair. Advocates on both sides have painted their positions with extremely broad brushes. All too often, they have been content to rest their conclusions on sweeping, undocumented, and often unexamined assertions about the connection between rising insurance costs and the structure of tort doctrine. State legislatures (the chief engines of tort reform), and to some extent the courts, have responded in an equally broad-brush, reactive fashion, with a marked preference for the quick fix over the comprehensive solution. Inevitably pressed for time and strapped for resources, they have seldom investigated much below the surface of this complex topic.

Indeed, throughout much of its history, the insurance rationale has largely been treated by decision makers with this same haphazard abandon. In periods of expanding liability, it has served as a convenient rationalization. In periods when contraction of liability has become politically expedient, the insurance rationale has become an equally convenient scapegoat. Seldom, however, has it received anything more than the most cursory examination. Much has been done for or against its name, but with remarkably little attention to its real content. This has certainly been true in the latest round of tort reform, which swept the state legislatures of the nation during the second half of the last decade.

The high-water mark of the 1980s liability insurance crisis has passed, and with a turnaround of fortunes in the insurance industry much of the debate about tort reform seems to be temporarily quiet.[5] It has been renewed in part in connection with discussions about how to reform our health-care system, although in that context tort rules have figured somewhat less prominently than other factors, such as the institutional practices of health-care providers and the bureaucratic inefficiencies of government-run health-care systems. Nevertheless, the debate over tort reform is almost sure to revive, probably when we hit the next trough in the insurance business cycle. The depth and severity of the 1980s crisis, as well as the array of tort reform legislation it spawned, suggest that the lull in the discussion of tort reform is only temporary, and that in this decade pressure will soon begin to mount for another round of more significant and fundamental changes. If that surmise is correct, it is an appropriate time to evaluate with greater care, and in a less emergent and politically charged atmosphere, the arguments about the role of insurance in setting tort liability that underlie the debate over tort reform.

This book undertakes such a review in three parts. Part I examines theoretical discussions of the relation between insurance and tort law in legal scholarship over the past century. It gleans from scholarly writings on tort theory a mature description of both the insurance rationale and its current critique. The purpose of this inquiry is to cultivate an understanding of the preferences and assumptions on which the insurance rationale depends, the problems its widespread use allegedly creates, and the place the insurance rationale occupies in the decision-making process concerning tort doctrine.

Part II turns from the theoretical to the practical. It reviews judicial and legislative decisions addressing the relation between insurance and tort liability during approximately the same period. It describes the various stages in the growth of the insurance rationale as a component of our system of accident compensation, and it reviews the areas of tort doctrine in which the insurance rationale has had its greatest impact. Then it compares and contrasts the ways in which insurance has been used in practice with the ways it has been described in theory.

Part III uses the lessons of the first two parts to evaluate the strengths and weaknesses of the insurance rationale. For this evaluation, it is necessary first to consider the 1980s insurance crisis itself, in order to fix its true dimensions. With this social phenomenon placed in perspective, it is possible systematically to evaluate the contemporary validity and significance of the arguments for and against the insurance rationale. Conclusions drawn from this evaluation lead to a modified version of the insurance rationale, a version that defines more precisely the proper scope of its application under present circumstances. This modified insurance rationale, in turn, becomes a tool for determining the most promising directions for future tort reform.

The concluding chapter projects some arenas for future tort reform. It identifies areas in which the pressure for tort reform of the immediate past has been misplaced. More important, it suggests those areas in which significant changes consistent with the modern understanding of the insurance rationale are feasible. And it offers some specific proposals for tort reform that will, without sacrificing the benefits of cost spreading, contribute both greater coherence and some badly needed cost-consciousness to the development of tort doctrine.

Running throughout this commentary is my own view that the current call for major pro-defendant changes to tort doctrine—for today the term "tort reform" almost always means defendant-oriented reform—rests on a host of unstated and often questionable assumptions, value preferences that are often at odds with contemporary norms regarding injury compensation, and a considerable measure of profit-motivated self-interest. The claims of the tort reformers also depend on undocumented factual assertions, many of which, when closely examined, are contrary to common sense. Tort reform is thus very much a house of cards—lots of ingenuity, little substance. It is, however, dangerously seductive, because it offers a convenient scapegoat for the rising costs of accident compensation, because it feeds into legislative desires for quick fixes, and because it is so effectively reinforced by the political lobbying and campaign contributions of large corporations and insurers. The trial-lawyer apologists for the status quo are of course no less self-interested, no less averse to political lobbying. But between these groups there is no spirit of compromise, and the danger is that we will either do nothing or jump headlong into measures that will repeal too much of the progress of the common law.

Some reform is needed, but it must be selective and deliberate, resting on a careful assessment of the arguments for and against limits on liability or compensation. The aim of this book is to supply some of the thoughtful balance that up to this point has been so noticeably lacking in the tort reform debate.

I

The Insurance Rationale for Tort Liability in Legal Theory

For tort scholars, the issue of the connection between insurance and tort liability is by no means a novel concern. Of course, much of tort theory during the past century has had relatively little to do with insurance. Scholars who have labored to understand the emerging content of particular tort concepts or principles, such as privacy or causation or assumption of risk, have often been able to put insurance considerations to one side, either as a given or as a factor to be held in check so that other dimensions of the common law could be explored. Nevertheless, a succession of theorists have grappled with defining the proper relation between torts and insurance in scholarly work dating back to the nineteenth century.[1] Included in this group are some of the most prominent scholarly contributions in the field, ranging from the pioneering work of Oliver Wendell Holmes Jr. to the recent trenchant critiques by George Priest, as well as works directed to a more popular audience, such as the writings of Peter Huber.[2]

Scholarship on torts and insurance can be grouped into roughly four periods. In the earliest of these, the relevance of insurance to determinations of tort liability was largely rejected in preference to other rationales for liability. The work of Holmes, easily the most dominant American tort theorist of the nineteenth century, led the way toward a laissez-faire model of tort doctrine that denied the public value of assured compensation and cost spreading.

After this period of rejection, there followed a time of grudging acceptance, in which a few scholars were willing to consider insurance as at least one factor to be weighed in setting tort policy. During this period, however, the force of the insurance rationale was confined to limited domains within tort law, most notably the workplace. It became the basis for the workers' compensation movement, but those who advocated assured compensation for workers were either unready or unwilling to extend the rationale elsewhere. Meanwhile, other leading voices in tort law, such as Jeremiah Smith and Francis Bohlen, the Reporter for the first Restatement of Torts, vigorously opposed adopting the insurance rationale and warned against its potential encroachment on traditional tort doctrines.[3]

The third period corresponded to the growth of Legal Realism. It was a period in which leading influential scholars began to treat insurance as a key, sometimes even a dominant, factor in defining liability. This was particularly evident in the work of Fleming James, Jr., although others, including William O. Douglas, Leon Green, Lester Feezer, and Albert Ehrenzweig, also made important contributions.[4] A generation later, their work formed the cornerstone of the products liability movement,[5] and it was incorporated into the tort theory of many legal economists, most notably Guido Calabresi.[6] Through these consumerists and latter-day realists, the insurance rationale finally achieved broad scholarly acceptance as a legitimate component of tort theory.

Finally, in the wake of spiraling liability costs, many scholars have recently shown a renewed skepticism about the role of insurance in tort law. Just as their realist forebears developed an elaborate rationale for the use of insurance considerations in setting tort liability, these contemporary theorists have developed an even more elaborate critique. Leaders in this countermovement have included Kenneth Abraham, Richard Epstein, Peter Huber, and George Priest.[7] They have argued that liability should be significantly scaled back, in part through abandonment of the notion that cost spreading is a desirable social goal. Others, such as Jeffrey O'Connell and Stephen Sugarman, have used similar arguments as a springboard for proposals to move to a "no-fault," or "first-party," insurance system.[8]

In each of these periods, scholars have emphasized different themes in arriving at their contrasting judgments about the torts-insurance relation. Together, they describe the growth of an idea, from birth to maturity and perhaps to eventual demise.

ONE

The Early History of the Insurance Rationale

In the common law we inherited from England, torts was a subject that received remarkably little attention.[1] This was probably due in large measure to the fact that substantive tort doctrine was vastly overshadowed in influence by the "forms of action"—arcane rules of pleading that governed the progress of tort suits in English and early American courts.[2] Compensation for injuries caused by another had been a feature of the common law since the Middle Ages. But in many of the leading common-law cases, procedure rather than substance determined outcomes. Cases were won or lost over whether they belonged in one or the other of two elusive pigeonholes of pleading—trespass or trespass on the case—into which, under the forms of action, all tort suits had to fit.

This lack of attention to tort doctrine persisted into the first half of the nineteenth century. Leading legal scholars of that period devoted their energies to other fields, most notably commercial law. This was true, for example, of both Joseph Story and James Kent, the leading legal writers in the first half of the nineteenth century.[3] Thus, in the United States, it was not until after the Civil War that the subject of torts began to attract the attention of legal scholars.

Some of the early efforts at development of tort theory proceeded by analogy to criminal law. This view proceeded from the premise that a tort judgment of liability was a civil "wrong." Thus, like a criminal conviction, it represented society's moral disapproval of a defendant's conduct. This seemed clear enough in cases involving intentional torts, such as battery, where civil and criminal law did in fact parallel each other. But early tort scholars also extended the idea of a moral rationale for torts to the new, rapidly expanding category of compensation for accidental harm.[4]

From this moral perspective, insurance is at best irrelevant and at worst pernicious to the structure of tort law. If the purpose of tort law is to punish, deter, or show reprobation for socially unacceptable conduct, compensation of the victim is more or less an incidental by-product of the system. Insurance to fund that compensation involves a separate, private contract that either is not germane to the purposes of tort law or, worse, positively interferes with them by letting the wrongdoer avoid the consequences of his or her wrongful act. Thus, theorists adopting this view tended to reject the idea that insurance ought to have any role to play in setting liability rules.

Oliver Wendell Holmes Jr.'s *Common Law*

The strictly moral view of tort law, however, soon began to give way to tort theory of a more pragmatic cast that consciously recognized tort law as a tool for effectuating public policies more economic than moral in nature. This emerging view of tort law as a form of social engineering received its most influential rendering in Oliver Wendell Holmes Jr.'s famous Lowell Institute lectures, which he later expanded and published in *The Common Law*.[5] Although Holmes repudiated an insurance rationale for tort law, he at least treated the issue as one worthy of some discussion.

Holmes was an unabashed advocate for the negligence standard that American courts had fairly recently embraced for cases involving accidental harm. One objective of his first lecture on torts was to persuade his audience that the negligence standard represented a better fit with the public values supporting liability than the strict liability principle that had reigned under the forms of action and that the negligence principle had fairly recently supplanted. The key feature of Holmes's defense of negligence was his focus on the functional impact of liability. He recognized that a decision to impose liability had the immediate effect of shifting the cost of injury from the plaintiff to the defendant. He believed that such loss shifting ought to occur only when it served some public good. In his lecture, he tried to determine the public good served by imposing liability for accidental harm and to use that determination as a mechanism for showing that "fault," defined as a failure to observe an objective, average standard of safe conduct, was the proper substantive liability standard.

Holmes's discussion of insurance in his lecture on torts is characteristically brief—but a single paragraph. It is worth quoting in full.

> The state might conceivably make itself a mutual insurance company against accidents, and distribute the burden of its citizens' mishaps

> among all its members. There might be a pension for paralytics, and state aid for those who suffered in person or estate from tempest or wild beasts. As between individuals it might adopt the mutual insurance principle *pro tanto,* and divide damages when both were in fault, as in the *rusticum judicium* of the admiralty, or it might throw all loss upon the actor irrespective of fault. The state does none of these things, however, and the prevailing view is that its cumbrous and expensive machinery ought not to be set in motion unless some clear benefit is to be derived from disturbing the *status quo*. State interference is an evil, where it cannot be shown to be a good. Universal insurance, if desired, can be better and more cheaply accomplished by private enterprise. The undertaking to redistribute losses simply on the ground that they resulted from the defendant's act would not only be open to these objections, but, as it is hoped the preceding discussion has shown, to the still graver one of offending the sense of justice. Unless my act is of a nature to threaten others, unless under the circumstances a prudent man would have foreseen the possibility of harm, it is no more justifiable to make me indemnify my neighbor against the consequences, than to make me do the same thing if I had fallen upon him in a fit, or to compel me to insure him against lightning.[6]

Despite its brevity, this paragraph is remarkably complex. In a few sentences, it manages to consider a variety of alternative compensation systems, including some that have a strikingly post-Victorian ring. Thus, Holmes was willing to entertain novel possibilities ranging from government-sponsored social insurance (the state as "mutual insurance company") to something roughly akin to the Clinton administration's idea of "managed competition" ("universal insurance" by "private enterprise"); he was willing to evaluate a variety of alternative structures for liability, ranging from pure fault to comparative fault ("divid[ing] damages" between the parties "when both were in fault") to strict liability ("throw[ing] all loss upon the actor irrespective of fault").[7]

In some respects, however, Holmes's analysis is also both rather casual and somewhat dated. At key points it equates what is with what should be,[8] and it rejects out of hand forms of public compensation for loss (such as social insurance against "tempests") that have since become an indelible part of the social fabric.[9] Nevertheless, Holmes's analysis effectively sets the terms of debate for succeeding generations of tort scholars by touching on several key problems surrounding the insurance rationale.

Holmes insisted that shifting losses is generally undesirable because such loss shifting cannot be accomplished without incurring the "cumbrous and expensive machinery" of state interference—what legal economists today refer to as "transaction costs" or, more specifically, "transfer costs."[10] Litigation (the typical method for shifting accident costs) was then, as it is now, a very expensive process. Because of these high transfer costs, Holmes concluded that law should not be used to shift accident costs unless there was a substantial reason for doing so.[11] Moreover, this reason had to be a fairly powerful one because its benefits must more than offset the expenses of tort litigation.[12]

Holmes thought the main reason for shifting loss was to create an incentive for safety. But he was at least willing to consider the possibility that providing victims with access to insurance also might serve as such a reason. By doing so he raised, if only to strike it down, the prospect that victim compensation might serve as an independent goal of tort law, rather than a mere accidental byproduct.[13]

Although Holmes did not elaborate, the connection between insurance and the goal of victim compensation is implicit in his analysis. Without insurance, compensation of the victim through tort liability would be haphazard. It would depend entirely on the means of the tortfeasor. If the defendant were rich, the plaintiff would recover. But if the defendant were poor (or clever enough to hide its assets), the expensive machinery of state interference would go for nought. The plaintiff would have a judgment, but compensation would never follow. Thus, if compensation were society's objective, without insurance we could never be sure that imposing liability would actually achieve it. With widespread insurance, however, there would be a fairly reliable and certain source of funds for compensation, making the pursuit of victim compensation and the spreading of losses for the first time feasible goals.

Holmes also implicitly realized that adopting an insurance principle for tort liability would threaten the validity of the fault concept. Although he did not say so directly, his analysis implied a linkage between the idea of assured compensation through the redistribution of losses and the idea of strict liability. Indeed, that seems to be the point of the excerpt quoted above. If assured compensation were in fact a sufficiently important goal, it could potentially support "redistributing the losses simply on the grounds that they resulted from the defendant's act." Holmes, in other words, recognized that he needed to defeat the goal of assured victim compensation if he were to succeed in his defense of the fault principle.

Not surprisingly, then, Holmes ultimately rejected this goal as an unacceptable basis for structuring tort liability.[14] He reasoned that a defendant's ability to absorb and spread accident costs did not outweigh the burdens of litigation, because (1) it was less important to society than other potential goals, especially safety,[15] and (2), if loss compensation were desired, it could be more efficiently administered by other means, such as voluntary insurance provided through private enterprise.[16] Holmes asserted that the absence of widespread private or public accident insurance in his contemporary society demonstrated the relative unimportance of insurance against loss as a factor in tort theory.[17]

How much Holmes's analysis influenced contemporary or subsequent jurisprudence is impossible to say,[18] but his lectures framed the terms of scholarly debate over the insurance rationale in several important ways. Preliminarily, Holmes explicitly linked tort doctrine with general economic and social policy objectives. He did not accept the notion that tort doctrine existed simply as a means for ordering private relations. Rather, he embraced the premise that tort doctrine can be and even should be manipulated to accomplish some broader set of desirable social goals.[19] Without such a premise, it would be impossible to entertain the idea that tort doctrine should be structured to achieve victim access to insurance funds.

In addition, Holmes apparently recognized that the set of potential social goals for tort law included both those goals (such as safety) that focus on using the law to influence defendants' conduct[20] and those goals (such as compensation) that focus on using the law to serve plaintiffs' needs.[21] The effect of the tort system on plaintiffs, in other words, was potentially as important in assessing policy issues as the effect of the tort system on defendants. Unfortunately, Holmes may not have fully recognized that it is the mix of burdens and benefits upon both sides of the litigation that ultimately defines the social consequences of tort doctrine, not just the impact upon one party alone. Rather, he saw the issue of tort policy in binary terms—either victim compensation or safety—and thus did not fully examine the prospect that both of these goals could be integrated into a common scheme.

Beyond these preliminary observations, Holmes also established compensating victims as a potential policy objective, and he implicitly recognized that insurance plays a pivotal role in accomplishing this objective.[22] The validity of the insurance rationale thus depends upon the relative primacy of compensation as a social goal. The more important the compensatory function of tort law, the more appropriate it is to let insurance considerations influence the development of liability rules. The less important compensation is, the more likely it is that the insurance rationale for tort liability will be subordinated to other concerns.

Of equal significance, however, Holmes also perceived that a compensatory purpose for tort law existed in some tension, and might ultimately conflict, with other purposes.[23] In particular, Holmes posited the need to choose, at some level, whether compensation or safety should be the dominant goal of tort doctrine.[24] Holmes himself opted for safety as the preferred goal, although he qualified that goal with countervailing considerations having to do with the cost of loss shifting and the social desirability of defendants' injury-causing activities.[25] He erected his defense of the negligence principle on the foundation of that qualified preference.[26]

Finally, Holmes recognized that the desirability of pursuing any social goal under tort law cannot be established in a vacuum but must be measured against the costs of shifting loss through litigation.[27] These costs, in turn, must be measured against other alternative forms of accomplishing the same objective. In the case of compensation, in particular, Holmes suggested that tort law be compared for its effectiveness against systems of social and private insurance, especially if these alternatives would eliminate or reduce the litigation-related expenses of loss shifting.[28]

The tort lectures in *The Common Law* did not exhaustively or systematically develop these considerations. Indeed, Holmes's dismissal of the insurance rationale and his assertion of a safety rationale for tort law were incomplete and rather abrupt. But the terms of his analysis gave more credence to the *possibility* of an insurance rationale for tort law than can be found in other tort scholarship of the period,[29] and it planted ideas for the use of torts to spread costs, which a new generation of scholars would develop into a coherent theory.

The Insurance Rationale and Workers' Compensation: The Noble Experiment

Although nineteenth-century tort theorists generally found little role for insurance in setting the contours of tort law, there was one area in which the insurance rationale took a surprisingly early, firm, and strong hold: the workplace. There, a combination of nineteenth-century tort doctrines—including especially the "unholy trio" of assumption of risk, contributory negligence, and the fellow servant doctrine—produced what came to be perceived as an unacceptable failure of the compensation system, which led to a general call for reform.[30]

Under nineteenth-century law, a worker who was injured on the job seldom received compensation from his or her employer. This was true even if the employer or a fellow worker were negligent. In such cases, employers had three powerful defenses. First, they could argue that the injured worker knew of the danger and thus "assumed the risk" by voluntarily staying on the job. Second, under the "fellow servant rule" they could argue that workers shared responsibility for one another's torts, preventing the employer from assuming vicarious liability in cases where one worker was injured through another's negligence. If these two defenses did not suffice (and they usually did), the employer could argue that the injured worker was contributorily negligent by failing to take precautions against workplace danger. This legal triple punch assured that victims of workplace injury rarely received compensation.[31]

This harsh treatment of worker injuries found support in commonly held contemporary notions of personal responsibility and economic relations. As courts applying the trio of employer defenses often observed, workers were individually responsible for the safety of the workplace. Since they had a primary obligation for their own safety, imposing liability on the employer would be unjust. Moreover, workers were regarded as mobile free agents, under no compulsion to enter or remain in the master's employment. Their willingness to contract their labor for a specified wage under dangerous circumstances was thus itself evidence of a willingness to assume the risk. If they did not care for the danger, workers could either quit their jobs or demand higher compensation as a reward for facing the risk. If they failed to do either, they should not be heard to complain to the courts.

The attitudes of the time are reflected in *Lamson v. American Ax & Tool Co.*,[32] a case made famous by the fact that the opinion was written by Holmes, who by 1900, the year of the decision, was serving as chief justice of the influential Supreme Judicial Court of Massachusetts. The plaintiff was a worker at a hatchet-manufacturing plant. His job was to paint the hatchets. About a year before the accident, the employer installed a new drying rack, upon which the plaintiff was to put the hatchets after painting them. The plaintiff, who was experienced at his work, soon complained that the new drying rack in his opinion was dangerous because it created a risk that the hatchets would fall on him. The employer, however, refused to make any changes. "He was answered, in substance, that he would have to use the racks or leave."[33] The plaintiff continued to work, and eventually the accident he had foreseen occurred.

The court found that the plaintiff had assumed the risk of injury. He "appreciated the danger more than any one else" and "perfectly understood what was likely to happen." When told to choose between his safety and his job "[h]e stayed, and took the risk." And as Holmes sharply put it, "[h]e did so none the less that the fear of losing his place was one of his motives."[34] The fact that the employer had complete control over the design of the drying rack, knew the danger, and clearly was in the best position to avoid it made no difference. Nor did the fact that the employer profited from the danger. Indeed, one suspects that the employer's adamant insistence on using the new rack probably stemmed from the prospect that it would speed up the painting process, lowering the manufacturer's marginal cost and improving its profit margin.

In the early decades of the twentieth century, workers fought back against this system through their new champions, the labor unions. At first, the unions tried to deal with the problem by sponsoring "mutual aid societies," in which workers would pool resources to provide compensation for those who sustained workplace injury.[35] But as these measures proved inadequate, and as labor unions began to gain political clout, the unions successfully lobbied state legislatures in several key industrial jurisdictions to address the problem by statute.[36] The legislatures were persuaded to adopt systems of workers' compensation similar to those that had been developed in Europe during the final decades of the previous century. The unions' rallying cry in this effort was that "the cost of the product should bear the blood of the workman."[37]

Workers' compensation, as conceived both then and now, was an extraordinary social experiment. Most important for our purposes, it was an explicitly insurance-driven system. The idea was that employers, who controlled the workplace and who profited from employees' safety risks, would assume strict liability for compensation of work-related injuries and would fund that liability through insurance. Payments would be more or less automatic, eliminating the need for litigation in most cases, and they would often proceed according to predetermined schedules of benefits for particular injuries. Defenses against liability, especially the trio of common law defenses—contributory negligence, assumption of risk, and the fellow servant rule—would be eliminated.[38]

Proponents of this system, including some contemporary tort scholars, argued for it on a variety of grounds. Among them was an explicit insurance rationale.[39]

Advocates for workers' compensation asserted that workers seldom had insurance for workplace injuries.[40] As a consequence, such injury often produced catastrophic consequences for an injured worker and his or her family. These catastrophic consequences could be avoided if compensation through insurance were available, and the most certain way to make it available was through the employer. Requiring the employer to purchase the insurance, moreover, was not unfair, since the cost of the accident was in any event a "cost of doing business" that, like any other such cost, could and should be treated as a cost of production and ultimately factored into the price of the employer's product or service. Also, since all employers within an industry would be subject to common obligations, providing the benefit of workers' compensation would not put any single employer at a competitive disadvantage.

In the circle of academic law, this argument found surprisingly broad acceptance,[41] although the old common-law regime continued to have its defenders.[42] Yet despite the fact that workers' compensation represented a major assault on the fault principle, which was the darling of current tort theory,[43] many scholars accepted the notion that workers' compensation was, in its own sphere, a good idea.[44]

The idea of assured compensation for industrial injury, however, was confined by even its most ardent proponents to the workplace, which they regarded as distinct from other social contexts. The belief that employers could insure against workplace accidents better than their employees did not generalize into a belief that other institutional defendants could insure better than those who were injured by their activities. The extraordinary social experiment known as workers' compensation thus became something of a footnote to general tort law. It eliminated some of the harshness of the nineteenth-century common-law regime, and it removed from its purview a pesky class of troublesome cases of negligence. But it left the mainstream application of the negligence principle to most accidents untouched.[45]

The workers' compensation idea nonetheless added important elements to the developing insurance rationale. First, it adroitly finessed the issue of choosing between socialism and private enterprise in a way that largely comported with Holmes's preference for private insurance arrangements. Under workers' compensation, the state effectively required the insurance and set its terms, as well as the terms of the compensation that workers received under it, but the administration of the system was usually left to private enterprise. Employers purchased their insurance from private companies, which set premiums and handled claims under limited governmental supervision. This hybrid approach reinforced the notion that insurance against loss could be accomplished efficiently through a private system of loss compensation. The complete socialism of public welfare for the injured was unnecessary.

Second, the workers' compensation experiment focused attention on third-party insurance as a preferred mechanism for cost spreading. Its advocates justified placing the obligation to insure on the employers through the argument that the costs could be passed on to the consuming public through higher prices on the employers' goods or services. Moreover, providing the insurance through the employer eased the burden of administration for the state, and it took advantage of the employers' relative advantages at effective risk management. Instead of requiring each worker to purchase his or her own policy (something many workers might well be unable to afford), it seemed to make sense to have the employer purchase the insurance for everyone.

Third, on grounds of administrative efficiency and certainty of compensation, workers' compensation linked the insurance rationale to substantive changes in tort doctrine. Perhaps the most dramatic was the move away from negligence and toward the principle of strict liability—a factor that initially met some resistance in the courts.[46] Equally important, however, was elimination of traditional defenses, especially the fellow servant doctrine and assumption of risk.[47] In theory, at least, this approach had the effect of streamlining the system. Instead of a multitude of legal issues, such as duty, negligence, causation, contributory negligence, assumption of risk, and the like, there was a single, fact-based inquiry: whether the injury occurred during the course of employment. In most cases, this issue would be relatively easy to resolve, so that lengthy trial proceedings to determine liability would be eliminated.

Finally, workers' compensation rested, fairly explicitly, on the belief that employers would do a better job of insuring their workers than the workers would or could do for themselves. The system of assured compensation through third-party insurance rested on an empirical judgment that employers could more cheaply and effectively insure against workplace injury than could employees.

In retrospect, what seems most interesting about the idea of workers' compensation is the degree to which its proponents were unaware of its implicit radicalism. It postulated a model of liability that was fundamentally at odds with most current notions of tort law. Even to the degree that it pursued the Holmesian goal of safety, tort doctrine remained premised on notions of personal responsibility. One was obliged to pay compensation only if one personally had failed to meet the requisite standard of care. There were, to be sure, some exceptions, such as the doctrine of vicarious liability (respondeat superior) and the emerging strict liability tort for ultrahazardous activity. But workers' compensation represented a much more fundamental assault on the notion of personal responsibility, in what was then a major sector of tort litigation.

A few commentators, most notably Jeremiah Smith, perceived the sharp dissonance between workers' compensation and the foundations of the fault principle. One of the leading tort scholars of the day, Smith observed in a highly visible article in the *Harvard Law Review* that the strict liability principle of workers' compensation and the negligence principle of the general common law were at war with one another, and he reluctantly predicted that the strict liability idea was likely to spread.[48] But his warning that workers' compensation was fundamentally at odds with the rest of the tort system went largely unheeded. Scholars and legislatures alike remained content to experiment with bold new ideas in the workplace at the same time that they staunchly adhered to the traditions of fault-based liability—including its basic rejection of the insurance rationale—in most other arenas of tort law.

TWO

Emergence of a General Insurance Rationale: The Triumph of Legal Realism

It seems curious that the enthusiasm for the insurance rationale with respect to workplace injuries did not immediately spread to other aspects of tort law. Yet most tort scholars, like most courts, remained content with the negligence principle and with the baggage of evidentiary burdens, immunities, and defenses that it had acquired. They continued to view liability in highly individual terms, and they refused to draw any significant distinctions between the liability of individuals for negligent action and that of corporate or institutional actors. Indeed, much tort scholarship during the first half of the twentieth century was devoted to concerns other than developing a theoretical connection between tort doctrine and insurance.[1] Many scholars, including some of the most prominent, accepted the predominance of the negligence principle as a given and devoted their efforts to working out a coherent and systematic rationale for effective application of that principle.[2]

Nevertheless, the example of workers' compensation profoundly influenced the generation of tort scholars who participated in the Legal Realism movement, which came to dominate American legal thought during the middle period of the twentieth century. In essence, these scholars tried to demonstrate that the ideas workers' compensation applied to the workplace could be generalized to other settings in which accidents frequently occurred.[3] Their work finally brought the insurance rationale into mainstream tort theory.

Realist Tort Theory

It is beyond the scope of this book to discuss the jurisprudence of legal realism in any significant detail. For our purposes, it is sufficient to note that the realists opposed the late nineteenth-century view of Harvard Law School dean Christopher Columbus Langdell and his followers, that law proceeded from fixed and unchangeable root principles that could be "scientifically" determined through the systematic study of judicial opinions. Instead, the realists believed (with varying degrees of radicalism) that law proceeded from the exigencies of practical experience, so that legal principles could and should change as experience dictated. As a consequence, the legal realists objected to legal formalism, preferring functional or instrumental rationales for legal principles. They objected to many existing legal doctrines, both because of the formalism of these doctrines and because the doctrines failed to address the realities of contemporary human experience. Their scholarship consisted in identification of outmoded legal rules that had lapsed from practical significance into empty formalism and in the proposal of alternative principles better suited to serving current needs.[4]

Several important realist scholars, including Leon Green, Lester Feezer, Fleming James, and Albert Ehrenzweig focused their attention on the law of torts.[5] Their general view of the realist scholarly enterprise, as applied to torts, is well captured in the preface to the first edition of Harry Shulman and Fleming James's influential torts casebook, which was first published in 1942:

> While the focus of tort law is the adjustment of relationships between individuals, the quality of the adjustment here, as in all law, is referred to its effects upon the social good. Otherwise it would seem wasteful to spend social wealth and energy merely to shift money from the pocket of the defendant to that of the plaintiff. Accordingly in tort cases, as elsewhere, liability or immunity is sought to be justified by its larger effects. . . .
>
> A live, dynamic law must, of course, always be ready to appraise and reappraise the quality of its adjustments,—to be at least aware of the effects, even if it may be unwilling or unable to change at a given time. Yet tort cases are so numerous and various, so common to the experience of all people whether lawyers or laymen, and so redolent of merely individual controversy and morality, that their social significance and the potentialities of possible adjustments are easily overlooked or unquestioningly assumed in a stereotyped assertion. . . .
>
> [W]e have tried to present the material in such a fashion as to em-

> phasize social consequences and to invite inquiry and criticism as to underlying assumptions. . . . [T]he law is concerned not so much with rule or doctrine as with problems in human relations, [and] the problem must be understood before rule or doctrine can be properly fashioned or applied."[6]

Working from this perspective, the realist tort theorists criticized existing tort doctrine as based on a false assumption that liability decisions involve a choice between two individuals who are equally able to bear the risk. Instead, they argued, strictly as an empirical matter, the choice more often must be made between an individual uninsured plaintiff, for whom the cost of the accident would be catastrophic, and an institutional insured defendant (such as a business corporation), capable of shifting and spreading the risk through participation in an insurance pool. Even where liability decisions are made between individuals, they argued, it is often the case—as, for example in automobile accident and landowner liability litigation—that one such individual is insured, while the other is not.[7]

The realist tort theorists argued that introduction of such an insurance factor radically altered the public policy concerns behind tort doctrine. First, the presence of insurance substantially reduced the force of the traditional moral and safety justifications for tort liability. Where the defendant could indemnify against the risk of liability, the moral connotations of tort liability virtually disappeared. The party who ultimately paid the damages was not the party who engaged in the "wrongful" conduct. Liability became simply another cost of a particular activity, a cost reflected in the amount charged for insurance premiums.[8] Consequently, using tort liability to express public disapproval of certain activities became virtually pointless.[9] Even using tort law to deter unsafe conduct would be undermined if, after the insurance premiums were paid, the activity remained economically advantageous. Where the costs of an accident could be spread to others through the mechanism of an insurance pool, the deterrent effect of imposing those costs on a particular defendant would be substantially dissipated.[10]

Second, if most tort actions involved institutional or insured defendants and individual uninsured plaintiffs, the social impact of placing the loss on the plaintiff would be very different from the impact of placing the loss on the defendant. For the plaintiff, the effect would be catastrophic, involving major social and economic dislocation for both the plaintiff and his or her family. A serious injury could well reduce a productive and economically self-sufficient individual to a helpless pauper. For the defendant, on the other hand, bearing the same cost would not be catastrophic at all. At the most, it might require the defendant slightly to restructure its activities or modestly to increase the price of its goods or services.

Because of the corporate and/or institutional defendant's ability to insure, the cost associated with an injury would be spread temporally through regular payment of insurance premiums, and it would be spread to a pool of other insureds as well. The cost would be simply a measurable and, through actuarial science, predictable cost of the defendant's activity. The defendant's social and economic dislocation following any particular accident would be only minor—a small increase in insurance premiums—as opposed, say, to an injured plaintiff's loss of livelihood.[11] Moreover, in the case of businesses even this economic impact would be only temporary, since the defendant would be able to pass that premium cost on to consumers of its goods or services.[12] Instead of a few people experiencing personal disaster as a result of an accident, a great many people would experience an often barely noticeable increase in cost or inconvenience.

Because of these considerations, tort theorists of the realist school argued that the real costs of an accident to society were generally greater if a loss was permitted to remain with the plaintiff than they would be if the same costs were shifted to the defendant and then spread through insurance. In their view, it followed that in most cases, regardless of defendant's fault, it made social sense to shift the loss from plaintiff to defendant.[13] This conclusion led the realist theorists into a full-scale attack on the fault principle, which they regarded as a romantic anachronism held over from earlier days in which the bulk of tort cases had involved two uninsured individuals.[14] That world, they wrote, was gone, and with it should go the idea of liability limited to circumstances of defendant's negligence.[15]

Beyond negligence, the realists also attacked a broad array of other tort doctrines similarly incommensurate with insurance realities. They called for elimination of charitable, governmental, and even intrafamily immunities, which, they asserted, were rendered unnecessary by the ability of such defendants to insure against their losses.[16] They attacked defenses such as contributory negligence and assumption of risk as archaic technicalities used by insurers to avoid paying out on risks they had already underwritten.[17] They attacked variations in standards of care based on assessments of a party's personal capacity.[18] They sought revision in the doctrine of proximate cause, to eliminate artificial barriers to insurance compensation. And they argued for expansion of tort duties to establish legal obligation for risks on the part of those who could best insure against them.[19]

In place of these outdated doctrines, some of the more extreme tort realists proposed that tort law should be structured in as many instances as possible to pursue a single main objective: placing (shifting) the loss onto the party best able to insure against its occurrence.[20] Such a party, they believed, should be strictly liable for compensation of others injured by its activities, with virtually no defenses to that liability other than proof that some other party could better insure. They argued that such a simple and straightforward insurance-driven system would eliminate most costly litigation, since liability would be clear and most defendants would promptly settle claims against them; it would effectuate maximum victim compensation; it would minimize social and economic dislocation caused by accidents; and it would bring about an effective level of safety through insurance rating and risk classification and through insurance company self-interest in promoting safety among insureds.[21]

The realist argument for adoption of an insurance rationale rests on some important judgments and assumptions. Initially, it reflects an empirical belief that most tort plaintiffs are individuals and most tort defendants are corporations or other comparable institutions. Except, perhaps, in the arenas of automobile accident and landowner liability litigation, the realist insurance rationale carries little force in cases of individual-versus-individual tort suits. In addition, the argument reflects the belief that defendants, as a group, are both more able and more likely to insure against accident costs than are plaintiffs. Were plaintiffs either equally or better situated for purchasing insurance, the logic of the realist critique would either diminish in force or even push in favor of defendant immunity rather than strict liability.

Two other important assumptions of the realist argument are that accident costs of defendant activity are both measurable and predictable, rendering insurance against those costs feasible, and that a spread loss is less severe in its social consequences than a loss that falls entirely on a single individual.[22] Finally, the argument reflects a belief either that maximizing cost spreading will not interfere with use of the tort system to promote safety or (in the insurance rationale's most extreme version) that an insurance/compensation goal is to be preferred over a safety goal in cases where the two conflict.

For scholars who proposed an insurance-driven tort system, there remained, of course, the question whether other alternative systems—in particular Holmes's hypothetical system of social accident insurance—would be a more efficient mechanism for accomplishing the same objective. Many realists registered frank preference for a social insurance alternative, although as time progressed they increasingly recognized the political barriers to such a choice. Indeed, much of the work of the realists during the 1920s and 1930s was devoted to proposals to institute a social insurance plan for traffic accident victims that would supplant tort law in a fashion following the workers' compensation model.[23]

The issue of motor vehicle compensation also sparked a flurry of proposals in the 1950s and 1960s.[24] Nevertheless, the realists also promoted developments within tort law that would lead to a private insurance-funded compensation system as an imperfect, yet perhaps more politically feasible and attainable, alternative.[25]

Integration of the Insurance Rationale into Mainstream Tort Theory

The theoretical contributions of the realists had a profound impact on tort thinking during the middle decades of the twentieth century, and they may be credited with bringing the insurance rationale into the mainstream of tort law debate. Their ideas, however, were not universally accepted. Most notably, William Prosser, who became the reporter for the Restatement (Second) of Torts and was one of the most influential tort scholars of the period, remained skeptical of the insurance rationale as anything more than a "makeweight" argument that could not stand on its own as a justification for significant change in tort doctrine.[26] Prosser went to some length to demonstrate that in his view insurance should and did have relatively little to do with the structure of tort doctrine.[27] Other leading tort scholars also made relatively little use of insurance in their work.[28]

The integration of the insurance rationale into mainstream tort theory, achieved during a period spanning the two decades from the mid-1950s to the mid-1970s, finally came about in three steps. First, the insurance rationale was converted from a perspective for critique into a tool for explanation by the publication in the mid-1950s of Fowling Harper and Fleming James's influential tort treatise.[29] This work systematically examined all aspects of tort law, and it persistently made the case in each area for use of an insurance criterion to resolve doctrinal confusion. Harper and James argue:

> It is the principal job of tort law today to deal with these [human] losses. They fall initially on people who as a class can ill afford them, and this fact brings great hardship upon the victims themselves and causes unfortunate repercussions to society as a whole. The best and most efficient way to deal with accident loss, therefore, is to assure accident victims substantial compensation, and to distribute the losses involved over society as a whole or some very large segment of it. Such a basis for administering losses is what we have called social insurance.[30]

By using the principle as a vehicle for organizing the law of accidental harm, Harper and James built on and incorporated much of James's earlier work, making it accessible to practitioners and jurists. As a result, James's relentless advocacy of the insurance rationale gained wide currency in the courts.

Second, the insurance rationale was incorporated into an economic theory of tort law by some prominent contributors to the law-and-economics movement that swept much of tort law in the 1960s and 1970s.[31] Most notably, insurance received substantial attention in the work of Guido Calabresi. Calabresi restated the insurance rationale in more economically rigorous terms, explored in greater detail the processes by which economic actors can spread accident costs, set up a framework for relating insurance concerns to other public-policy considerations of tort law, and began to particularize the issues to be addressed in evaluating alternative types of insurance-based compensation systems.[32]

Calabresi explicitly relegated cost spreading to the role of a "secondary" goal, one less important in his design for liability rules than the "primary" concern of optimizing safety, and to that extent he parted company with his realist predecessors.[33] Indeed, Calabresi opposed social insurance schemes and (to a lesser extent) first-party insurance, principally out of a concern that such schemes could allocate accident costs to parties other than the "cheapest cost avoider," an allocation that would "externalize" the costs and thus interfere with safety goals.[34] But he nevertheless made cost-spreading considerations an important component of his argument for strict liability as a more satisfactory standard of "general deterrence" than negligence.[35] As the idea of blending tort law with economics gained adherents, Calabresi's recasting of the insurance rationale in economic terms broadened its scholarly acceptance.

Finally, and perhaps in some respects most significantly, the insurance rationale was drawn into the consumerist thinking of tort theorists such as Page Keeton and John Wade, who sought to explain developments in products liability.[36] They justified the movement in the 1950s and 1960s toward strict liability of manufacturers for product defects in part by reference to the manufacturers' superior capacity to bear and distribute the risks of product-related injury. Since the development of product liability was very possibly the most striking development in tort law since the advent of negligence itself more than a century before, the link between this new category of tort law and the insurance rationale added significantly to both the insurance rationale's familiarity and its apparent legitimacy.

Through the cumulative effect of these three steps, by the 1970s it became commonplace for tort scholars to presume that cost spreading was an important function of tort law and that much of the pro-plaintiff development of tort law in recent decades could be explained as an undertaking by courts to accomplish cost-spreading goals. Whether they agreed or disagreed with the developments produced in its name, tort scholars thus acknowledged the insurance rationale as a factor to be reckoned with in setting the terms of tort liability.

Principal Themes

Running through this period of insurance-oriented tort theory are several important themes regarding the advantages of importing an insurance rationale into tort law. Since the durability of the insurance rationale ultimately depends in heavy measure on the validity or invalidity of these themes, I recapitulate them here.

Access to Insurance

Perhaps the most important theme is that liability rules should reflect judgments about who in society has superior *access* to insurance against accident costs. The key tenet of the insurance rationale is a belief that some parties to tort disputes have better access to insurance than others. Typically, in the past, this argument has had both empirical and structural components. It is based on the existing structure of insurance markets, in which some groups—businesses, automobile owners, landowners, employers, or the like—have had an easier time obtaining liability insurance than private individuals and thus have been able to insure more comprehensively against accidents. The access theme posits that this state of affairs is an empirical reality that the tort system, if it is to achieve goals of adequate victim compensation, simply cannot afford to ignore.

The access argument, however, is also based in part on more structural claims. Those who in fact have better access to insurance do so in part because of social and economic forces that determine who will and who will not be able to insure. Proponents of the insurance rationale thus have argued that in our society institutional actors are in fact "better" insurers against accident costs than individuals, for a variety of reasons. They are better predictors of those costs, both because they possess the information needed to make those predictions and because they lack certain psychological barriers to risk assessment. They are also more efficient risk managers, capable of achieving certain economies of scale in the purchase and maintenance of insurance. They often have greater financial ability to purchase insurance and thus are more attractive customers to whom the insurance industry targets its services. And they can, at least to some extent, exert the kinds of bargaining power that allow them to insist on kinds of insurance coverage that best suit their needs.

Likelihood of Purchasing Insurance

A second, closely related theme has been that insurance-driven tort law should reflect a judgment about the likelihood that certain typical parties to tort suits carry insurance. This theme obviously overlaps with the access theme. Yet it is sufficiently distinct to deserve separate mention because it emphasizes not just empirical and structural advantages in insuring, but also statistically verifiable propensities to make use of these advantages. A major objective of the proponents of the insurance rationale has been to push liability in the direction of parties who actually carry insurance. This emphasis has been dictated by their desire to achieve real assured victim compensation. All the theoretical advantages in the world will be to no effect unless they produce real insurance against loss. Thus, even more than the access theme, this likelihood theme stresses purely factual considerations. Liability should be assigned to the individuals or groups who do insure, or the advantages of cost spreading will not be achieved.

In our society as it is currently structured, the argument runs, some people or groups insure against accidents in adequate amounts, while others do not. Generally speaking, corporations and institutional actors do insure against accidents; private individuals, with limited exceptions, do not. If tort liability is to accomplish the goal of loss compensation, it will do so effectively only if the costs of accidents are shifted to those who do insure.

Although this theme rests principally on empirical observation, there may be a structural foundation lurking behind this claim as well. Some activities, such as automobile ownership or product manufacture, may be of a type that inevitably impels the actor to seek insurance protection against accidents, whereas other activities, for example, joyriding or buying a toaster, do not. Since corporate and institutional actors are more likely (again, with limited exceptions) to engage in the activities that impel purchase of insurance, we can infer that they will be more likely to possess means for adequate injury compensation.

This theme for the insurance rationale sometimes gives it a "deep-pocket" appearance, especially when advocates have written loosely about assigning liability to parties "best able to bear the loss." It has made the insurance rationale vulnerable to criticism by those who see it as a thinly disguised and extremely awkward attempt at redistribution of wealth. It is important to note, however, that the focus was never on wealth alone as a criterion of liability. The desire of proponents of the insurance rationale was not to impose the financial burdens of liability on those with ability *to pay,* but to relieve and reduce the financial burdens of liability by imposing them on those with ability *to spread*—those who would redistribute them through insurance.

Cost Effectiveness

Proponents of the insurance rationale have stressed differences between the parties to tort suits not only in their relative access to and likelihood of maintaining insurance, but also in the relative cost to them of such insurance if it is maintained. This theme, which dovetails with the access and likelihood themes, asserts that large institutional actors, through economies of scale, enhanced bargaining power, marketing efficiencies, superior informational resources, and better mechanisms for accident cost control, will be better able than individual actors to reduce the costs of insuring against accidents. In addition, with respect to such institutional actors, the insurance industry itself will be able to pool and classify risks in a more cost-effective fashion. Thus, liability rules should be structured to shift accident costs not only to those parties with greatest access to insurance and greatest likelihood of having insurance, but also to those who can insure most cheaply. Given the relatively low costs of liability insurance for most enterprises prior to the 1980s, this theme had considerable popular appeal during the time when the insurance rationale made its way into mainstream tort theory.

Treating Accidents as a Cost of Business

If there has been a single unifying theme to the arguments for an insurance rationale, it has probably been the idea that the costs of accidents resulting from profit-making activities should be treated as a "cost of business" to be borne by business enterprise. This idea, borrowed from the workers' compensation milieu, gave the insurance rationale its identity as a pro-plaintiff, antibusiness theory. It also gave it the popular but rather misleading name "enterprise liability."[37]

Often, this cost-of-business theme has been little more than a convenient shorthand capsulation of the access, likelihood, and cost themes discussed above. But sometimes it has contained an additional component that both asserts an enterprise's superior risk-distributing capacity and draws an explicit link between insurance and safety.

One facet of this theme is the idea that placing liability on an enterprise, which in turn would shift and spread it through liability insurance, would have the effect of spreading the costs even more effectively than individual insurance.[38] Thus, an insured enterprise could spread some of its accident costs by contractual arrangements to other participants in the enterprise, such as suppliers, wholesalers, and retailers, who would in turn spread that portion of the costs through their own insurance. The enterprise could also spread a portion of its costs, through insurance pools, to competitors in the industry in which the enterprise operated. This would happen when insurers, because of the enterprise's loss, raised premiums for all participants in the particular insurance pool. And the enterprise (together with its suppliers, wholesalers, retailers, and competitors) ultimately could spread any increased insurance costs to the consumers who purchased the goods or services of that enterprise/industry.[39] The result, according to proponents of the insurance rationale, would be that the dislocating effects of accident costs would be minimized through maximum spreading.

Yet at the same time those costs would also stand a better chance of being "internalized" as a cost of engaging in an injury-producing activity.[40] This would happen when the costs of accidents (or at least some portion of them), figured in terms of insurance premiums, would be added to the price of injury-producing goods or services, thus influencing the demand for the product or service in question. Consumers of that product or service would have to weigh their benefits from purchase against the "real" costs of the good or activity, including its accident costs. This in turn would create pressure toward an optimal balance between cost spreading and increased safety.[41]

As such, the cost-of-business idea presses beyond cost spreading alone to suggest that if done by the right parties, cost spreading also ultimately may coincide with at least some cost avoidance. In this view, Holmes may have been wrong: cost spreading and cost avoidance, if properly structured, may work as complementary, not conflicting, goals of tort law.

Risk Management

Indeed, the complementary relation between insurance and safety deserves mention as a distinct theme of insurance-oriented tort theory. Few, if any, proponents of the insurance rationale directly opposed the notion that tort liability should also be structured to promote safety, although they sometimes doubted its effectiveness in achieving that goal.[42] Some went so far as to suggest that directing liability toward insurance actually would bring about a positive contribution to safety, as a result of the insurance industry's capacity to promote safety among insureds. The idea here, which draws force from the example of workers' compensation, is that insurance companies can provide institutional insureds with a substantial pool of expertise in risk management and risk control. Given an adequate incentive, the insurance companies will put pressure on their insureds to institute safety programs that reduce both the insured's and the insurer's exposure to liability losses. To bolster this argument, advocates of the insurance rationale sometimes pointed to insurer-initiated workplace safety programs that developed after the institution of workers' compensation.[43]

Equity

Those who argued for an insurance-driven tort system often coupled their empirical and economic arguments with a moral overtone of equity. There is no reason, they asserted, to provide insurance-backed assured compensation to employee victims of industrial accident but to deny comparably assured access to insurance-funded compensation to nonemployees who are injured by the same enterprise.[44] Recognizing the disparity in treatment between employees and others who are injured by business activity does not, of course, by itself compel the conclusion that equality should be achieved by bringing the relatively disadvantaged group up to the higher level of protection. It could just as easily be achieved by eliminating workers' compensation and thrusting employees back into the fault system. But any such response probably would have been politically unacceptable during the period when the insurance rationale developed; and in an era of expanding national wealth the equity argument bolstered the insurance rationale's claim to popular attention.[45]

Reducing Transfer Costs

From the perspective of the 1990s, it would seem that any system requiring resort to personal injury lawsuits could hardly find justification as a means of reducing transfer costs, but such a theme occasionally has been advanced in favor of the insurance rationale. The argument is that an insurance-oriented tort system, by transforming tort liability from a moral issue to an economic one, by simplifying proof of liability, and by effectively transferring control of defense to insurers, would reduce the number of cases that actually went to trial and would promote expeditious settlement of claims. Instead of refusing payments and attempting to defeat the plaintiff at trial, corporate actors facing virtual certainty of ultimate liability would be motivated to avoid the costs of litigation by voluntarily compensating victims before litigation ensued.[46]

Inevitable Risk

A final important theme underlying the push toward an insurance-oriented tort system concerns the inevitability of safety risks in a modern industrial society. This theme, unlike the others, stresses not so much perceived advantages of the insurance rationale as perceived limits on its most likely competitor, a safety rationale. In this view, even with an emphasis on safety, there would be in modern enterprise an irreducible core of "inevitable" accidents. Unless insurance to cover these accidents were made available through the mechanism of tort liability, society would still experience the social and economic dislocations of individual uncompensated catastrophic loss.[47]

Indeed, one detects in some of the literature supporting the insurance rationale a sort of fatalistic pessimism that even imposition of strict liability, let alone negligence, would have relatively little impact on the exponential growth of danger inherent in modern society. Consequently, imposing liability in order to achieve safety would amount to little more than a Quixotic quest. From this perspective, the only meaningful benefits that tort liability can confer on society are compensation and spreading of losses.

THREE

The Insurance Rationale Decried: The Theoretical Underpinnings of the Current Movement for Tort Reform

In legal scholarship, the insurance rationale probably reached its heyday sometime during the early or mid 1970s. But even before it reached that point, some tort scholars, particularly some participants in the law-and-economics movement and supporters of so-called no-fault insurance, launched a salvo of criticism that cut sharply against the grain of the insurance rationale.[1] That critique enjoyed a building crescendo of support through the 1980s, and it ultimately supplied the recent tort reform movement with its theoretical underpinnings.

The Two Leading Schools of Tort Reform

Critics of the insurance rationale have fixed most of their attention on two issues: (1) the choice between negligence and strict liability as the primary standard of care in tort law, especially as applied to the burgeoning law of product liability, and (2) the choice between first-party and third-party compensation systems, especially as applied to motor vehicle liability. Two distinct and sometimes conflicting schools of thought have coalesced, each around one of these two issues. Both groups have shared the view, however, that an undue emphasis on third-party, insurance-backed compensation through expanded tort liability has produced a fundamentally misdirected and grotesquely inefficient accident compensation system. Both groups have advanced recent dramatic increases in the costs of liability insurance, together with restraints on availability of such insurance in certain sectors, as evidence that the system has deteriorated to the point of collapse and is in need of fundamental change.[2]

Using data of the 1980s insurance crisis,[3] these critics have argued that what they see as the cost-spreading experiment of the second half of the twentieth century has largely failed. The experiment was designed to produce, by manipulation of tort liability rules, a relatively cheap and responsive accident compensation system similar in function, if not in structure, to workers' compensation. Instead, the experiment has produced a horribly expensive, extremely inefficient and unresponsive system in which many accidents go significantly undercompensated, while others are grossly overcompensated. The failure, they assert, has occurred for at least three reasons: because compensatory, cost-spreading theories of tort liability do not in fact supplement but rather conflict with the primary tort function of securing optimum levels of safety;[4] because cost spreading has been pursued through highly inefficient means;[5] and because the absolute liability toward which the insurance rationale presses produces unpredictable risk that ultimately cannot be insured.[6] The result, according to the critics, is a self-destructive system that ends up producing less rather than more safety, that deters innovation, and that leads to substantially greater social and economic dislocation than would either a tort system structured without regard to cost spreading or a cost-spreading system structured without regard to tort liability.

The Law-and-Economics Critics

The first group of tort critics owe much of their inspiration to the law-and-economics movement of the 1960s and 1970s, specifically to such "Chicago school" theorists as Ronald Coase and Richard Posner.[7] Building upon microeconomic elaborations of Learned Hand's famous calculus of risk in *United States v. Carroll Towing Co.*,[8] these theorists have often pressed vigorous arguments in favor of negligence as the theoretically preferred formula for liability. A negligence standard, they have asserted, creates precisely the impetus needed to motivate rational cost-benefit determinations about safety. Under that standard, actors will weigh the social benefits of injury-producing activity against the social costs of accidents to produce an optimal balance between them. They will be burdened with liability only in cases where accident costs exceed the benefits of the injury-producing activity. They will be relieved of liability, and the huge transfer costs that go with it, when additional investments in accident avoidance fail to achieve net benefits in safety. Thus, theoretically at least, the negligence standard, if properly understood as an economic, rather than a moral, assessment, achieves the optimum balance between injury-producing activities and accident avoidance, from society's point of view.[9]

Strict liability, on the other hand, fails to take such cost-benefit determinations into account and therefore results in suboptimal allocation of resources with respect to safety issues.[10] This is especially true if any defense based on victims' negligence is eliminated, because under such a regime any incentive for the consumer of a product or service to engage in safe conduct is virtually eliminated.[11] The producer of that product or service would bear the cost of accidents even in circumstances where the consumer failed to take advantage of efficient cost-avoidance alternatives available to him or her.[12] To use a familiar but extreme (and probably apocryphal) example, suppose the purchaser of a lawn mower decided to use it to cut hedges, causing injury. Strict liability would make the manufacturer responsible, even though the operator of the mower could easily have avoided the accident. Accordingly, the law's push toward strict liability and the insurance rationale behind it are fundamentally at odds with the safety optimization that a rigorous application of the Hand formula would achieve.[13]

In addition to opposing strict tort liability, some critics have also asserted the superiority of private contractual arrangements over tort liability rules as a means of allocating risks from productive activities. Richard Epstein has been a particularly strong advocate of this viewpoint, especially in the product liability and medical malpractice areas.[14] Critics taking this perspective argue that parties to contractual arrangements can distribute risks more efficiently than courts applying rigid legal formulas. "Default" rules allocating liability in the absence of contractual arrangements may be necessary, but the system should be designed to allow deviation from the default pattern where it is economically efficient for individual contracting parties to do so.[15]

From the springboard of this critique, the law-and-economics theorists and their allies have advocated a series of substantive reforms, including (1) substantial cutbacks on, or even elimination of, strict product liability, especially in cases involving defects in design or inadequate warnings;[16] (2) elimination of liability for the actions of third parties, especially joint tortfeasor liability, where one defendant can be held financially responsible for another's share of a judgment;[17] (3) scaling back of "unreasonable" tort duties;[18] (4) renewed emphasis on defenses based on plaintiffs' conduct;[19] (5) reducing the magnitude of tort judgments, especially by cutting back or eliminating punitive damages;[20] and (6) strict adherence to traditional rules of causation.[21] Their work has received substantial attention of late, in part because of its influence on the proposals of the Working Group on Tort Reform that operated under the auspices of the Reagan administration Justice Department.[22] Their views also received substantial attention in the Reporters' Study *Enterprise Responsibility for Personal Injury,*[23] sponsored by the American Law Institute, the organization responsible for revising the Restatement of Torts.

The No-Fault Critics

The second group, the no-fault theorists, have been less concerned about choices between alternative liability rules than about choices between alternative compensation systems and the need for any liability rules at all.[24] They focus attention on the structural differences between third-party insurance, in which a plaintiff must sue a defendant and establish its legal responsibility (in a negligence system, its "fault") in order to receive the benefits of coverage under the defendant's liability insurance, and first-party insurance, in which each individual insures him- or herself against accidents, without regard to the question who was at fault, and without a judicial finding of legal liability as a predicate for insurance coverage. To the extent that an insurance-backed system for compensation is either desirable or inevitable, this group of contemporary theorists has argued that a first-party system—often somewhat elusively termed a "no-fault" system (a term that sometimes promotes confusion between first-party compensation and strict liability)—is preferable to the third-party liability insurance system that the triumph of the insurance rationale has put in place.[25]

These proponents of no-fault insurance argue that a first-party system would avoid the costly litigation process and render liability rules virtually superfluous. They have asserted that although such a first-party system may not have been feasible in earlier times, current widespread availability of relatively inexpensive health and accident insurance makes such insurance a workable alternative now.[26] And even if first-party insurance does not currently exist in a given sector, it can be established by legal mandate (as in the case of the "no-fault" automobile insurance that several states introduced during the 1970s) or by private contract.[27] Critics belonging to this school have suggested widespread adoption of no-fault insurance plans in areas involving recurrent serious accidents.[28] Much of their work has been devoted to automobile accidents, but they have also proposed no-fault plans for such other areas as consumer products and medical services, and they have envisioned expansion of the idea to cover other kinds of injury-producing activities as well.[29]

In some of its more extreme versions, this argument perceives a virtual withering away of most tort liability and its replacement with an administratively efficient, highly responsive first-party insurance system more akin in structure to fire or marine insurance than to liability insurance. Alternatively, it takes on the form of a governmentally mediated social insurance scheme. In this latter form, modern no-fault proposals often resemble compensation schemes advocated generations earlier by the scholarly advocates of the insurance rationale.[30]

Even a casual evaluation of these two theoretical perspectives suggests that there are important issues with respect to the role of insurance on which they are at odds. The law-and-economics group seems to prefer a tort system that relegates insurance to an incidental role, whereas the no-fault group arguably seeks a system in which insurance is an even more dominant force than it is today and in which liability rules fade into insignificance. Indeed, proponents of first-party insurance embrace many of the arguments of the early legal realists and sometimes share their enthusiasm for social accident insurance. Nevertheless, in their common critique of the existing system, both the legal economists and the first-party theorists share an abhorrence for using cost-spreading considerations to shape the structure of third-party liability. Thus, they have joined forces in their assault on the insurance rationale as it is currently employed.

The legal economists and the first-party theorists are by no means the only schools of contemporary tort scholarship. Other groups have also made substantial contributions, including the corrective-justice theorists, who have attempted to resurrect a moral foundation for tort law;[31] critical legal studies theorists, who have challenged the tendencies of tort law to reflect and reinforce the dominant corporate structure of American enterprise;[32] and feminist theorists, who have argued that tort law often reflects male stereotypes regarding harm and its redress.[33] Nor, of course, are these various schools of thought completely compartmentalized; many theorists blend perspectives in their work. But it is a reasonably fair assessment that the most trenchant and sustained attacks on the insurance rationale have come from the legal economists and the first-party advocates.

Principal Themes of Current Tort Criticism

As in earlier segments of this discussion, I do not attempt to set out in elaborate detail all the arguments advanced by these two groups of critics of the insurance rationale. Rather, I extract the essence of their leading criticisms, together with some of the primary assumptions on which they rest.

Forced Insurance

One of the most frequently voiced criticisms of the insurance rationale is that it hampers individual decision making by essentially forcing consumers of products or services to purchase an insurance component along with the product or service they think they are buying.[34] This argument proceeds from the belief that individuals have different levels of risk aversion and would accordingly, if given the choice, assess their insurance needs differently.[35] By placing the obligation to insure on the producer, insurance-oriented tort doctrine cuts off this opportunity for choice, since the producer insures all consumers at the same level and forces them to "buy" the insurance by passing the insurance costs on as a fixed cost of the product.[36] Moreover, the argument goes, if such insurance were truly desired by a large number of consumers, it would probably be available and would be purchased on a first-party basis.[37] The fact that it is not suggests that insurance is of secondary importance to most consumers. Note that this argument is very similar to Holmes's assertion a century ago that the need for universal accident insurance can be disproved by the absence of any market for such a product.

Finally, this argument is based on the idea that the price of third-party insurance, indiscriminately passed on to all consumers, fails to reflect variations in the safety level of consumer conduct.[38] Thus, safe consumers inevitably subsidize risky ones through their purchases.[39] This is unfair, because it fails to reward consumers for their safe conduct. It is also unwise, because it engenders a "why worry?" attitude that increases consumer carelessness.

The Advantages of First-Party Insurance

Another leading theme of the current critique is that a primary defect in insurance-based tort law is its dependence on third-party insurance to the exclusion of superior first-party alternatives.[40] This argument rests in significant part on the empirical assertion that realistic first-party alternatives in fact exist, or can be easily made to exist, and are underused as mechanisms for accident compensation.[41] First-party health and/or accident insurance is now widely available to many potential victims, usually through the relatively efficient mechanism of group policies maintained by employers. First-party insurance for accidental death is also widely available. Life insurance of one form or another is very common. Disability insurance is also widely available and usually very inexpensive, although it is notably underused. Together, these kinds of insurance could cover the most immediate costs that accidents cause.

Critics sounding this theme argue that these forms of first-party insurance can do a better job of compensating for accident costs than third-party liability insurance, which is accessible only through the expensive process of tort litigation.[42] Alternatively, they argue that even if these existing forms of first-party insurance are inadequate, new lines of insurance can be devised.

Jeffrey O'Connell, a longtime advocate of no-fault alternatives, has been particularly creative in devising new kinds of no-fault protection.[43]

Of course, health, accident, life, and disability insurance compensate only for specific economic forms of loss. They do not compensate for pain and suffering, which is often a leading component of modern tort damage awards. Accordingly, an essential element of the first-party insurance theme is the belief that pain-and-suffering losses are unimportant and unworthy of compensation in any event.[44]

There are many factors cited to support this belief. Some critics point out that pain-and-suffering awards tend to correlate with economic loss, suggesting that they are disguised attempts to compensate for economic loss.[45] Others assert that they reflect jury understanding of the reality of contingent fees and thus that they represent an attempt to "pad" damage awards to assure that enough will be left for the plaintiff after the lawyers draw off their share.[46] Still others object to the awards on the ground that pain and suffering cannot be translated into dollars, so that such awards are inherently arbitrary and unpredictable.[47] Finally, some critics assert that from society's viewpoint it is the economic costs of accidents that matter most, that pain-and-suffering awards represent a throwback to moralistic conceptions of tort law, which ought to be discarded, and that one of the current system's vices is its tendency to overcompensate pain and suffering relative to economic loss.[48]

The critics who attack pain and suffering have even less regard for punitive damages, which first-party programs would also eliminate. They see punitive damages as essentially an unabashed appeal to juror sentiment and prejudice, in which awards bear virtually no relation to any of the aims of tort law, including victim compensation.[49] Since plaintiffs receive full compensation first, before punitive awards are assessed, the awards represent a windfall—extra compensation the plaintiff does not deserve. Furthermore, although punitive damage awards are meant to deter future tortious conduct, they in fact grotesquely overdeter, since under broadly accepted economic principles a full compensatory award itself should provide adequate deterrence and since multiple juries may well award punitive damages for the same conduct. Thus, in the eyes of the critics, punitive damages are a particularly pernicious element in the tort system. They add nothing of value, but they do a great deal of harm by impairing predictability and unnecessarily escalating cost.

Even if first-party insurance is widely available for the kinds of loss that tort liability now covers, there remains the question whether it is a superior vehicle for covering those losses. The argument for first-party insurance attempts to answer this question by focusing attention on the huge portion of third-party insurance that is, under our present system, used to cover transfer costs rather than to compensate victims. Its proponents argue that first-party insurance would eliminate most of those transfer costs, thus leaving a much larger portion of the insurance dollar to go directly into loss compensation.[50]

The primary reason for such savings, of course, is that resort to a first-party system would eliminate the costs of litigation. In our present system, the critics assert, lawyers are enormously expensive intermediaries who, by pursuing costly and unnecessary litigation, bog the system down in hopeless inefficiency.[51] Secondarily, the proponents of first-party insurance also stress the vulnerability of the present system to "bogus" elements such as unjustified pain-and-suffering awards, nuisance claims, and windfalls produced by overlapping compensation from collateral sources.[52]

A few critics have gone beyond these transfer-cost arguments to suggest that first-party insurance is also superior in its amenability to effective risk classification.[53] Risk classification is the process by which insurers separate relatively dangerous from relatively safe activities and insure the former at higher premium rates than the latter. A simple, familiar example of this process is the modern life insurance practice of classifying smokers and nonsmokers separately, so that smokers (who have a predictably shorter life expectancy) must pay substantially more for comparable life insurance. Third-party liability insurance can classify risks only according to producer activities, and even this form of classification is hampered by the tendency of modern corporations to engage in a wide range of different productive activities. Third-party insurance of this kind thus cannot classify according to the relative risks of consumer activity.[54] First-party insurance, on the other hand, can sort out consumers according to their relative accident propensities.[55] Thus, it can eliminate the present system's tendency to make safe consumers subsidize unsafe ones.[56] Lurking in this argument is an assumption that consumer behavior has more ultimately to do with safety risks than producer behavior, so that classification by consumer characteristics will produce a more finely tuned and more predictable system of risk assessment than will classification by producer products or services.

Unpredictability

Another major theme of the current onslaught against the insurance rationale is that expansion of liability produces an unacceptably high level of unpredictability regarding accident costs, and this in turn threatens the effective operation of insurance markets.[57] This argument begins with the observation that prediction is essential to insurance rate making. Insurers cannot set fair rates for insurance premiums unless their actuaries can accurately assess the likelihood that a covered risk will materialize. Actuaries use past loss statistics, of course, in their efforts to predict future occurrences. But if losses (in the form of liability to accident victims) are progressively and unpredictably escalating, actuaries will not be able to assign a satisfactory "credibility factor" to past loss experience.[58] The more volatile the situation is, the less credible the past numbers become, and the more actuaries end up relying on subjective perceptions and speculation about the future rather than hard data drawn from the past. The more this occurs, the less likely it is that premiums will accurately reflect losses, with the result that insurance becomes a less effective tool for spreading losses.[59]

This argument obviously assumes that we are currently experiencing a period of unpredictable escalating liability. To justify this assumption, critics point to several factors.

First, they stress the tremendous volatility of jury-awarded damages, which can vary dramatically for comparable loss situations.[60] Moreover, the volatility of damage awards is further aggravated by the availability of punitive damages, which can be grossly disproportionate to a plaintiff's actual pecuniary losses.

Second, they point to barriers to accurate prediction posed by doctrines that tend to divorce liability from the specific actions of a particular defendant.[61] These include such doctrines as joint tortfeasor liability, where one defendant may be held responsible for another defendant's share of a common judgment against them; market-share causation, where a defendant's liability is assessed in terms of its share of a relevant market, instead of in terms of the injuries its goods or services actually caused; and successor liability, where a corporation that obtains the assets of a predecessor also assumes its tort liabilities.

Third, they note the difficulties in predicting "long-tail" liability, in which liability from a particular activity (for example, the use of a cancer-causing substance, such as asbestos or DES) can arise many years after the activity has ceased. They observe the tendency of modern legal doctrines that often generously extend or toll statutes of limitations to aggravate the length of the tail.[62] The result is that liability falls on the defendant long after the injury-producing conduct, with the result that the liability and damages are assessed according to legal rules and economic conditions that are radically different from those that existed at the time the defendant insured.

Finally, they argue that "socio-legal risk" itself has become unpredictable. Because courts are constantly changing old doctrines and adding new ones in the direction of increasing liability, then applying these doctrines retroactively, underwriters of future risk must hedge their bets by assuming the emergence of new and unforeseen pro-plaintiff legal developments. Actuarial "predictions" of such unforeseeable legal developments are sure to fluctuate wildly.[63]

The product of all these developments, critics contend, is an environment in which actuaries are baffled in their efforts to predict future liability from current producer activities.[64] In some instances, this phenomenon has aggravated already dramatic insurance premium hikes as actuaries "fudge" to cover the inherent weakness of their predictions. In other instances, it has led insurers to withdraw from certain markets altogether, reportedly because the impossibility of predicting loss has rendered any underwriting at all imprudent.[65]

One leading critic, George Priest, has carried these arguments still further by asserting that unpredictability is aggravated to an even greater degree by a high correlation of these socio-legal risk factors within certain insurance classification pools.[66] Insurers typically control risk within a classification by playing the relative riskiness of one actor's conduct against the relative safety of another's to achieve an average and relatively constant risk level. Thus, for example, life insurance might be classified by age and smoking habits; but within a single such classification (say, for example, nonsmokers thirty-five years of age) there will be some insureds who have relatively safe occupations (say, law professors) and others who have relatively dangerous ones (say, construction workers). In such a scheme the insurer has controlled for occupation-related risks by lumping them together in a single pool. But where the same risk is shared by every member of the pool (for example, if every thirty-five-year-old nonsmoker were a construction worker), this form of risk control becomes impossible. According to Priest, this is what happens with socio-legal risk in the tort system. Regardless of how the insurance pool is defined, all the insureds within it face a common risk of rapidly escalating liability. In his opinion, this inability to control socio-legal risk by means of risk classification has been a leading factor in insurers' decisions to withdraw from underwriting in certain markets where the extent of socio-legal risk has proven extreme, and it is causing risk-classification pools to "unravel" in other markets.[67]

Adverse Selection

Just as current critics of the insurance rationale find in it a threat to insurers' ability to predict, so they also find in it a threat to insurers' ability to control for adverse selection.[68] The concept of adverse selection, well known to students of insurance, is the danger that the "best" risks will find it advantageous to drop out of an insurance pool, leaving only the "worst" risks in the pool. For example, in life insurance, adverse selection would occur if only the sick and elderly applied for life insurance, while the young and healthy did not. When such a phenomenon occurs, it interferes with the insurer's ability to control risks by spreading them among pool members—in effect getting the good risks to subsidize the poor ones in a fashion that produces a moderate premium for all pool participants. Thus, for insurance to work, it is important that factors contributing to the process of adverse selection be minimized.

Adverse selection is a problem inherent in insurance of any kind, and it probably cannot be completely eliminated from any voluntary insurance system. Nevertheless, it can usually be brought within acceptable limits if the insurer is able by classification of risks to differentiate to some degree among insureds, based upon their risk potential, without entirely sacrificing the concept of a risk pool.[69] Thus, to resort once again to life insurance for an illustration, insurers typically classify risks by age and by some factors relating to health (such as whether applicants smoke), and they charge applicants in the different risk groups varying rates for comparable amounts of protection. This reduces (though it does not eliminate) the degree to which some insureds must subsidize others, and it keeps the insurance product attractive to the lower risks. Thus, for example, a young, healthy nonsmoker may be persuaded to purchase life insurance because for him or her it is so relatively cheap.

In liability insurance, similar controls for adverse selection would be available if insurers could differentiate among insureds according to their propensity to be subject to tort liability.[70] Historically, of course, insurers have done just that. To cite one well-known example, doctors who are surgeons or anesthesiologists typically have paid much higher liability insurance premiums than doctors who are general practitioners, because insurers have determined that the former are engaged in much more dangerous activities than the latter, and thus they are exposed to a far greater risk of tort liability. Similar risk-classification systems have been employed by liability insurance underwriters in a broad array of industries.[71]

According to its critics, however, the insurance rationale for tort liability has positively interfered with insurer ability to control adverse selection by effective risk classification, because it has severed the connection between liability and the relative safety of the insured's conduct.[72] If liability rests solely on the need for compensation and the defendant's ability to absorb and spread the loss, it does not necessarily vary with the relative prudence or caution of the defendant. It becomes accordingly much more difficult for the insurer to distinguish different risk classifications, making it necessary for the insurer to charge an unvarying high premium to all insureds. This, in turn, causes the "better" risks, over time, to drop out of the insurance pool, usually by electing to self-insure.[73] The disappearance of the better risks will leave only the "worse" risks in the pool, driving the premiums still higher and thus exacerbating the exodus from the pool of the more desirable insureds. Critics sounding this theme have cited evidence of some typical defendants electing to "go bare"—that is, drop their insurance coverage entirely—or to self-insure as support for the thesis that this process of adverse selection is well under way.

Moral Hazard

Another argument against the insurance rationale is that it tends to promote what in insurance circles is known as the "moral hazard."[74] Moral hazard, another problem inherent in all insurance, is the tendency of the fact of insurance itself to influence the behavior of the insured. A simple example is the possibility that a person owning fire insurance on a dwelling might be less cautious about handling inflammable material, because of the knowledge that insurance will cover the damage if any fire ensues. With automobiles, moral hazard has been the occasion for a joke; some people drive cars sporting bumper stickers saying, "Hit me, I need the cash." Insurers surely are unamused.

Once again, the moral hazard can never be completely eliminated from any insurance system, but an effective insurance system must allow some mechanism for its control.[75] The most common means of controlling for moral hazard involves structuring the insurance relationship so that the insured retains some portion of the risk and thus shares an incentive to minimize the risk.[76] One common way of doing this, familiar to nearly all in the field of health insurance, is the idea of copayment. For a covered risk, the insurer will bear some portion—say, 80 percent—but the insured must bear the rest. The idea is that the insured will retain some incentive to control the costs. Another well-known method of avoiding moral hazard is experience rating, where after the period of insurance expires the original premium may be modified either up or down to take into account the actual loss experience.[77] Experience rating gives the insured an incentive to control losses in hopes of receiving a partial premium refund.

Opponents of the insurance rationale argue that it aggravates the moral hazard associated with liability insurance for two principal reasons. First, the insurance rationale interferes with the effectiveness of typical controls for moral hazard because it divorces the purchase of insurance from control of the accident-causing situation.[78] Copayment or experience rating can, of course, be used to give the producer-insured a safety incentive. But the consumer, who puts a product or service to use, arguably has greater control over the environment in which an accident with respect to that product or service may arise. Yet the consumer has no direct role in maintaining or paying for the insurance from which he or she will benefit if an accident does in fact occur. Consequently, the consumer has no interest in keeping the cost of premiums for that insurance down, and thus no particular incentive toward safety.[79] Nevertheless, in our information age, consumers are very likely to be aware that such insurance does in fact exist, and they may well take risks in their use of a product or service because they assume they will be compensated if something goes wrong. When this occurs, a moral hazard with respect to liability insurance arises that the insurer is powerless to control.[80]

Second, in part because of strict liability and in part because of consumer moral hazard, producer-insureds may lose their own incentive toward safety.[81] Despite their efforts to improve the safety of their products and services, the strict liability principle that the insurance rationale supports will ensure that they continue to be held liable when accidents occur. And even their best efforts at safer product design will not keep pace with consumer inventiveness in taking safety risks. As a result, producers over time will become jaded about their ability to control liability costs and will give up on their efforts to do so.

The moral hazard theme is closely allied and shares important assumptions with the first-party, adverse selection, and predictability themes discussed above. Like the first-party theme, it essentially assumes that consumers have more to do with the safety of products or services than producers. Like the adverse selection and predictability themes, it also assumes a world in which liability insurers find it exceedingly difficult to make significant differentiations among producers based upon their loss characteristics.

Regressive Taxation

One of the more unusual arguments advanced by a few critics of the current tort system is that pursuit of the insurance rationale effectively subsidizes the rich at the expense of the poor.[82] This assertion rests on the notion that the rich, if injured, collect larger damage awards because tort compensation correlates highly with income. Thus, if accident rates are the same for the rich and for the poor (and advocates of this view assert that there is no evidence to show that they are different), a larger portion of the liability insurance dollar is paid to wealthy claimants than to poor ones. Yet the poor have to pay the same forced "insurance premium" when they purchase products or services as the rich do. The result, effectively, is a transfer of wealth from the poor to the rich, a transfer that further widens the gulf between them. Critics sounding this theme observe that such a regressive effect runs absolutely counter to the social predilections of the realists who popularized the insurance rationale.[83]

Economic Stagnation

A final theme in the arguments of current tort law critics harks back to the central thesis of the Holmes paradigm discussed in Chapter One. Holmes preferred negligence to strict liability because he believed strict liability would deter socially beneficial productive activity.[84] The modern version of the same argument contends that the insurance rationale, by creating liability beyond what can be justified by safety considerations, is effectively diverting into compensation money that could be spent with greater social utility on further technological development.[85] To put the argument in other terms, compensation through tort liability carries with it a significant opportunity cost, in the form of lost development opportunities, that must be factored into any honest assessment of social preferences.

In variations on this theme, critics also sometimes argue that money spent to avoid liability would be better spent on new technology to improve products or services in other ways, or that producers lack courage to put new technology into use, because of fears about the potential liability it might generate.[86] The latter of these two arguments has been particularly apparent in attacks on product liability. It is also a centerpiece of Peter Huber's provocative work, which attempts to make a popular case for substantial tort reform.[87] By these accounts, multitudes of new products and services that might make dramatic improvements in the quality of life—new medicines, new building materials, new machinery, and the like—may never be marketed, because corporate decision makers cannot reliably predict their liability exposure and do not want to risk the kind of liability catastrophe that materialized with asbestos, DES, or the Dalkon Shield. Thus, the liability fostered by the insurance rationale interferes with productivity and creates technological stagnation.

FOUR

The Role of Insurance in Tort Liability: Some Preliminary Lessons from Scholarship

One cannot accurately gauge the proper function of the insurance rationale without making at least some attempt to discern how it has been used in practice. I take up that subject in Part II. Nevertheless, the preceding discussion of the insurance rationale in tort scholarship yields some important preliminary judgments that are worth recording before delving into statutes and case law. Indeed, from the differing scholarly perspectives discussed above, one can assemble a kind of "decision tree"[1] with respect to the role of insurance in setting tort liability, which itself may serve as a helpful framework for measuring actual legal developments. The idea at this stage is not to come to closure on any given issue; that undertaking—to the extent it is possible at all—is reserved for Part III. Rather, my purpose at this phase is to set out the issues themselves in a more or less systematic fashion and to identify the points on which advocates and critics of the insurance rationale lock horns.

By combining the various contributions of the four scholarly periods treated above, it is possible to identify seven clusters of issues concerning the relation between tort doctrine and insurance. Some resolution of each set of issues, roughly in the order in which they are presented below, is necessary for a thorough examination of the torts-insurance relation. On a few of the issues, there has been substantial agreement among tort scholars. On many, however, the different perspectives discussed above establish sharply differentiated, and occasionally even completely opposite, views.

The first group of issues to be addressed in determining the role and force of the insurance rationale bears on the question whether tort doctrine should be structured to serve public-policy objectives or is better treated simply as a private-dispute resolution mechanism in which public concerns have at most a minor role. On this question—in this century at least—most scholars seem to be in relative accord. The view that tort law is, as Leon Green put it, "public law in disguise" has long since been settled.[2] Although a few theorists have argued recently for the view that tort law should be treated as a private system of "corrective justice" in which public-policy concerns are of diminished significance,[3] most participants in the tort reform debate have agreed that tort doctrine should be developed according to *some* policy objective or set of objectives. The debate is about which objectives matter.

There is, however, a more controversial subsidiary question, which concerns the relative roles of courts and legislatures in setting the policies of tort doctrine. Typically, of course, the development of tort law (one of the last remaining bastions of the common law) has been primarily the job of the courts. Courts have woven the main fabric of the law, with legislatures acting relatively interstitially, as they did when they enacted workers' compensation. Current proposals for tort reform, however, tend to envision a much more powerful role for the legislatures.[4] They generally call for state legislatures, and perhaps even Congress, to engage in much more active and thorough oversight of the tort system, either by enacting legislative provisions that directly revise tort doctrine or by replacing torts with legislatively mandated first-party compensation schemes. Accordingly, resolution of the subsidiary question regarding the relative roles of court and legislature will be essential to decisions about implementing tort reform.

The second basic set of questions to be addressed concerns identification of the policies that matter in setting tort doctrine, assessment of their importance to society, and determination of their relative priority. The tort scholarship reviewed thus far is deeply divided on this set of issues. Much of the difference in outcome regarding the ideal structure of tort law is attributable to fundamental differences about the policies tort law ought primarily to serve.

The scholarly literature specifically poses six principal policy goals whose relevance and priority must be evaluated: safety, efficiency, compensation for loss, distribution of loss, technological development, and freedom of choice.[5] To make reasoned choices among alternative directions for tort law, it is necessary to determine how important each of these goals is, both in absolute and relative terms. It is also necessary to decide whether they are complementary or conflicting goals and, if they conflict, to determine which goals should predominate.

It seems likely that most tort scholars would accept each of the six goals specified above as relevant to tort law in some degree.[6] Sharp differences arise over their *relative* roles and importance in structuring tort doctrine. For our purposes, it is important to note in particular that scholarly attitudes toward the insurance rationale depend heavily on prior judgments regarding the importance of compensation as a goal and on the degree to which compensation is either paramount or subordinate to other policy concerns. These attitudes about the importance of compensation in turn tend to drive judgment about the significance of loss distribution.

Those who favor the insurance rationale tend to elevate the importance of compensation. Positing the need for effective compensation leads them to emphasize the value of widespread loss distribution as a means for making compensation effective and assured. In contrast, those who oppose the insurance rationale usually view compensation as a distinctly subordinate concern. For them, interests in safety, efficiency (usually thought of almost exclusively in terms of producer efficiency), technology, or freedom of choice (or some combination thereof) counter the value of compensation, and they justify sacrificing compensation in some substantial portion of cases. To put the matter in oversimplified but perhaps nonetheless useful terms, support for the insurance rationale flows from a "victim" perspective, which emphasizes effective handling of the needs of the injured as the primary policy concern of tort law; opposition to the insurance rationale flows from a "producer" perspective, in which the needs of institutional defendants and their uninjured customers are paramount. Just as attitudes in the plaintiffs' and defense bar toward the insurance rationale can be explained by reference to self-interested choices between these two perspectives, so also the attitudes of tort scholars can be largely explained by the same competing perspectives, although one hopes the scholars have arrived at their views in a somewhat more disinterested fashion.

A third preliminary but nonetheless fundamental decision concerns what we mean by compensation for loss. Since the insurance rationale depends heavily on the goal of compensation, judgments about how it ought to influence tort doctrine cannot be made without a fairly particular idea what compensation for loss involves. The relative importance of economic loss, pain and suffering, and other components of traditional tort damage awards is one important inquiry.[7] Another is an assessment of the relative impact, in terms of potential social dislocation, of losses falling on different groups. This assessment, moreover, must proceed on both sides of the traditional tort suit. One must determine whether the risks of catastrophic loss to the individual victim that proponents of the insurance rationale stressed a generation ago are of equal significance today. One must also determine what forms of social dislocation, if any, flow from shifting those losses to insurance-backed corporate and institutional defendants.[8] In other words, we must know both the costs of compensating loss and the costs of not compensating loss, before we can decide in any given context which we want to do.

If the resolution of these first three sets of inquiry identifies compensation of loss for individual accident victims as an important feature of tort doctrine, then *some* role for insurance in setting tort liability becomes unavoidable. This is true for at least two reasons. First, unless we expressly forbid it, those whom we ask to provide compensation will naturally turn to insurance as a form of financial self-protection. Second, a decision to provide compensation necessarily engenders a need to decide how to finance that compensation, and insurance is among the most readily available alternatives for doing so. Exactly what the role of insurance should be, however, depends on resolution of four more sets of inquiries.

The fourth basic question one must ask in determining the role of the insurance rationale is how important it is to maintain a *private* system of insurance for loss compensation. The present regime and any modifications of it must ultimately be measured for efficacy against the alternative of some socially mandated system of public insurance against accidents.[9] Such a system may, of course, prove to be politically infeasible (although social insurance is much more common today than it was fifty or one hundred years ago); or it may prove too vulnerable to bureaucratic inefficiency and excess; or it may suffer from other vices, such as a tendency to externalize costs.[10] But even Holmes recognized that the possibility of using the state as a universal mutual assurance society could not be simply ignored.[11]

The fifth set of inquiries has probably been the sharpest point dividing the proponents of the insurance rationale from its critics. It bears on the question who in society (or within particular subcategories of social activity) is the *best* insurer against the costs of accidents. The contributions of tort scholarship identify several subsidiary factors that go into this determination.[12] Among the groups to which liability may be assigned, one must determine: (1) who has superior access to insurance; (2) who is more likely to insure; (3) who can insure more cheaply; (4) who has superior information about risks, and superior risk management capacity; (5) who has better power to spread costs, and to whom they will spread; and (6) who ultimately has greater control over insurable risks. Even if an insurance rationale for tort liability is accepted, how it ought to shape liability rules cannot be determined without an answer to these questions. Furthermore, any tentative answer to the question who is best insurer is likely to pose implications for other noncompensatory goals of tort law.

A sixth set of inquiries, identified in some of the more recent tort scholarship, concerns what is needed to preserve what might be termed an "insurable environment"—one in which insurance functions of risk classification and cost spreading will operate effectively.[13] This inquiry requires attention to the problems of moral hazard, adverse selection, and unpredictability of risk, which can interfere with effective insurance against loss.[14] This inquiry has been one of the main foci of recent criticism of the insurance rationale.

Finally, the seventh set of issues concerns whether the other six inquiries can be resolved uniformly across the range of accidents, or whether particular types of accidents should be treated differently.[15] As we have seen, accidents in the workplace and, to a lesser extent, accidents from products are already treated separately. Among other candidates for different treatment are automobile accidents, medical accidents, accidents on occupied premises, and accidents from toxic substances. One must decide whether the insurance rationale, to the extent it applies at all, applies in these different accident environments in the same or in different ways.

It would be premature at this point to attempt even provisional resolution of these issues. Indeed, they are so broad, are so intricately interwoven, and make such enormous informational demands that one is tempted to despair of ever resolving them at any level more satisfying than mere assertion of one's own largely untutored predilections. Yet resolve them in some fashion we must, for in this context, as in so much of law, both action and inaction constitute taking a position. If we move forward toward tort reform, we must have some reason for doing so and some blueprint for what we want to accomplish. If we oppose tort reform, we must offer some justification for preferring the status quo. Either way, the pose we eventually strike will have to be explained in terms of our judgments on these seven issue clusters.

II

The Insurance Rationale for Tort Liability in Practice

Adequate consideration of the insurance rationale for tort liability, especially as it relates to questions of tort reform, cannot take place in a scholarly vacuum. Much depends on whether and how the insurance rationale is used by courts and legislatures in the actual process of setting liability rules. The contemporary criticism of tort doctrine that constitutes the linchpin for tort reform is not merely theoretical. It rests on the assertion that the insurance rationale is overused in practice, especially by the courts, and that this overuse is harmful to the health of the accident compensation system. Thus, it is essential to take a fairly careful look at decisional and statutory law in order to assess the validity of this and other claims that the scholars have made about the ways in which tort doctrine and insurance interact.

Such a review fails to elicit a very clear picture, because even in modern times legal decision makers all too rarely disclose openly the policy grounds for their decisions. But the outlines that do emerge hardly suggest an insurance rationale rampant and in danger of running amok. To the contrary, although courts and legislatures have over time become more comfortable and familiar with the idea that insurance considerations should influence judgments about tort law, their embrace of the insurance rationale has always been and continues to be relatively tentative and uncertain, if not downright reluctant.

Even in recent years insurance has seldom achieved the kind of dominant, driving force as a decisional factor that one might imagine from reading the scholarly literature. When it figures in decisions at all, it is usually as one of several factors given relatively equal weight—a matter calling for balances and tradeoffs against other policy concerns rather than an objective for headlong pursuit. Throughout, courts have remained willing to subordinate insurance to other policy factors, especially safety, if they could be persuaded that there was a true conflict between them. They have also remained sensitive to cost concerns, and to the impact of tort liability on the activities of defendants. Where courts (and sometimes legislatures) have embraced the insurance rationale, they usually have done so in a cautious, qualified fashion.

With those limitations in mind, however, it is still fair to suggest that trends in practice reflect a profile similar to, though more subdued than, the trends of scholarship. The role of insurance in practice follows a course that is roughly parallel to its role in scholarship, although there is a decided lag between theory and practice during most periods. Thus, the scholarly ideas of one generation make their way into the courts and legislatures of either that generation or the next, but they do so gradually and imperfectly. They often bear practical fruit a decade or two, sometimes even longer, after the scholarly seeds have been planted.

The first chapter of this part traces the historical development of the insurance rationale in tort practice, providing an overview of the ways courts and legislatures have used insurance to shape liability rules. The second examines in greater detail some cases that exemplify the range of doctrinal developments that have been influenced by insurance considerations. The third summarizes the principal themes of the insurance rationale in practice and attempts to discern where the courts and legislatures have placed us on tort doctrine's decision tree.

FIVE

Judicial and Legislative Approaches to the Insurance Rationale

Throughout the nineteenth century and during much of the twentieth century, courts and legislatures either refused to recognize the insurance rationale at all or gave it grudging acceptance and extremely limited scope. Courts initially viewed the very idea of insuring against one's liability to another with skepticism, although by the close of the nineteenth century the pressures of business necessity allowed liability insurance to develop. Nevertheless, well into the twentieth century, most courts held to the view that tort liability ought to be developed without regard to the method by which compensation was financed; it was an article of faith with courts of this period that any doctrine that would render one party an "insurer" of another's injuries ought to be rejected. Somewhat more adventurous were the legislatures, which began to experiment with linking liability and insurance through workers' compensation, automobile financial responsibility laws, and other measures. Eventually, some courts began to use the insurance rationale as a foundation for modest reforms of tort law, such as the elimination of charitable immunity. But it was not until the development of strict liability to consumers for injuries caused by defective products, a phenomenon of the 1960s, that the insurance rationale became a prominent element in tort jurisprudence. That prominence has proven to be remarkably short-lived, as the rationale has faced increasingly intense judicial and legislative opposition during the past fifteen years.

Early Judicial Skepticism Toward Insurance-Based Liability

To understand the nineteenth-century judicial attitude toward insurance as a factor in tort law, one must bear in mind the basic structure of insurance as it then existed. In the mid-nineteenth century, insurance was far from being the kind of widespread, multifaceted phenomenon it is today. In the United States, social insurance of any kind was virtually nonexistent. Life and property insurance for individuals were available, but only a relatively small segment of society—the wealthy and sophisticated few—were likely to purchase it, except in tiny amounts. Fire and marine insurance had established a firm foothold in the business community.[1] But liability insurance, as we understand it today, was unknown.[2]

As a consequence, insurance to the nineteenth-century mind was fundamentally first-party insurance. It was a mechanism for the insured to transfer his or her own risks of personal loss to a corporate or mutual insurance pool. The idea of transferring, not one's own loss, but one's contingent risks of liability for another's loss was, for much of the nineteenth century, not only virtually unknown but probably contrary to prevailing notions of the legal limits on "insurable interest."[3]

Insurance against liability to third parties did not develop until fairly late in the nineteenth century.[4] It occurred through an evolutionary process from first-party insurance for uncontrollable loss, to first-party insurance for personal loss occasioned by one's own negligence, to insurance for the benefit of third parties whose losses were occasioned by one's negligence to others.

As mentioned above, marine insurance was one of the most prevalent commercial lines of insurance during this period. This is the kind of insurance that merchants maintain on the goods they ship in commerce. It derives its name from the fact that it was first used in England to protect against loss of goods at sea, but by the nineteenth century similar insurance, termed "inland marine insurance," was also maintained for land-based commerce in goods conducted by all sorts of common carriers, warehousers, and others involved in the handling of merchandise.[5]

During the middle third of the nineteenth century, policies of marine insurance began to include coverage for losses occasioned by negligence. Thus, for example, the owner of cargo on board a ship that was lost through the negligence of the captain could, through an appropriately drafted marine policy, recover from the cargo's insurer for losses from this mishap, just as he or she could recover for losses occasioned by fire or storm. Insurers were willing to provide this form of insurance even in circumstances where the captain was the owner's employee, so that under established principles of vicarious responsibility the captain's negligence could be attributed to the owner.

From this beginning, insurers gradually expanded to provide similar forms of first-party protection of the insured against his or her own negligence.

Eventually, this practice spread from marine insurance to other first-party lines, such as property and casualty or fire insurance. By this means, the practice of underwriting for risks that were the responsibility of the insured became established within the business community.

One place where this practice was of particular import involved common carriers. Under this form of insurance, carriers, such as the railroads, which had become such a dominant force in American economic life, could insure against loss the property they carried for others, even if that property was damaged through the negligent operation of the train. In effect, if not in form, this was essentially liability insurance, since in theory the owners of the property could have sued the railroad for negligence to obtain compensation for such a loss.[6] Railroads even occasionally insured the property of adjoining landowners, a development that forced courts to identify a new form of insurable property interest.[7]

Legal reception of the idea of insurance against losses occasioned by negligence was by no means immediately positive. Occasionally insurers refused to pay under these policies, on the ground that insuring someone against a want of due care was contrary to public policy. They argued from the premise that exculpatory contracts transferring the risk of negligence to others had been held void as against public policy; an insurance contract doing the same thing, they reasoned, should be equally unenforceable. This policy against transferring the risks of negligence to others was especially strong as applied to common carriers, the very businesses that were now availing themselves of insurance against their negligent acts. Moreover, allowing someone to transfer the risks of negligence to an insurer promoted careless behavior. This, in turn, introduced an unacceptable level of what we now term "moral hazard" in personal insurance. For these reasons, the insurers asserted, insurance provisions extending coverage to losses occasioned by negligence ought not to be enforced.

As the insurance coverage spread to include goods owned by others, the insurers added two other arguments. To permit coverage in those cases, they asserted, would frustrate tort law's purpose of deterring unsafe conduct. It would also essentially wipe out the insurer's own right of subrogation to defend the insured (usually a common carrier) against the owner's claim for negligence. By making these additional arguments, the insurers forged a perceptible link between notions of liability and scope of insurance coverage, although in this instance they did so for the perverse purpose of denying responsibility for coverage they had already sold.

These arguments were by and large rejected by nineteenth-century courts, although even in rejection the argument against insurance coverage for negligent losses remained remarkably persistent. As late as the early twentieth century insurers still sometimes resisted coverage on the grounds outlined above.

Nevertheless, rejection came in roughly three steps. First, under marine insurance, the courts accepted coverage for the insured's own loss due to negligence. Second, they expanded the doctrine allowing coverage for negligent losses to other lines of insurance, such as casualty and fire insurance. Finally, they accepted the notion that carriers (and presumably other businesses) could obtain such insurance for the benefit of their customers.

The first of these steps came quite early. In 1837, in *Waters v. The Merchants' Louisville Insurance Co.*,[8] the Supreme Court upheld marine insurance against loss due to negligence. Writing for the court, Justice Story concluded that "[t]here is nothing unreasonable, unjust, or inconsistent with public policy, in allowing the insured to insure himself against all losses from any perils not occasioned by his own personal fraud."[9] Since Story was one of the leading insurance-law experts of his day, his opinion carried great weight in leading American jurisdictions, such as Massachusetts and New York, which included the leading centers of trade and shipping.

The view taken in *Waters* was extended beyond the marine insurance milieu in two subsequent Supreme Court decisions. In *Phoenix Insurance Co. v. Erie & Western Transportation Co.*,[10] the Court held that a common carrier could grant an owner of goods a right of recovery under the carrier's insurance policy, even where coverage extended to loss occasioned by negligence. Justice Horace Gray declared, "No rule of law or of public policy is violated by allowing a common carrier, like any other person having either the general property or a peculiar interest in goods, to have them insured against the usual perils, and to recover for any loss from such perils, though occasioned by the negligence of his own servants. By obtaining insurance, he does not diminish his own responsibility to the owners of the goods, but rather increases his means of meeting that responsibility."[11] This passage is particularly noteworthy because of its emphasis on the public benefit of assured compensation ("means of meeting . . . responsibility") as an offset to any potential vice of moral hazard. The Court reaffirmed its holding in *Phoenix* and extended it to fire insurance four years later in *California Insurance Co. v. Union Compress Co.*[12] These decisions proved to be extremely influential in other common-law jurisdictions. They eventually turned the tide in favor of allowing insurance against risks occasioned by negligence, and they helped to set the stage for the development of true third-party liability insurance.[13]

Once these legal developments took place, it became possible for a few relatively large corporations (such as railroads) that were routinely subject to suit for negligent behavior to contemplate explicitly insuring against the risk of *liability* to others. The hazard—loss occasioned by one's own negligence—was by now a familiar subject of coverage. The only difference was that coverage was triggered, not by the injury-causing event, but by the judgment of legal liability that followed upon it. Moreover, such corporations and their insurers began to contemplate extending that coverage beyond property loss to include personal injury,[14] particularly in cases involving injury to employees, where the nineteenth-century defenses that had long worked so well were beginning to break down. Thus, by the last decade of the nineteenth century, many major corporations began purchasing employers' liability policies, and some, such as the railroads, were purchasing what was effectively liability insurance covering injuries to their customers as well. Occasionally, state legislatures helped out, as the Connecticut legislature did in the 1880s by passing legislation designed to ensure that railroads could insure against negligently inflicted property damage of their passengers and adjoining landholders.[15]

The development of true liability insurance did not begin until the latter decades of the nineteenth century. It did not mature into a familiar feature of the business landscape until the advent, at the turn of the century, of employers' liability insurance, which presaged the coming of workers' compensation.[16] And although liability insurance grew steadily from this point, it did not become a widespread phenomenon until well into the twentieth century, when it spread from employers' liability and the liability of common carriers to include other business risks. In a roughly contemporaneous development, insurers began to offer similar forms of liability insurance to operators of motor vehicles. Thus, in the 1880s, when Holmes contemplated and discussed the idea of a system of private liability insurance as an adjunct to the tort system, he was really looking at least two or three decades into the future. And in the late 1920s, when the tort realists began to argue for extension of the workers' compensation idea to other areas of tort law, the centerpiece of their argument—the widespread availability of insurance to cover the risks of legal liability—was in fact a remarkably new phenomenon.

The first cases to contemplate the relation of tort law and insurance were actually cases decided under insurance law. As with insurance against negligence in first-party marine insurance, liability insurance was sometimes attacked on public-policy grounds.[17] The argument ran that tort responsibility, like criminal responsibility, was personal and thus should not be allowed to be shifted to another, even by contract. To the degree that a tort judgment represented an attempt to punish a moral failure, it would undermine the law to allow an individual, by contracting with another, to avoid legal responsibility. And to the extent that a tort judgment represented an attempt to deter socially unacceptable behavior, allowing the judgment to be shifted to an insurer would destroy the intended deterrent effect.

These arguments must have carried a certain appeal, given what we know about contemporary scholarly and judicial views of tort doctrine. Nevertheless, most courts rejected these challenges in reliance on the earlier first-party insurance decisions. In addition, interestingly, these courts echoed Justice Gray's argument in the *Phoenix* case that the benefit liability insurance conferred on the public policy favoring full compensation of the injured victim at least offset, if it did not outweigh, the claimed interference with deterrence of unwanted conduct.[18] Thus, by the first decades of the twentieth century, the legality of third-party liability insurance was firmly established. But the fact that litigants, judges, and commentators still occasionally advanced public policy challenges to liability insurance suggests that insurance as a feature of the tort system was still regarded with considerable suspicion.

The Wall of Separation Between Insurance and Tort Doctrine

Even after liability insurance was accepted as a permissible form of protection against the financial impact of tort judgments, it was quite some time before courts recognized any role for insurance in shaping liability rules.[19] In individual cases, courts held firmly to the view (much as they do today) that *evidence* regarding insurance is generally irrelevant, and hence inadmissible, in a tort action. Then, as now, the rationale for this position was that jurors might be prejudicially motivated to find liability and award damages if they knew the defendant had a fund available to pay them.[20] From this principle, the courts jumped to the general view that what is inadmissible in the individual case as a matter of evidence for the jury is also inappropriate as a factor of general policy addressed to the court.[21]

As a matter of pure logic, this position was fundamentally flawed. Use of insurance to determine an individual party's liability in a particular case, and use of insurance to determine generally applicable liability rules, are, of course, quite different phenomena. Courts often consider matters in determining questions of law that, once those questions are settled, are inappropriate for a jury to consider in applying the law and finding the facts.[22]

Nevertheless, the judicial view that insurance considerations had no place in setting tort doctrine reflected the policy predilections of the period. It was consistent with the prevailing belief that liability rules constituted judgments about the relative safety and social propriety of defendants' conduct, not about the need for plaintiffs' compensation. It effectively erected a wall of separation between tort and insurance that took several decades to break down.

Indeed, from the late nineteenth century until well into the first half of the twentieth century, courts went to some lengths to resist pressures to shape the principles of tort to accomplish cost-spreading objectives. During this period, it was customary for courts to oppose any legal development that would, in their judgment, render the defendant an "insurer" of the plaintiff's safety.[23] In particular, courts for that reason resisted efforts to increase the standard of care from that of the reasonable person to any higher standard, and they often retained common-law defenses and immunities that allowed some defendants to escape liability even in the face of negligence, on the ground that the immunity was necessary to protect one party from becoming the "insurer" of another.

Implicit in this admonition against shaping the law to make one actor an "insurer" of another's injury is the idea that cost spreading is an illegitimate factor in the development of tort doctrine. That oft-repeated injunction encapsulates the basic assumption that tort doctrine and liability insurance should exist and develop on separate, if roughly parallel, tracks. There was, in the judicial mind of the early twentieth century, a barrier between tort and insurance that could not and should not be breached. In this view tort doctrine rested in large measure on largely intuitive notions of fairness, with a dash of morality and some concern for deterrence of dangerous conduct, but *not* in any significant way on compensation for loss. The law completely embraced the "producer" perspective, in which the fairness of outcomes was viewed almost entirely in terms of balancing the defendant's interests in freedom of action against the public desire to deter unreasonably dangerous behavior. Any impact on the "victim's" needs was a by-product, not a motivating factor, in the development of the law.[24]

Interestingly, the same courts that rejected use of insurance considerations to benefit plaintiffs also rejected use of those considerations to benefit defendants. Thus, they adopted the so-called collateral source rule, which prevented defendants from arguing to courts or juries that plaintiffs' insurance should be a factor in mitigation of damages.[25] Under this rule, once liability was determined, the defendant would be obligated to compensate the plaintiff for the full amount of damages, *even if* the plaintiff previously had obtained compensation from another "collateral" source, such as first-party insurance. Thus, for example, if a tort plaintiff possessed accident insurance, the compensation he or she had received under the policy would not be admissible in a suit against a tort defendant that had caused the injury, nor would the amount of the insurance recovery figure at all in the determination of an appropriate damage award if the tort defendant were found liable. Courts supporting this result reasoned that the defendant was not an intended beneficiary of the insurance policy, that the defendant ought not to "profit" from the plaintiff's foresight, and that the defendant should not be able to escape the consequences of its "wrongful" act.[26] Apparently, the wall of separation was not based on preference for one class of litigants over another. Rather, it stemmed from a firmly held belief that insurance considerations simply had no place in the mix of policy considerations behind tort doctrine.

Chinks in the Wall, Legislative and Judicial

The first evidence that the wall of separation between insurance and liability was beginning to break down came from legislatures. The two most significant legislative initiatives occurred in the fields of workplace and motor vehicle injury, areas where modern technological developments had greatly increased risk and had inflicted widespread injury.

By far the more dramatic developments occurred in the workplace. As mentioned in Part I, during the early decades of the twentieth century many state legislatures, and even Congress to a limited extent, joined the workers' compensation movement. That movement began during the 1880s in continental Europe, where workers' compensation was instituted in part to defuse socialist and communist labor movements.[27] It spread from there to Great Britain and finally crossed the Atlantic to the United States. The first attempt at a relatively comprehensive workers' compensation statute came in New York in 1910.[28] After some early setbacks, the movement spread quickly to other states, so that by the 1940s virtually every state in the union had some form of workers' compensation statute.

Although there were significant variations in the structure of workplace liability, in many of these statutes the legislatures thoroughly redesigned liability rules in order to produce an insurance-backed and insurance-driven system of compensation for industrial accidents.[29] Many systems, following New York's lead, dropped negligence and replaced it with strict liability. By statute, the legislatures curtailed many common-law defenses, especially the trio of contributory negligence, assumption of risk, and the fellow servant rule that had so drastically impeded worker recovery during much of the nineteenth century. They reduced evidentiary demands by requiring workers only to show that their injury "arose out of" or occurred "in the course of" their employment. Often, they replaced judicial resolution of disputes with an administrative system of enforcement. And they structured damage schedules that specified in advance the level of compensation for certain kinds of recurring injuries. All these changes were undertaken to simplify the determination of liability and to facilitate quick, efficient delivery of compensation.[30]

These changes in the tort liability framework were accompanied by changes on the insurance side. In most systems employers were given the freedom to purchase employers' liability insurance from private insurers. In some "elective" systems employers were given the choice whether to participate in the compensation system at all. Nevertheless, for employers within the compensation system, the legislatures both expected and effectively required that they maintain liability insurance or its functional equivalent.[31] The insurance and tort systems were both completely overhauled in an effort to integrate them into a single system that had assured and immediate (albeit incomplete) compensation of the injured worker as its *primary* goal.

Although the drafting of these statutes included many political compromises that produced significant limitations and gaps in coverage, the workers' compensation statutes, taken in toto, were nonetheless remarkable. To date, there has never been a more thoroughgoing affirmation of the insurance rationale than that embodied in the adoption of workers' compensation. Nor has a legislative compensation scheme ever stood in such stark contrast to the contemporary common law.

Although the most significant, workers' compensation was not the only example of legislative attraction to the insurance rationale. As the nation became motorized in the 1920s, interest turned to the increasingly vexing problem of motor vehicle accidents. This interest culminated in publication of a study conducted by a blue-ribbon panel known as the Committee to Study Compensation for Automobile Accidents, under the auspices of Columbia University.[32] The committee proposed a workers' compensation type of statutory plan to provide assured compensation for victims of motor vehicle accidents. The committee advocated the plan on an explicit insurance rationale.

Although the Columbia plan was widely praised and supported in the academic community, it did not succeed in the legislatures.[33] Instead, legislatures took a more modest approach, albeit one that similarly linked tort law with insurance. Massachusetts led the way in the 1920s by enacting a law requiring owners of automobiles to purchase liability insurance.[34] While other states resisted the idea of compulsory insurance, many did adopt "financial responsibility" laws that required some owners of licensed motor vehicles either to maintain certain specified levels of liability insurance or to provide some alternative evidence of financial responsibility. In these instances, the legislatures did not attempt, for the most part, to alter common-law liability rules. But they did attempt to provide some guarantee that when those rules yielded liability, there would be an insurance fund (or its equivalent) available to supply at least minimally adequate compensation.[35]

At about the same time, legislatures also experimented with other measures of more limited application. One of these involved the so-called Dram Shop Acts, in which taverns and other dispensers of alcoholic beverages were subjected to liability for injuries caused or sustained by their obviously intoxicated patrons.[36] Dram shop liability probably had as much to do with social mores about drinking as it did with insurance; but it is at least worth noting that the extension of liability was partly justified on the ground that taverns would be better able to insure against the loss occasioned by such injuries.

Early legislative measures intended to draw torts and insurance closer together met with initial resistance in the courts. Surely the most notable example of such judicial resistance was *Ives v. South Buffalo Railway Co.*[37] In this case, the New York Court of Appeals struck down, on constitutional grounds, the New York legislature's first attempt to enact workers' compensation. The court not only found the adjustment of tort liability rules on an insurance rationale to be undesirable, it also concluded that such an effort was beyond the purview of government because it constituted a deprivation of liberty and property without due process of law. The court essentially held that absent some specific, extraordinary danger to workers, employers had a constitutional right to have liability set according to the fault standard. *Ives*'s impact was short-lived, however, as the people of New York soon passed a state constitutional amendment to allow workers' compensation, and the Supreme Court of the United States, in *New York Central Ry. v. White,*[38] upheld a second New York workers' compensation scheme as a matter of federal constitutional law.

Eventually, courts were persuaded to accept the goals of cost spreading and effective compensation of accident victims as legitimate governmental purposes that were relevant to *legislative* structuring of liability. They remained unconvinced, however, that courts should themselves act in a similar fashion in their development and application of common law. Judicial skepticism about the role of insurance in setting tort doctrine remained the norm.

Perhaps educated by the legislatures' example, a few courts began in the 1930s and 1940s to evaluate on their own the relevance of insurance in structuring tort doctrine. During this period, however, judicial applications of anything approaching an insurance rationale remained cautious and highly selective.

One of the first areas in which courts gave insurance considerations substantial play was the question of charitable immunity. The charitable immunity doctrine had been fashioned in the nineteenth century as a bar against tort recovery from eleemosynary institutions. It rested on a number of arguments, among them the notion that subjection of charitable agencies to tort liability would divert funds from charitable uses and deter future donations, thus leaving the charities with substantially less money to spend on their charitable activities. Thus, the burden of tort liability ultimately would fall on the beneficiaries themselves, a result inconsistent with their probably impecunious status. This result was socially undesirable, courts reasoned, because the beneficiaries were probably more needy and deserving than the tort victims.[39]

Beginning in the 1930s, some courts began to oppose this reasoning and to cut back on charitable immunity. Although movement in this direction was initially slow, by the 1960s most major jurisdictions had either eliminated charitable immunity entirely or at least limited it substantially. Courts in these jurisdictions disputed the thesis that the tort liability burden would fall so heavily upon needy beneficiaries. Instead, they argued that the ability of charitable institutions to obtain liability insurance would spread the costs and minimize the impact of tort judgments on the charitable institution's activities. Interestingly, in a few jurisdictions, courts (or sometimes legislatures) withdrew charitable immunity only *to the extent* that the charity was insured. Thus, in this area the courts drew explicit connections between liability rules (here, nonliability rules) and insurance.[40]

Use of insurance considerations to eliminate charitable immunity does not, by itself, betoken broad embrace of the insurance rationale for tort liability. Indeed, one could argue with some force that it is in fact consistent with the wall of separation between insurance and tort. The earlier rule granting charitable immunity was itself, in a way, a breach of the principle of separation because it explicitly took an institution's ability to pay tort recoveries—which the courts presumed to be slight—into account in fashioning liability rules. Arguably, then, withdrawal of immunity simply restored the system's purity by insisting that tort determinations be made without regard to the parties' relative abilities to cover the cost of injury or their methods for doing so.

But contemporary developments in related areas of tort law, such as intrafamily and governmental immunity, suggest that the change in judicial attitude toward charitable immunity was in fact an early signal of a new trend. Case law from the 1930s through the 1950s includes numerous examples of courts that continued to maintain and repair the wall of separation between tort and insurance, but it also discloses a gradual yet steady increase in judicial willingness to let a party's capacity to distribute risk play a role in determining whether a party should be subject to liability, at least under a negligence standard.[41]

It is beyond the scope of this book to explore in any detail the reasons for the shift in perspective. But one observation may be pertinent. This period in judicial history roughly coincided with the period in American politics that began with Franklin Roosevelt's New Deal and ended with Lyndon Johnson's Great Society. It was a period of extraordinary change in the role of American government. One important legacy of that time in American politics was a fundamental shift in public attitudes toward the role of government in assuring personal security. Since the 1930s, we have become increasingly accustomed to governmental institutions—and hence, by derivation, to legal rules—that have as their main focus assuring the personal financial security of individuals against various forms of danger, harm, or loss. Often these take the form of the government either providing directly or sponsoring programs of insurance.[42] In a political climate where individuals were beginning to receive governmentally established compensation for retirement, disability, unemployment, and the like, the view that assurance of compensation for loss from personal injury was irrelevant to the tort system must have seemed out of step with the new direction of public policy.[43]

The Insurance Rationale Coming of Age: The Era of Product Liability

Until the advent of the post–World War II consumer economy, and the concomitant rise of product liability, reference to insurance considerations in tort cases remained sporadic. Although some commentators during the period prophesied a new trend toward insurance-based tort doctrine, the case law, taken *ensemble,* fails to make a case for broad judicial acceptance of the insurance rationale. Near the end of the war, however, Justice Roger Traynor of the Supreme Court of California ushered in a new generation of judicial tort thinking with his landmark concurrence in *Escola v. Coca Cola Bottling Co.*[44] Traynor took the occasion of an exploding soda bottle case to advance his argument that manufacturers of mass consumer goods should be held strictly liable for injuries caused by defective products. His opinion represents a remarkable departure from the past for many reasons, not the least of which is his explicit advocacy of an insurance rationale.

Traynor offered many arguments to support his position, but his thesis centered on four key points. First, he contended that liability for negligence alone had failed to produce a sufficient deterrent to the manufacture of unsafe products, so that strict liability was needed to supply an adequate motivation for safety.[45] Second, he argued that strict liability was justified by the superior ability of manufacturers to absorb and spread the losses occasioned by defective products—that is, he advanced an insurance rationale.

> Those who suffer injury from defective products are unprepared to meet its consequences. The cost of an injury and the loss of time or health may be an overwhelming misfortune to the person injured, and a needless one, for the risk of injury can be insured by the manufacturer and distributed among the public as a cost of doing business. . . . However intermittently such injuries may occur and however haphazardly they may strike, the risk of their occurrence is a constant risk and a general one. Against such a risk there should be general and constant protection and the manufacturer is best situated to afford such protection.[46]

Third, he argued that strict liability would eliminate artificial barriers to proof of liability caused by the inaccessibility, in mass production contexts, of evidence of specific negligence.[47] Finally, he asserted that in modern times, as a result of mass manufacture and marketing techniques, consumers lacked the resources independently to investigate the safety of the products they purchased, being forced instead to rely upon manufacturers' implicit or explicit representations regarding product safety.[48]

Because of its subsequent influence, some aspects of Justice Traynor's *Escola* opinion and its use of insurance are worth further consideration. Initially, Justice Traynor apparently did not regard any one argument as conclusive support for strict liability. He treated deterrence, issues of proof, consumer reliance, and insurance as factors that worked together to press toward strict liability. In particular, he interwove his arguments based on deterrence and his arguments based on insurance into a single paragraph that moves back and forth between these two themes.[49] More generally, his view was that all four justifications cut in the same direction.

Justice Traynor did not venture any thoughts about what should be done in circumstances where these factors pulled in different directions. One can perhaps draw some inference, however, from the order of his arguments and the emphasis he gave to each. Apparently his primary concern was the ineffectiveness of the negligence principle, as then applied, to produce what in his judgment was an adequate measure of deterrence for unsafe products. His chief animating concern was that even with a negligence principle firmly in place, dangerous and defective products would still enter the market, and they would still wreak havoc upon the lives of unsuspecting victims. In his view, a stronger deterrent than the negligence principle was required to guard against these dangers.

The superior ability of product manufacturers to insure against loss was for Traynor a related yet apparently secondary consideration, one that justified imposition of liability only in those few circumstances where even the utmost care would fail to prevent injuries. Most likely, then, insurance considerations were subordinate in Traynor's mind to the other arguments he offered. Indeed, the insurance rationale in *Escola* is probably most accurately regarded as something of a "fudge factor." Traynor wanted strict liability for injury from defective products because he thought that product manufacturers were probably, in nearly all cases, the most efficient cost avoiders. He justified adopting a categorical rule—one that might impose liability even in those rare cases where the manufacturer was not the most efficient cost avoider—by observing that the manufacturers were also probably the best cost spreaders. In this way, the manufacturer's relative ability to insure might justify resolving uncertainty about optimum deterrence in the direction of producer strict liability. But it could not alone support strict liability, nor could it be used if there were clear evidence that optimum deterrence of product danger could be better accomplished by some other principle. Thus, for example, Traynor cautioned that "[t]he manufacturer's liability should . . . be defined in terms of the safety of the product in normal and proper use, and should not extend to injuries that cannot be traced to the product as it reached the market."[50] In these situations, one could categorically presume that the manufacturer was *not* the most efficient cost avoider, so that liability would be inappropriate despite the manufacturer's risk-distributing abilities.

Another noteworthy aspect of Traynor's insurance rationale is its empirical foundation. Justice Traynor based his insurance rationale on the observation that product manufacturers usually did insure against liability, while victims of product defects usually did not insure against accidents. To some degree, then, his reliance on the insurance rationale was grounded in social relativism. His argument depended on the validity of an empirical assertion about insurance. If insurance markets and practices were to change substantially from what he understood them to be, the strength of his insurance rationale for strict liability would change as well.

In summary, Justice Traynor's reliance in *Escola* on an insurance rationale was qualified. Though certainly bolder than any judicial use of insurance-oriented tort thinking that preceded it, his *Escola* opinion continued to reflect a cautious judicial stance concerning the degree to which insurance considerations ought to shape or determine tort doctrine.

Nevertheless, the explicit reference to insurance in *Escola* ultimately had an enormous impact on the acceptance of insurance considerations in tort law. The effect was not immediate, since strict tort liability for product defects did not take hold until nearly two decades later. Yet as strict product liability took root and spread during the 1960s and early 1970s, court after court in jurisdiction after jurisdiction turned to Justice Traynor's *Escola* opinion—including its insurance rationale—for support.[51] Thus, by the mid-1970s, most jurisdictions had, in one way or another, incorporated insurance considerations into the set of policy factors to be considered in setting one important group of common-law liability rules. They used the belief that a class of defendants (manufacturers) was better able to spread the costs of accidents than a class of plaintiffs (consumers) as at least a secondary reason for imposing liability. To play upon Judge Benjamin Cardozo's famous metaphor, which William Prosser applied to the advance of strict product liability, the same forces that conquered the "citadel of privity" also tore down the wall of separation between insurance and tort doctrine.[52] The insurance rationale finally had come of age.

From its now solid base in product liability, the insurance rationale began during the 1960s and 1970s to gather momentum. Since these decades, references to insurance have become increasingly common not only within but also outside the domain of product liability. As a result, the insurance rationale has had an impact on a wide range of important tort law developments.

Insurance considerations have figured in numerous product liability developments, including the initial adoption of strict product liability;[53] determination of who qualifies as a "seller" subject to such liability;[54] determination of whether strict product liability applies in cases involving only "economic loss" to the purchaser;[55] extension of product liability to include injuries to individuals other than the ordinary consumer (in particular, the establishment of so-called bystander liability);[56] the determination of what constitutes a product "defect," especially in the area of design defects;[57] determination of what damages are recoverable in product liability;[58] the application of Section 402A's exception from strict liability for sellers of "unavoidably unsafe" products;[59] availability in products cases of defenses, particularly the defense of comparative negligence[60] and the so-called government contractor defense;[61] and the availability, in cases involving failures to warn, of the so-called state-of-the-art defense.[62]

Beyond product liability, other tort-law developments influenced by insurance considerations include treatment of other traditional zones of strict liability, such as liability for "ultrahazardous activities";[63] expansion of the scope of duty in negligence law;[64] reduction or elimination of municipal, spousal, and other tort immunities;[65] extensions of vicarious liability;[66] liberalization of requirements for proof of causation (especially the development of the market share theory);[67] adoption of comparative negligence;[68] the development of toxic torts;[69] extension of liability to successor corporations;[70] interpretation and application of dram shop laws and related issues of liability for alcoholic intoxication;[71] constitutionality of legislative measures limiting liability, such as automobile guest statutes;[72] and application of choice-of-law principles to tort cases.[73] In most of these areas, reference to and reliance on the insurance rationale has been both less common and more subdued than in the product liability field, but in each instance the references are sufficiently frequent and widespread to permit the inference that insurance considerations have exerted significant influence on development of the law.

It would be a mistake, however, to surmise from this catalogue of developments influenced by the insurance rationale that it has always exerted an expansionary, pro-plaintiff effect. Nor would it be accurate to assume that the insurance rationale has overwhelmed other policy considerations in the areas where it has played a role. To the contrary, both within product liability and beyond it, courts have often recognized ways in which insurance considerations support limits on liability. And they have been prepared to let other factors serve as effective counterweights to their desire to achieve effective spreading of accident costs. Moreover, at key points along the way, concurring or dissenting judges have voiced strong reservations about headlong pursuit of risk spreading as a primary function of tort law. They still often counsel against tort rules that would make defendants "insurers" of the safety of their products and services.

Signs of Recent Judicial and Legislative Skepticism

Just as in scholarship, tort practice during the 1980s has been marked by a decline in judicial and legislative enthusiasm for the insurance rationale. To be sure, in cases where courts have adopted expansive liability rules, they have continued the habit developed in the 1960s and 1970s of referring to insurance considerations as one of several factors supporting their decisions. But in many of these cases, dissenting judges have begun to voice the concern that the costs of liability insurance may be getting out of hand. There have also been noteworthy instances where the courts themselves have cut back on liability. And in these instances courts have not infrequently mentioned the escalating cost of liability insurance and the so-called liability insurance crisis as reasons for either containing or limiting liability rules. These developments suggest that courts, like contemporary scholars, have become wary about the dangers of runaway liability.

Skepticism has been even more evident in the legislatures. As a result of a sustained campaign during the 1980s by a coalition of insurers and large corporations, nearly every state legislature has been persuaded to enact at least a few of an array of contemporary measures that insurers, corporations, and others have advocated under the rubric "tort reform."[74] These measures have as their explicit purpose scaling back the monetary burden of tort liability on defendants. It is fair to say, however, that most tort reforms enacted during the 1980s have fiddled at the edges of the tort compensation system, amounting to little more than what one commentator has called a band-aid response.[75] So far at least, most legislatures have resisted pressure to overturn the more expansive liability rules set by courts in the 1960s and 1970s. Instead, they have been content primarily to focus attention on methods for limiting or reducing damages awardable on a finding of tort liability, or on other similar measures designed to reduce the cost of liability, without altering the basic legal structure.[76] Most of the judicial developments mentioned above that depended in part on the insurance rationale have remained intact.

SIX

Some Prominent Examples of the Insurance Rationale in Practice

It would unduly lengthen this study to describe in detail all the legal developments that have been influenced by the insurance rationale. Thirty years ago the published judicial opinions using or discussing the insurance rationale still amounted to a relative handful. Today, they probably number in the hundreds, representing a diverse span of courts and jurisdictions. Nevertheless, it may be possible to convey some of the flavor of judicial use of the rationale, in particular, by examining a few leading examples of the insurance rationale in action. Justice Traynor's use of the rationale in *Escola* I have already discussed. In this chapter I briefly examine several other cases that illustrate the insurance rationale across a range of uses over several decades: *President and Directors of Georgetown College v. Hughes,*[1] one of the earlier cases eliminating charitable immunity; *Rowland v. Christian,*[2] which adopted a general standard for determining the existence of duties of care; *Reyes v. Wyeth Laboratories,*[3] which extended the duty to warn of product dangers to pharmaceutical drugs administered in a nationwide vaccination program; *Sindell v. Abbott Laboratories,*[4] which initiated the concept of market share liability; *Beshada v. Johns-Manville Products Corp.,*[5] which imputed knowledge of unknowable dangers in cases involving product liability for failure to warn; and *Anderson v. Owens-Corning Fiberglas Corp.,*[6] which returned to a negligence standard for product failure-to-warn cases in California. The first five decisions all represent expansive uses of the insurance rationale. The final case exemplifies a major retraction.

President and Directors of Georgetown College v. Hughes

As noted above, it was common in the tort law of the early twentieth century for courts to treat charitable nonprofit organizations as immune from liability. The reasons for this view were discussed in the previous chapter. They all rest ultimately on a concern for the financial impact that liability might have on the charitable functions of the institution. The courts were concerned that a crippling tort judgment might seriously impair the organization's ability to perform its charitable mission, and that fear of such liability (and the resulting financial drain on the institution) might deter potential donors from lending their financial support.

This reasoning obviously presumed that a charitable institution would have to pay any tort judgment against it directly out of its assets or operating revenues. Otherwise, if there were other sources for compensation of tort victims that would permit the assets and operations of the charity to remain intact, there would be no need to fear that tort liability would have such an immediate deleterious impact on the organization's charitable functions. If, in particular, a charity could insure against liability, there would be no reason why it would be any less able than a profit-oriented corporation simply to treat liability as a cost of its charitable business and to spread that cost.

This is essentially the counterargument against the traditional view that the District of Columbia Court of Appeals advanced in the *Georgetown* case. The case involved an action by a special duty nurse who was injured when she was struck in the back by a swinging door at Georgetown College's hospital. She claimed that a student nurse who was hurrying to get an article that had been requested by her instructor negligently opened the door without checking to see if the corridor into which it opened was clear. The plaintiff sought damages from the college on grounds of vicarious liability. On appeal, the only question before the court was whether the college was immune from such liability because it was a charitable corporation. The court unanimously agreed that the defendant should not be immune, although it split evenly on the question whether liability should be limited to "strangers" or should be extended to include all potential tort victims.

Writing for the court, Judge Wiley Rutledge rejected the argument that tort liability would lead to "dissipation" of charitable assets, because "insurance is now available to guard against it and prudent management will provide the protection. It is highly doubtful that any substantial charity would be destroyed or donation deterred by the cost required to pay the premiums." Judge Rutledge stressed insurance's "prevalence and low cost" as "important considerations" in disputing fears of dissipation. "What is at stake, so far as the charity is concerned, is the cost of reasonable protection, the amount of the insurance premium as an added burden on its finances, not the awarding over in damages of its entire assets."[7]

In addition to minimizing fears of adverse impact on the activities of charities, the *Georgetown* court also stressed the positive benefits of compensation. The court observed that granting immunity would impose a "cost to the victim of bearing the full burden of his injury," which must be offset against any benefits immunity would extend to charitable functions. In this context, the court specifically mentioned "the general extension of workmen's compensation and social security legislation to include the employees of charitable institutions" as evidence of public policy in favor of assured compensation to the victims of charitable activities. The court also argued that "much of modern charity or philanthropy is 'big business' in its field. It therefore has a capacity for absorption of loss which did not exist in the typical nineteenth century small hospital or college." Thus, the court found it equitable to impose on charities the same tort obligations as their profit-making counterparts.[8]

To these arguments based on the ability of the modern charitable organization to insure against liability, the court added a significant safety consideration. It identified "the tendency of immunity to foster neglect and of liability to induce care and caution" as an independent consideration militating against the extension of blanket charitable immunity. The court also added what may be termed an equity argument, when it stressed "the injustice of giving benefit to some at the cost of injury to others." In this same vein, the court also argued that it would be unjust for the victim "to bear the loss wrongfully inflicted upon him, at a time when the direction of the law is toward social distribution of losses through liability for fault, liability without fault, and legislation which gives the person disabled to work what is commonly but inaccurately called 'social' security."[9]

Based on this argument, the court concluded that charitable immunity was an anachronism out of step with the modern realities of nonprofit enterprise:

> We think . . . that charitable corporations should respond as others do for the wrongs inflicted by persons who act in their behalf about their business and within the course of their duties, actual or apparent. Immunity, whether full or partial, is to be granted only when compelling reason requires it. If there [ever] has been, there is no longer such reason.

> The rule of immunity is out of step with the general trend of legislative and judicial policy in distributing losses incurred by individuals through the operation of an enterprise among all who benefit by it rather than in leaving them wholly to be borne by those who sustain them.[10]

Stressing once again that the elimination of immunity would impose financial detriment only to the limited extent of relatively modest insurance premiums, the court held that "[t]he incorporated charity should respond as do private individuals, business corporations and others, when it does good in the wrong way."[11]

The reasoning of the *Georgetown* decision reflects many of the main themes of the insurance rationale. It treats existing immunity rules as anachronisms based on erroneous assumptions about the nature of tort liability, the structure and function of charities, and the validity of compensatory goals. It also summons the example of workers' compensation as a model for the use of risk-distribution principles to structure liability. Nevertheless, the reasoning of the *Georgetown* case does not rely exclusively on the insurance rationale, nor does it fully explore the potential liability implications of that form of thinking. The court coupled insurance considerations with an interest in promoting safety, and it assigned as one of the chief defects of charitable immunity its theoretical tendency to foster neglect. Moreover, the court was content to halt its reasoning at the point of an obligation to refrain from negligence, and it persisted in employing descriptions of negligence liability that accentuated its moral overtones. The charity should bear and distribute the victim's loss, but only where the charity has occasioned that loss through "wrongful" conduct.

Rowland v. Christian

A persistent source of controversy in the law of torts has been the question of the degree to which owners and occupiers of land (for convenience, I will call them collectively "occupiers") owe duties of care to persons who enter upon their property. During the nineteenth century, courts worked out a relatively elaborate series of distinctions that varied the level of the occupier's duty according to the status of victim and the purpose of his or her visit. Thus, if the person entering the property had the status of an "invitee" and was there for a business purpose, the occupier owed the visitor a substantial duty of care. On the other hand, if the victim was a "licensee," who was on the property for a more casual purpose, the occupier owed a considerably less stringent duty. And if the victim was a "trespasser," who was on the owner's property without his or her consent, the victim was treated as entering the property for a "wrongful" purpose, and (except in a few rare instances, usually involving trespassing children and so-called attractive nuisances) the occupier owed him or her no duty of care at all. Over time, courts developed numerous qualifications and exceptions to this scheme, as well as an elaborate jurisprudence attempting to define the various categories. Even though it often produced what seemed like unduly harsh results and was frequently the subject of critical scholarly commentary, this basic approach remained remarkably stable through the first half of the twentieth century.

The *Rowland* case involved a direct challenge to this scheme. The plaintiff in the case was a social guest at the defendant's apartment. While he was there he used the bathroom, and he was seriously injured when the porcelain handle of a water faucet broke, injuring the nerves and tendons in his right hand. The plaintiff sued his host, who had been aware that the faucet was cracked but had failed to fix it. The defendant argued that since the plaintiff was a social guest, he was a "licensee" to whom the host owed no general duty to secure the safety of the premises. Since the defendant had not engaged in any willful injurious act, she could not be held liable.

The California Supreme Court rejected this contention. More important, in the course of doing so it discarded the traditional common law distinctions between invitees, licensees, and trespassers. Writing for the court, Justice Raymond Peters began his analysis by asserting as a basic premise that absent special circumstances, every individual owes a general duty of care toward every other person. Thus, he argued, if a landowner or occupier owes any lesser duty to licensees, it would be as a result of a judicial decision to deviate from the general duty of care. Such a deviation, in reality, is nothing more than a form of qualified immunity from liability. Like other immunities, it must be justified, if at all, by reference to countervailing policies that override the common law's concern for protection of the victims of negligence. "[N]o such exception should be made," Justice Peters asserted, "unless clearly supported by public policy."[12]

Whether such an exception would be appropriate in the case before the court, then, did not depend on the status of the victim or the purpose of his visit. Instead, the court held that it involved

> the balancing of a number of considerations; the major ones are foreseeability of harm to the plaintiff, the degree of certainty that the plaintiff suffered injury, the closeness of the connection between the defendant's conduct and the injury suffered, the moral blame attached

> to the defendant's conduct, the policy of preventing future harm, the extent of the burden to the defendant and consequences to the community of imposing a duty to exercise care with resulting liability for breach, and the availability, cost, and prevalence of insurance for the risk involved."[13]

In making this change from status to policy as the defining source of the land occupier's duty, the court stressed the arbitrariness and confusion that had developed in common law attempts to apply the invitee-licensee-trespasser distinctions and the numerous exceptions to limits on liability that had grown up around them. "Without attempting to labor all of the rules relating to the possessor's liability," the court concluded, "it is apparent that the classifications of trespasser, licensee, and invitee, the immunities from liability predicated upon those classifications, and the exceptions to those immunities, often do not reflect the major factors which should determine whether immunity should be conferred upon the possessor of land."[14] In particular, the court stressed the lack of connection between these traditional categories and insurance considerations. "The last of the major factors, the cost of insurance, will, of course, vary depending upon the rules of liability adopted, but there is no persuasive evidence that applying ordinary principles of negligence law to the land occupier's liability will materially reduce the prevalence of insurance due to increased cost or even substantially increase the cost."[15]

Applying these principles to the facts of the case, the court found it to be an easy one for liability. The defendant was aware that the faucet was defective and that the defect presented an unreasonable risk of harm. The defendant also knew that persons in the plaintiff's position would be likely to be subjected to the risk. In these circumstances, she had a duty either to repair the faucet or at least to warn her guest of its danger. The court observed that it probably could have reached the same result by manipulating the traditional common-law rules, but it saw no point in doing so. "[T]o approach the problem in these manners would only add to the confusion, complexity, and fictions which have resulted from the common law distinctions."[16]

Rowland has had a substantial impact on the development of the law, both in California and beyond, although it would be premature at best to say that the common-law distinctions it purported to discard have entirely disappeared. For our purposes, what is noteworthy about *Rowland*'s approach is its explicit use of a set of policy factors, including an insurance rationale, as a substitute for traditional common-law categories as a means of addressing the question of tort duties. But *Rowland*'s reliance on insurance was decidedly cautious in at least two important respects. First, the court treated insurance as only one of several factors to be considered, and the court made it clear it was by no means the most important. Rather, the court treated other considerations such as foreseeability, moral blame, and "the policy of preventing future harm" as matters of at least equal and (judging from the order of presentation) perhaps even greater rank.

Second, even to the extent insurance figured into the court's policy mix, it did so not as a basis for expanding liability but as a potential reason for contracting it. As the court structured its inquiry, the question was whether land occupiers should enjoy a qualified immunity from the general duty of care—whether they should enjoy a freedom from potential liability that others in society do not receive. The court was willing to entertain the possibility that substantial evidence establishing difficulty in procuring insurance, or evidence that liability would trigger exorbitant premiums, might serve as a justification for reducing the level of duty below the standard of ordinary care. It did not suggest, at least in this decision, that it was prepared to use insurance considerations as a basis for *increasing* the level of care beyond that set by the generally applicable negligence standard.

The impact of *Rowland* was ultimately expansive. The decision's expansive influence was due in part to the fact that it led to the elimination of long-standing common-law immunities. In addition, in cases such as *Tarasoff v. Regents of University of California,*[17] its analytical approach was used to expand affirmative obligations of care beyond traditional common-law boundaries. But *Rowland*'s use of the insurance rationale was nonetheless more cautious and conservative than was its use in the scholarly literature from which the insurance rationale was drawn.

Reyes v. Wyeth Laboratories

As mentioned above, probably the most fertile territory for the insurance rationale has been in the field of product liability. From its appearance in the 1960s until very recently, product liability was universally recognized as a species of strict liability, and most courts applied it more or less according to the terms of Section 402A of the Restatement (Second) of Torts.[18] One persistent question under the regime of Section 402A has been whether certain products involve sufficiently unique circumstances that they should be exempt, either in whole or in part, from the requirements that Section 402A establishes. In the mid-1970s, the courts addressed one such claim for special treatment in cases involving drugs administered in the course of mass immunization programs.

Reyes v. Wyeth Laboratories was such a case. The plaintiff received a dose of the defendant's oral vaccine for polio, which had been developed and was administered pursuant to a nationwide, governmentally supervised immunization program established in an effort to stamp out poliomyelitis. Within two weeks of taking the vaccine, the plaintiff, then an eight-month-old child, contracted the disease. Her parents filed suit on her behalf against the manufacturer of her vaccine. They claimed that her ingestion of the live polio virus contained in the oral form of the vaccine actually caused her disease and that the defendant had failed to warn her parents that there was a known, albeit small, risk that this might occur. The plaintiff alleged both negligence and strict liability.

The defendant advanced a host of defenses against these claims. Among them was a contention, bolstered by arguments from a variety of professional medical groups, that in cases involving national immunization there should be no duty to warn, because government, acting on behalf of the public, had already determined that the social benefits of immunization outweighed the minimal risks to individual victims. Since the matter had already thus been wrested from individual determination, no socially valuable purpose would be served by imposing liability for a failure to warn.

The court rejected this argument. Writing for the United States Court of Appeals for the Fifth Circuit, Judge John Minor Wisdom rested his conclusion on three policy factors. First, he noted that the risk of contracting polio from the vaccine, though extremely small, was foreseeable and was generally shared by the whole population. In these circumstances, he concluded that requiring manufacturers to advise recipients of the risk would convey "a basis for rational choice" about whether they should undergo vaccination. Second, he observed that the manufacturer's argument erroneously presumed an absence of individual choice regarding immunization. In fact, he argued, individuals concerned about the risk of contracting polio from the live virus could choose an alternative vaccine (one administered by injection) that used a killed virus and did not present the same risk, or in some circumstances they might even rationally choose to forgo immunization entirely. Since these choices had not been prohibited by law, they could not be foreclosed by the manufacturer's unilateral decision not to warn.

The third argument Judge Wisdom advanced against the manufacturer's position entailed use of the insurance rationale. The court relied on a passage from an earlier products case, *Helene Curtis Industries, Inc. v. Pruitt,*[19] for the conclusion that issues of risk distribution are relevant to setting the principles of liability: "Until Americans have a comprehensive scheme of social insurance, courts must resolve by a balancing process the head-on collision between the need for adequate recovery and viable enterprises. . . . This balancing task should be approached with a realization that the basic consideration involves a determination of the most just *allocation of the risk of loss* between the members of the marketing chain."[20] Striking the required balance in the case before him, Judge Wisdom concluded, "Statistically predictable as are these rare cases of vaccine-induced polio, a strong argument can be advanced that the loss ought not lie where it falls (on the victim), but should be borne by the manufacturer as a foreseeable cost of doing business, and passed on to the public in the form of price increases to his customers."[21] In other words, the "just allocation of the risk of loss" in this case was to the party with superior cost-spreading capacity.

This use of the insurance rationale is notable because it represents a situation in which, at least arguably, the court could not rely heavily on a safety rationale as an allied reason for imposing liability. Judge Wisdom implicitly accepted the manufacturer's contention that the product could not be made safer, as well as the notion that the statistically minuscule risk of contracting the disease from the vaccine was substantially less than the risk of contracting it from a "wild" source if the child were not immunized. Thus, the injury in the case arguably fell into the category of "inevitable risk."[22] Nevertheless, the court relied on the fact that the incidence of the risk was statistically predictable, and on the prospect that the manufacturer could effectively spread that risk, as a satisfactory foundation for liability.

Yet even here the insurance rationale did not operate without support from other policy factors. The court gave at least as much emphasis to the well-established policy of tort law that in medical decision making individuals should be given control over their own bodies. The court insisted that the party subjected to the risk of contracting a disease from the injection (or, in the specific case before the court, her parents) should be the party to make the choice. Since the manufacturer possessed information material to making a rational decision whether to subject oneself to such a risk, it was the manufacturer's obligation to pass that information on, even if the predictable result was that the vast majority of people would choose to receive the vaccination anyway. Protection of this value of personal autonomy, as well as cost-spreading considerations, thus supported the court's decision.

Sindell v. Abbott Laboratories

Just as *Rowland v. Christian* had used the insurance rationale to rethink issues of duty, another leading California case, *Sindell v. Abbott Laboratories,* employed the insurance rationale to rethink principles of causation as applied in a mass tort context. The case involved a class action against manufacturers of a pharmaceutical product, diethylstilbestrol, popularly known as DES. The action was brought in California by a "DES daughter" on behalf of herself and others similarly situated. The action specifically named as defendants eleven drug companies that had manufactured and sold DES as a pharmaceutical product. The complaint alleged that the plaintiff's mother had ingested DES during pregnancy because it had been prescribed by her obstetrician to prevent miscarriage. It further alleged that DES was a carcinogenic substance, which caused cancer in the female offspring of mothers who ingested the drug during pregnancy. The cancer had a long latency period; it did not appear in the female offspring until a minimum of ten to twelve years after birth. The complaint alleged various theories of liability, including the claim that drug manufacturers knew or should have known of DES's carcinogenic properties yet failed to issue adequate warnings of the danger.

A critical difficulty in the case was that the plaintiff could not prove which of the numerous drug companies that manufactured DES and sold it for prescription use in California actually manufactured and sold the drugs her mother ingested. Because of the long latency period, records that might have disclosed the identity of the manufacturer had long since disappeared. The same would be true for other similarly situated DES daughters seeking to establish liability for their injuries. Without this critical element of proof, under traditional common-law principles none of these plaintiffs would be able to prove which defendant was the "cause in fact" of her injuries. Without this evidence her case would fail. Thus, unless the requirements for proving causation were altered, manufacturers would be able to escape liability entirely in nearly every case, even though it was obvious in each instance that one of them did manufacture the product that caused the plaintiff's injuries.

Struck by the inequity of this outcome, the court determined that the unique facts of this case called for an adjustment of the traditional rules of causation. Instead of requiring each plaintiff in the class to show which company or companies supplied her mother with DES, the court adopted what has come to be known as a "market share" approach to causation. Writing for the majority, Justice Stanley Mosk declared, "[W]e hold it to be reasonable in the present context to measure the likelihood that any of the defendants supplied the product which allegedly injured plaintiff by the percentage which the DES sold by each of them for the purpose of preventing miscarriage bears to the entire production of the drug sold by all for that purpose." The court required the plaintiff, however, to join as defendants companies whose sales of DES reflected a "substantial share" of the market. It reasoned that this requirement, by increasing the likelihood that one of the named defendants was the actual manufacturer of the DES in question "significantly diminished" any "injustice of shifting the burden of proof to defendants to demonstrate that they could not have made the substance which injured plaintiff." The court also reasoned that having a substantial share of the market represented in each case would provide "a ready means to apportion damages among the defendants," since "each defendant will be held liable for the proportion of the judgment represented by its share of that market unless it demonstrates that it could not have made the product which caused plaintiff's injuries."[23] The court further noted that defendants would be free to cross-claim against other manufacturers that the plaintiff had failed to join in the action.

The court justified this approach in part on the ground that, in the aggregate, "each manufacturer's liability would approximate its responsibility for the injuries caused by its own product."[24] It was, however, content to tolerate on policy grounds what it forecast to be minor variances between aggregate liability and actual aggregate causal contribution. As its primary support for this position, the court argued the injustice of making injured victims bear the cost of an uncertainty in proof of causation for which they were not responsible: "The most persuasive reason for finding plaintiff states a cause of action is that . . . as between an innocent plaintiff and negligent defendants, the latter should bear the cost of the injury. Here . . . plaintiff is not at fault in failing to provide evidence of causation, and although the absence of such evidence is not attributable to the defendants either, their conduct in marketing a drug the effects of which are delayed for many years played a significant role in creating the unavailability of proof."[25] To this reasoning, Justice Mosk appended a set of policy considerations that included an insurance rationale:

> From a broader policy standpoint, defendants are better able to bear the cost of injury resulting from the manufacture of a defective product. As was said by Justice Traynor in *Escola,* "[t]he cost of an injury and the loss of time or health may be an overwhelming misfortune to the person injured, and a needless one, for the risk of injury can be insured by the manufacturer and distributed among the public as a cost of doing business." . . . The manufacturer is in the best position to discover and guard against defects in its products and to warn of harmful effects; thus, holding it liable for defects and failure to warn of harmful effects will provide an incentive to product safety. . . . These considerations

> are particularly significant where medication is involved, for the consumer is virtually helpless to protect himself from serious, sometimes permanent, sometimes fatal, injuries caused by deleterious drugs."[26]

In *Sindell,* as in the cases previously discussed, the insurance rationale played an important yet limited role. The court's main concern in *Sindell* was to construct a rule that would approximate in aggregate outcomes the liability burden that would occur if the facts regarding causation were known in individual cases. To the extent that objective could not be achieved—and only to that extent—the court attempted to allocate litigation risks (specifically, the risk that parties would be unable to turn up certain required forms of proof) to the parties that, though not "at fault" for the uncertainty, nonetheless had the greater control over the processes that produced it, as well as a greater capacity to spread the losses.

This thinking led the court to a relative preference for manufacturers over consumers as the parties better able to bear the risks of causal uncertainty. In making this choice, the court self-consciously echoed the multiple strands of reasoning used by Justice Traynor in *Escola.* The court argued that the defendants are better able to control product safety and that market share liability is necessary to give them adequate incentive to do so. The manufacturers of a drug like DES create the manufacturing and distributing practices that produce the evidentiary gap. They both cultivate and profit from consumer reliance on the safety of pharmaceuticals. And they possess superior capacity for risk distribution.

The insurance rationale arguably figures more prominently in the reasoning of *Sindell* than it did in *Escola.* Notably, it is the first broad policy argument the court mentioned. Moreover, the court's need to rely on insurance as a "fudge factor" is more immediately apparent here, since it is obvious under the *Sindell* approach that some defendants will bear a portion of liability for accidents that (because they did not supply the DES in question) they were in fact powerless to avoid. Yet in *Sindell,* as in *Escola,* the insurance rationale continues to operate in concert with other arguments, including an explicit reliance on safety. The court remained unwilling to rest its decision solely on insurance grounds, and it did its best in the way it structured market share liability to minimize dependence on insurance considerations.

The decision in *Sindell* was highly controversial, and the court was narrowly divided on the outcome. In dissent, Justice Frank Richardson specifically attacked the majority's use of the insurance rationale to support its holding:

> The majority attempts to justify its new liability on the ground that defendants herein are "better able to bear the cost of injury from the manufacture of a defective product." . . . This "deep pocket" theory of liability, fastening liability on defendants presumably because they are rich, has understandable popular appeal and might be tolerable in a case disclosing substantially stronger evidence of causation than herein appears. But as a general proposition, a defendant's wealth is an unreliable indicator of fault, and should play no part, at least consciously, in the legal analysis of the problem. . . . Moreover, considerable doubts have been expressed regarding the ability of the drug industry, and especially its smaller members, to bear the substantial economic costs (from both damage awards and high insurance premiums) inherent in imposing an industry-wide liability."[27]

This passage is noteworthy evidence that by the time *Sindell* was decided in 1980, some judges were becoming uncomfortable with widespread reliance on the insurance rationale. Justice Richardson's dissent attacked the rationale in the main by resurrecting the time-honored theme that it is a form of deep-pocket thinking that wrongly makes wealth a criterion of liability. In other words, Justice Richardson would at least partly rebuild the wall of separation between liability and insurance. Beyond that, however, Justice Richardson also maintained that the majority should take into greater account the *magnitude* of the insurance burden. In cases involving relatively modest increases in the cost of business due to insurance, use of the rationale might be tolerable. But in cases where the insurance costs (and resulting premium increases) promised to be massive, concern for the effect on defendants' activities ought to outweigh the court's desire to accomplish cost spreading through liability.

Beshada v. Johns-Manville Products Corp.

One of the most prolific sources of tort law during the 1970s and 1980s has been the asbestos disaster. For several decades, asbestos, a natural mineral substance, was widely used as a fire retardant, insulator, and construction material in a wide variety of products. In the early 1970s, however, it became clear that the product was extremely toxic, causing a variety of seriously debilitating, often fatal diseases in persons exposed to substantial amounts of the substance. The result of this disclosure was a massive wave of lawsuits by victims of asbestos injury that has engulfed the courts and has driven several once-thriving firms and their insurers either near or over the precipice of bankruptcy.[28]

Beshada v. Johns-Manville Products Corp. was one of these asbestos cases. Several plaintiffs, workers and survivors of deceased workers who had been exposed to substantial amounts of asbestos in their jobs and had suffered resulting injuries and death, filed suit against several corporations that manufactured asbestos. The suits claimed that asbestos was a defective product for which the manufacturer should be held strictly liable under the principles of Section 402A. As evidence of the defect, plaintiffs claimed that defendants had failed to give adequate warning of the toxic effects of asbestos exposure.

The companies sought to argue as a defense that they should be exonerated from failure to warn, because, in view of the "state of the art" of asbestos manufacture, the dangers of asbestos were technologically "unknowable" at the time of the plaintiffs' exposure. The defendants argued that it would be both illogical and pointless in terms of policy to hold them to a duty to warn that they could not possibly have fulfilled.

The Supreme Court of New Jersey, which had long been a leader in developing product liability, unanimously rejected this state-of-the-art defense. The court, in an opinion by Justice Morris Pashman, advanced several reasons for its conclusion. Initially, the court observed that it was "misleading" under 402A to speak of a "duty to warn," because "[s]trict liability focuses on the product, not the fault of the manufacturer." The issue, then, was not whether the defendants did anything "wrong" by failing to warn, but whether the product (asbestos) was dangerous if it was manufactured and sold without a warning attached. "[A] major concern of strict liability—ignored by defendants—is the conclusion that if a product was in fact defective, the distributor of the product should compensate its victims for the misfortune that it inflicted on them."[29]

Proceeding from this observation, the court reasoned that the critical question was not the blameworthiness of the defendant but "whether imposition of liability for failure to warn of dangers which were undiscoverable at the time of manufacture will advance the goals and policies sought to be achieved by our strict liability rules."[30] The court identified three policies it thought would be served by imposing liability: risk spreading, accident avoidance, and streamlining the fact-finding process.

With respect to risk spreading, the court identified it as "one of the most important arguments generally advanced for imposing strict liability." It concluded that the risk-spreading capacity of defendants firmly supported liability for unknowable dangers:

> The premise is that the price of a product should reflect all of its costs, including the cost of injuries caused by the product. This can best be accomplished by imposing liability on the manufacturer and distributors. Those persons can insure against liability and incorporate the cost of the insurance in the price of the product. In this way, the costs of the product will be borne by those who profit from it: the manufacturers and distributors who profit from its sale and the buyers who profit from its use. "It should be a cost of doing business that in the course of doing that business an unreasonable risk was created."[31]

Under this view, the propriety of treating the dangers of asbestos as a spreadable cost of the business of asbestos manufacture was unaffected by the alleged unknowability of the danger.

The court concluded that imposing liability for unknowable dangers would also serve the cause of accident avoidance. The court observed that the defendants had conceded that it would be appropriate to impose liability for dangers that were scientifically "knowable" but that the manufacturers had not in fact discovered. The reason for imposing such liability, they agreed, was to create an incentive for manufacturers to stay abreast of technology and to act swiftly when dangers in their products came to light. Yet the state of scientific knowledge, the court reasoned, was very much a function of the defendants' own willingness to invest in safety research. "The 'state-of-the-art' at a given time is partly determined by how much industry invests in safety research. By imposing on manufacturers the costs of failure to discover hazards, we create an incentive for them to invest more actively in safety research."[32]

Finally, the court stressed the practical difficulties and potential for confusion that would flow from a state-of-the-art defense. The court observed that what is "knowable" is a very different inquiry from what is in fact "known" at any given time, and it would require introduction of very sophisticated expert testimony to determine what dangers were "knowable" by a defendant when it manufactured the asbestos in question. "We doubt," the court said, "that juries will be capable of even understanding the concept of scientific knowability, much less be able to resolve such a complex issue. Moreover, we should resist legal rules that will so greatly add to the costs both sides incur in trying a case." In addition, since knowability was in part a function of manufacturer investment in safety research, it would be necessary, in assessing knowability, to pass judgment on "whether defendants' investment in safety research in the years preceding distribution of the product was adequate." This inquiry, in turn, would create opportunities for the jury to become confused into thinking that the critical question was "whether it was defendants' fault that they did not know of the hazards of asbestos." But that would convert the issue from one of strict liability to one of negligence.[33]

In many ways, *Beshada* represents one of the most aggressive uses of the insurance rationale to date. In the time-honored tradition of *Escola,* the court avoided relying solely on insurance considerations, and it sought to team cost-spreading policies with safety and issues of proof. That linkage works best, however, only for dangers that are theoretically "knowable," even if under the current regime of safety research they have not in fact been ascertained. In the case of truly "unknowable" dangers, the strength of the safety rationale is greatly diminished. It is difficult to maintain that liability creates a greater emphasis on safety, since by hypothesis an "unknowable" danger is one that even "adequate" safety research will not disclose. The interests of safety are served by imposing liability without regard to the state of the art only in circumstances where allowing the defense is likely to confuse the jury into setting an artificially low standard of adequacy for safety research; in all other instances, allowing the defense and denying the defense theoretically produce roughly comparable incentives for safety research.

Streamlining the trial process remains a legitimate consideration, yet that rationale, standing alone, would prove too much, since the same goal could be advanced to eliminate many other difficult issues of proof, such as the issues of defect or causation, which the court was undoubtedly content to retain. One would only streamline trial processes if one were confident that doing so would significantly serve, or at least not seriously jeopardize, other important policy objectives. Thus, it seems clear that the court's analysis depended on the conclusion that streamlining the process here would not only save litigation costs but also produce social benefits sufficient to outweigh the additional costs of liability that eliminating the state-of-the-art defense would place on producers. The chief benefit available, and the one on which the court ultimately placed its principal reliance, was the superior capacity of asbestos manufacturers to spread the costs of asbestos injury. This factor supported a comparative judgment that between a victim who neither knew nor could have known of the danger, and a manufacturer who (by hypothesis) also neither knew nor could have known of the danger, the manufacturer was the party better able to bear the cost of injury.

The court reinforced this conclusion by returning in its closing summary to the language of the insurance rationale to support its holding.

> The burden of illness from dangerous products such as asbestos should be placed upon those who profit from its production and, more gener-

> ally, upon society at large, which reaps the benefits of the various products our economy manufactures. That burden should not be imposed exclusively on the innocent victim. Although victims must in any case suffer the pain involved, they should be spared the burdensome financial consequences of unfit products. At the same time, we believe this position will serve the salutary goals of increasing product safety research and simplifying tort trials.[34]

Thus, even more than in *Reyes*, this is a case where the court, contemplating the prospect of "inevitable harm" (here in the form of unknowable danger), allowed the insurance rationale to loom large as a factor driving the decision to shift liability from victim to manufacturer.

Interestingly, *Beshada* has been among the most controversial of recent tort decisions.[35] Few other courts have been willing to impose strict product liability for unknowable dangers. Only two years after *Beshada*, the New Jersey Supreme Court itself withdrew from the implications of its own reasoning, concluding in *Feldman v. Lederle Laboratories*[36] that state-of-the-art evidence should be relevant in most product-warning cases and that *Beshada*'s ruling should be limited, for some unexplained reason, to cases involving asbestos. Thus, the story of *Beshada* illustrates by exception the general rule of judicial practice regarding the insurance rationale. Although most courts have accepted risk distribution as one of the policy reasons for adopting strict product liability, few (including the New Jersey Supreme Court itself) have been willing to accord the rationale the degree of prominence it exhibits in *Beshada*'s reasoning. When drawn to the brink of unabashed and single-minded reliance on the insurance rationale, courts tend to back away.

Anderson v. Owens-Corning Fiberglas Corp.

The failure-to-warn issue, which precipitated heavy reliance on the insurance rationale in *Beshada*, also produced one of the sharpest judicial attacks on the rationale in the California Supreme Court's recent decision in *Anderson v. Owens-Corning Fiberglas Corp*. As in *Beshada*, the case involved an action for injuries caused by exposure to asbestos. As in *Beshada*, the plaintiff sought recovery on the ground that the manufacturer had failed to warn of the product's dangerous propensities. As in *Beshada*, the parties became locked in a dispute over the admissibility of state-of-the-art evidence. In this instance, however, the court sided with defendants and concluded that state-of-the-art evidence should be allowed. In doing so, the court eliminated imputation of knowledge from product liability cases in California generally, a move that returned design defect and product-warning cases from strict liability to what is functionally a negligence standard.[37]

Anderson drew heavily on an earlier California decision, *Brown v. Superior Court,*[38] which had exempted prescription drug manufacturers from strict product liability for design defects. In the course of that decision, the *Brown* court had also exempted pharmaceutical manufacturers from liability for failure to warn of "unknowable" dangers. As *Anderson* explained, the court in *Brown* had reasoned that without such an exemption manufacturers "would be discouraged from developing new and improved products for fear that later significant advances in scientific knowledge would increase its liability."[39] The court in *Brown* had specifically alluded to the allegedly skyrocketing cost of liability insurance premiums as evidence supporting its contention that imposition of full strict liability on manufacturers of pharmaceuticals would interfere with the availability of some beneficial drugs and might push the cost of others to a level that the general public could not afford.[40]

Although *Brown* had carefully limited both its reasoning and its holding to pharmaceuticals, *Anderson* decided that *Brown*'s reasoning should be applied broadly to all products. Writing for the court, Justice Edward Panelli devoted most of his opinion to a defense of the propositions that negligence considerations were inevitable in a failure-to-warn case and that California law had tolerated the introduction of negligence concepts into product liability under Section 402A. Near the conclusion of his analysis, Justice Panelli also maintained that the court's decision "not only accords with precedent but also with the considerations of policy that underlie the doctrine of strict liability." In this context, he took the occasion to minimize the importance of the insurance rationale: "We recognize that an important goal of strict liability is to spread the risks and costs of injury to those most able to bear them. However, it was never the intention of the drafters of the doctrine to make the manufacturer or distributor the insurer of the safety of their products. It was never their intention to impose *absolute* liability."[41] In a footnote to this passage, he added:

> The suggestion that losses arising from unknowable risks and hazards should be spread among all users to the product, as are losses from predictable injuries or negligent conduct, is generally regarded as not feasible. Not the least of the problems is insurability. . . . Dean Wade stated the dilemma but provided no solution: "How does one spread the potential loss of an unknowable hazard? How can insurance premiums be figured for this purpose? Indeed, will insurance be available at all?

> Spreading the loss is essentially a compensation device rather than a tort concept. Providing compensation should not be the sole basis for imposing tort liability, and this seems more emphatically so in the situation where the defendant is no more able to insure against unknown risks than is the plaintiff."[42]

Although concurring and dissenting justices attempted to minimize *Anderson*'s impact,[43] the significance of the decision for product liability law is enormous. As Ellen Wertheimer has demonstrated, allowing issues of knowability of danger to shape the scope of product liability introduces a factor the logic of which, in manner roughly comparable to a computer virus, eats up the system of strict liability for products. Except for the relatively insignificant category of mismanufacture cases, it effectively returns product liability to a negligence-based system.[44] When the fallout from *Anderson* clears, there may well be no more strict product liability in the state that gave the product liability theory its birth.

Equally important for our purposes is the *Anderson* court's specific repudiation of the insurance rationale as a policy foundation for product liability. The court paid perfunctory homage to the role that insurance considerations played historically in the development of product liability. It then raised some serious doubts about whether losses from unknowable dangers were sufficiently predictable to permit insurance to function. But in the passages quoted above, especially the concluding sentences of the footnote, the court went much further. It explicitly rejected compensation as a proper goal of tort law, and it equated risk distribution with strictly compensatory goals. The result was effectively to banish cost-spreading considerations as an illegitimate factor in setting liability. Under this court's reasoning, in the absence of a clear safety justification, *no* imposition of liability could be justified on insurance grounds, even if more-effective cost spreading could thereby be achieved. In other words, in the view of the *Anderson* majority, insurance is the sort of "makeweight" argument that Prosser[45] long ago thought it to be: a sort of policy padding that can be added on as window dressing when other considerations (notably safety) would independently support liability, but a factor that on its own can support nothing because of the irrelevancy to tort doctrine of the compensatory goals from which the insurance rationale springs.

SEVEN

Summary of Principal Themes

Perhaps the best way to gather the modern strands of the insurance rationale together is to consider which arguments about the insurance rationale from scholarship have been accepted and put to use by courts and legislatures. This, in turn, will allow us to plot the point where contemporary practice places us on the tort "decision tree" set out at the end of Part I. Generally, courts and legislatures have absorbed the bulk of the realists' argument for adoption of the insurance rationale, albeit in more-simplified terms. Still, only rarely have they given those arguments detailed consideration, and they have resisted taking them to their logical extremes. The arguments of the insurance rationale's critics, on the other hand, have received only occasional attention, although opposition to the insurance rationale has grown in both courts and legislatures during the last decade.

At this point, it is fairly common for courts, both inside and outside product liability, to refer to corporate and institutional defendants' superior access to and likelihood of obtaining insurance. In practice, these factors are nearly always treated as empirical observations, and there is seldom any attempt to document them with any sort of precision. Courts simply assume, in a variety of contexts, that corporate and institutional defendants are in a better position to obtain insurance than the individual victims of accidents. Usually they couple that assumption with the assertion that such defendants can treat the cost of liability as a cost of business and can pass that cost on, presumably by charging higher prices to the consuming public for their goods or services. And courts have also sometimes added the claim that insurance could be purchased by the defendant at a relatively low cost. Thus, the access, likelihood, cost of insurance, and cost of business themes advanced by the realists in the first half of the twentieth century have, by the second half of the century, finally achieved a measure of practical acceptance.

The risk-management, transfer-cost, and inevitable-risk arguments also used by the realists have received less attention, although the last of these themes sometimes inhabits the shadows of judicial opinions. Courts applying the insurance rationale have generally assumed that cost spreading and deterrence of unsafe conduct move in corresponding directions, but they have not examined the interactions between insurance and safety in any detail. Similarly, they have given relatively little consideration to the problems of transfer costs. One finds occasional mention of the inevitable risks of a modern industrial society, but this theme is not nearly as prominent in practice as it was in realist scholarly writing.

In contrast to the realist position (which after all has been around a long time), most of the arguments of the recent critics of the insurance rationale have not yet penetrated extensively into judicial debate. When, in recent years, courts have either refused to extend liability or have cut back on existing rules, they have not infrequently referred to the high cost of insurance. And in a few cases, such as liability for defective pharmaceutical products, courts have listed the danger of technological stagnation as a factor counseling against strict liability. On rare occasions, they have also mentioned problems of insurability currently being experienced in some sectors, which can be interpreted as oblique reference to the problems of predictability. But the other themes of the insurance rationale critique—such as preference for first-party insurance, adverse selection, moral hazard, and regressive taxation—are almost completely missing from decisional literature.

Where, then, do the clusters of arguments advanced by courts and legislatures place us on the tort doctrine decision tree? In my view, the following observations represent a reasonably fair assessment:

Torts as public policy Courts and legislatures are virtually unanimous in accepting the idea that tort doctrine should be driven largely by considerations of public policy. As with most scholars, the debate is over which public policies carry the greatest force, not over whether policy considerations have a leading role to play.

On the subsidiary question of relative governmental responsibilities, there seems to be a tacit agreement that courts should serve as the principal architects of tort law, with the legislatures as overseers. Legislatures feel free to make exceptions and regulations with respect to judicially developed tort doctrine, and they may legislate compensation systems to complement or even supplant the tort system in discrete areas. But no legislature to date has had the temerity to undertake wholesale restructuring of the system.

Priority of policy objectives There seems to be remarkable unanimity among courts and legislatures about the relevance and priority of particular policy objectives. Even in fields such as product liability, where the insurance rationale has had the greatest play, deterrence of unsafe conduct remains firmly fixed as the primary purpose behind imposition of liability.[1] Adequate compensation for injured victims, however, has moved during the past century from an excluded consideration to the position of second most important goal. With only a few notable exceptions (such as *Anderson*), courts (with tacit legislative permission) tend to prefer compensation, and hence risk distribution, to either technological development or freedom of choice as a key policy component of the system. These latter values no doubt continue to delimit choices among alternative means of achieving compensation, but they seldom attain sufficient force in contemporary thinking directly to override compensatory goals.

As noted earlier, the importance assigned to compensation as a policy goal has had a profound impact on the significance and prevalence of the insurance rationale. Because tort rules are designed to promote effective compensation for loss, assurance of compensation becomes an important factor in evaluating alternative choices for liability. In our system, insurance has become the primary mechanism for assuring compensation for loss. Thus, a court or legislature determined to achieve effective compensation through liability simply cannot afford to ignore access to insurance as a decisional factor.

What constitutes adequate compensation The appropriate elements of compensation are more uncertain. In this area courts have largely deferred to juries, giving them a fairly free hand to fix compensation once liability for injury has been established. Perhaps because of this judicial laissez-faire attitude, legislatures have of late been more active regulators in this area. But they have regulated in an ad hoc, "blunt instrument" fashion—using such relatively arbitrary mechanisms as damage caps or limits on the type of damages recoverable—that has contributed little to a determination of appropriate forms or levels of compensation for particular injuries. In particular, the explicit trade-off between the degree of compensation and the standard for liability that is at the heart of the workers' compensation model has received scant attention outside that venue.

Neither courts nor legislatures have given much detailed consideration to questions of the *relative* impact, especially in terms of insurance, of placing costs on one party or the other. When they have addressed the issue at all, the courts usually have made the unexamined assumption that plaintiffs are probably uninsured and would suffer catastrophic loss if the burden of accident were not shifted, whereas defendants either are fully insured, are capable of self-insuring, or have fairly ready access to liability insurance. And until recently, they have also made the equally unexamined empirical guess that institutional defendants could cheaply insure against liability. Beyond these rudimentary assumptions, legal decision makers have done little to examine the financial implications, and attendant social dislocation, occasioned by tort liability.

Private versus public insurance Although attitudes have changed regarding the relevance of compensation and insurance in setting tort liability, one constant theme during the past century of tort jurisprudence has been a preference for a privately ordered compensation system. Public compensation for accidents does, of course, exist. Indeed, if one were to add together the variety of state and federal programs that include accident compensation in one form or another, they would no doubt amount to a very substantial investment of public funds. But these programs are discrete, unintegrated, unsystematic, incidental, and occasional. With but a few exceptions that are limited in focus, they do not really amount to alternatives to a privately funded tort system. Efforts to interest governmental decision makers in wholesale social insurance that would supplant a privately funded system of tort liability have failed. Public decision makers today share Justice Holmes's preference for a privately structured system,[2] even if they do not draw from that preference the same implications for tort doctrine that he did.

Best insurer As mentioned above, contemporary jurisprudence does reflect some judgments about who, in certain contexts, is likely to have superior capacity to insure, who is more likely to insure, and who has greater power to spread losses. But these judgments are not backed by careful analysis. The level of debate on these issues in practice does not even begin to approximate the level of debate in contemporary scholarship.

Insurable environment It follows from the lack of analysis of best-insurer issues that courts and legislatures have hardly even begun to scratch the surface on the question of what is needed to maintain a satisfactory insurable environment. Thus, where courts or legislatures have structured liability rules to promote access to third-party insurance, they have seldom paused to consider the extent to which their decisions might create a moral hazard, aggravate adverse selection, interfere with accurate loss prediction, or otherwise interfere with the operation of insurance markets. A few recent decisions, such as *Anderson,* have raised doubts about the predictability of liability costs under expansive rules of tort liability.

Accident typology There has been some modest movement in recent decades toward the view that different kinds of accidents ought perhaps to be handled by different sets of liability rules. The remarkable development of workers' compensation, of course, paved the way for this approach. And product liability—easily the most important tort development in the second half of the twentieth century—is itself an attempt to segregate a particular kind of accident from the general run of tort law and to treat it according to a "customized" set of liability rules. Also, there has been some similar effort to identify certain kinds of environmental harms and so-called toxic torts for separate treatment. But once again, there is a palpable lack of systematic approach. The separate veins of tort doctrine in evidence today are largely accidents of history, not the product of careful attempts to determine which kinds of accidents are best treated by what kinds of liability rules.

III

The Insurance Rationale, the Liability Insurance Crisis, and the Future of Tort Reform

With the theoretical and practical contours of the insurance rationale established, it is now possible to turn to the ultimate objective of this book—assessment of current claims that a liability insurance crisis has been caused by the adoption of the insurance rationale and that restoration of stability in insurance markets requires radical tort reform. This assessment proceeds in three stages. First, I examine the 1980s insurance "crisis" as a phenomenon and evaluate both its extent and the degree to which it is causally related to the judicial and legislative implementation of the insurance rationale. Second, I reconsider and redefine the insurance rationale itself in light of the insurance crisis, the critique it has spawned, and the contemporary movement for tort reform. Finally, from this reconsideration I distill a modified, somewhat more qualified version of the insurance rationale, which may be employed as a tool for assessing the validity and desirability of current tort reform measures. My aim is to arrive at a set of guidelines courts and legislatures can use to set the agenda for development of tort doctrine in the closing decade of the century.

EIGHT

The Insurance Rationale and the Late Liability Insurance Crisis

Before considering the developments that have prompted the tort reform movement, it may be helpful to dwell for a moment on the meaning of the much-overused term "crisis." My edition of the *Oxford English Dictionary*[1] offers three interrelated meanings that are potentially relevant to the present discussion, each of which connotes a different degree of urgency. In medicine, "crisis" sometimes takes on a relatively technical meaning. It is defined as the turning point for better or worse in an acute life-threatening disease—the point where, after medical science has done its utmost, the patient either begins to recover or dies. By metaphorical extension from this definition, the liability insurance system is in crisis if it is currently suffering from an acute and dangerous disease (the cancerous growth of the insurance rationale), so that, even with radical intervention in the form of tort reform, it is in great danger of self-destruction. This grim and apocalyptic vision of the situation is fairly rare in the literature, but it does appear occasionally.[2]

A second, related definition of "crisis," also medical in orientation, declares that it is a marked or sudden change in the progress of a disease, together with the physical symptoms that accompany it. Again metaphorically, this definition applies if the tort system, currently diseased with the insurance rationale, suffered a sharp and painful onset of symptoms when liability rates escalated during the 1980s—the kind of pain that only a fairly radical surgery to remove the cancerous growth will alleviate. References to this kind of "crisis" in the critical literature are quite common.[3]

Finally, a more general definition states that a "crisis" is any turning point or point of decision, a point where one must make final and relatively irremediable choice between at least two conflicting courses of action. The Cuban Missile Crisis of the 1960s is a classic example of a crisis of this sort. The 1990 United Nations authorization for use of force against Iraq represents another. The liability insurance situation presents a crisis of this sort if, to address the problems experienced during the 1980s, we must make fundamental and relatively permanent choices about the future direction of the tort system. The literature on tort reform abounds with this usage.[4]

My position is that the developments in liability insurance during the 1980s do *not* amount to a "crisis" according to any of these three definitions. Dire predictions of an unraveling and self-destructing insurance system are probably unfounded and at most premature. And although the precipitous increases in insurance premiums during the 1980s were undoubtedly acutely painful for some, there are too many potential causal contributors outside the tort system to permit a firm conclusion that the phenomenon was a symptom of serious disorder in tort doctrine. It is not even clear that fundamental and permanent changes in tort doctrine, specifically elimination of the insurance rationale, are needed to address the problems that do exist. Rather than permanent, irremediable, structural change, what is most needed is reliance on the fluidity and adaptability of common-law processes, together with continuation of the process of selective legislative intervention, to bring about a period of doctrinal stabilization that will facilitate market corrections.

Insurance Rate-Making Rorschach Blots: The Relative Roles of Perception and Reality in the Making of the Liability Insurance "Crisis"

To address these points, it is necessary first to obtain some grasp of the forces at work in the recent troubles experienced by the liability insurance market. That is no easy task. Indeed, definitive exposition is nigh impossible because, except for a few basic facts, the phenomena themselves are either unknown or hotly disputed, or both.

Some empirical research has been done in an attempt to describe what happened and why, but it is incomplete and fairly unrevealing.[5] Partly because of the way insurers report financial information, and partly because of the lack of data for longitudinal comparison, it is nearly impossible to tell (1) just what changes in real losses liability insurers have experienced, (2) to what sectors of the liability markets those changes in experience can be assigned, or (3) to what degree they have influenced changes in premium rates. The higher premium rates themselves tell us that rate makers are *perceiving* a higher level of exposure and risk.[6] What we do not know, and what insurers either cannot or will not tell us, is the extent to which those perceptions are founded in actual experience.

Indeed, much of the "evidence" purportedly linking liability premium rates with judicial developments is episodic and anecdotal. Especially in the popular literature of tort reform, commentators often cite individual examples of exorbitant verdicts or of extreme imposition of liability and then assert without systematic demonstration that such cases are becoming much more common and are symptomatic of a system run amok.[7] Then they draw the inference that this supposedly common prevalence of unwarranted liability has been the driving force behind escalating premium rates. Evidence of this sort fails to prove much, because the critical leap from the specific instances to the general conclusion is unsupported. Without more, we cannot tell whether the particular instances being cited are in fact representative of what happens in most cases or are merely an extreme aberration at one end of a long continuum of different outcomes.

There have been a few studies done from a larger case-file data base, some by the insurance industry itself, some by affiliated organizations, and a few by more-objective sources.[8] Instructively, they show much more modest increases in median recoveries in tort cases than one might expect from the anecdotal materials, as well as much less one-sided outcomes in cases that are actually taken to trial. Although comparable data from earlier periods does not seem to be available, so that it is difficult reliably to identify any trends, the more comprehensive data studies suggest that changes in the liability picture are more gradual than some alarmists assert.[9]

But if this is so, one might naturally ask how it could be that premium rates have gone up so sharply. The answer lies, at least in part, in the way that liability premium rates are set.[10] To be sure, the rate-setting process begins with an assessment of past loss experience. But liability insurance premiums are not (indeed, they could not be) simply a projection into the future of past trends. Rather, actual loss experience is discounted by what underwriters sometimes call a confidence factor or a credibility factor. This factor is nothing other than a rate maker's educated but ultimately subjective guess about whether past trends will continue into the future, whether they will change, and, if so, in what direction and to what degree. Consequently, even if present loss experience shows relatively modest increases in the degree of risk, premium rates could still skyrocket if rate makers *believe* that increased risk is about to escalate.

This information suggests that the sharp premium increases experienced during the 1980s may well have been based more on rate makers' *perceptions* about the probable future impact of tort doctrine than on any actual impact already experienced.[11] And those perceptions of increased risk may well have been driven by the psychological impact on the rate-making community of a relative few dramatic and well-publicized "surprise" verdicts as much as by increased loss experience in the run of cases.[12] This scenario would be a bit like a community's suddenly experiencing a sharp increase in demand for home burglar alarm systems after a highly publicized burglary, even though the community's rate of property theft had not gone up very much.

Over time, of course, one would expect rate makers' overreaction, if it existed, to be corrected by moderation or perhaps even reduction of rates—at least in a competitive environment. But the key words there are "over time" and "competitive environment." They prohibit drawing any very firm inferences from premium-pricing experience during a few years in the early 1980s in a fairly oligopolistic insurance market where certain frankly monopolistic pricing practices are legally permitted.[13]

Of Montagues and Capulets: Insurer and Trial-Lawyer Explanations for the Crisis

The difficulty of arriving at an objective assessment of the situation is compounded by the fact that most "information" on the 1980s liability insurance crisis has been disseminated by two warring camps—insurers and plaintiffs' trial lawyers—or their affiliates. These camps have offered two coherent and plausible, yet distinctly conflicting, accounts of what happened during the 1980s. Yet since each camp is obviously motivated by overwhelming self-interest, neither their explanations nor the data summoned to support them are wholly free from suspicion. The insurers want liability scaled back, so it is no surprise that their information points to an impending liability crisis. Trial lawyers want to preserve the existing system, with its promise of handsome contingent fees, so it is no surprise that they find no need for change in tort doctrine. As is so often the case in such adversary settings, the truth probably lies somewhere in between these two extremes.

Both camps begin with the only two facts that cannot be denied: a fairly sudden and sharp increase in liability insurance rates during the last dozen years, with particularly acute increases between 1982 and 1985; and, during the same period, selective withdrawal by insurers from some markets, where insureds suddenly found themselves unable to purchase liability protection at virtually any price.[14]

The insurer explanation for these phenomena ties them directly to changes in tort doctrine.[15] In this view, acceptance by courts of the insurance rationale produced two decades or more of unthinking, reflexively pro-plaintiff tort rulings by courts. At the same time, juries were set free to award wildly escalating damages to successful plaintiffs.[16] The result was an unending upward spiral of liability, especially for corporate or institutional defendants and their insurers. Much of this, moreover, has been so-called long-tail liability, incurred under insurance policies issued and covering activities that occurred long ago, when liability rules were different and underwriters were unable to foresee the doctrinal changes that would bring about massive new exposure.[17] Thus, past premiums, and the investment income from them, proved woefully insufficient to cover the costs of escalating liability.

Consequently, to remain solvent, insurers were forced to raise current premiums dramatically, both to cover existing, unanticipated liability outflow, and to guard against similar developments in the future. In a few circumstances, moreover, the uncertainties of exposure became so severe that insurance for some particularly risky activities has become effectively unavailable.[18] Even where insurance was available, premiums became so great that some firms simply could not afford to pay them. They were forced to contemplate a choice between ceasing certain liability-causing business activities, self-insuring (if they had the resources to do so), or "going bare" (that is, forsaking any form of insurance) and thus incurring the risk that a harsh adverse judgment (or a series of adverse judgments) might render them insolvent. At the same time, in some areas, notably the pharmaceutical industry, businesses were forced to avoid new undertakings because the risks of liability and/or the costs of insurance made marketing of new technology unprofitable.[19]

The root of all these developments, in the insurer view, has been the unbalanced, reflexively pro-plaintiff development of tort law during the relevant period, driven by the inherently "deep-pocket" orientation of the insurance rationale.[20] Thus, the only way to restore equilibrium in insurance is to eliminate the insurance rationale from tort doctrine and to revise the unwholesome liability rules it has produced.

The trial-lawyer explanation ties the phenomena of the 1980s to the way the insurance business is practiced in the United States. Trial lawyers begin by observing that the modern insurance industry is only partly devoted to underwriting and spreading risks. It is equally concerned with investing premium dollars in profitable ventures. The success of an insurance enterprise in the modern era depends as much, if not more, on its ability to get a high return on investment as it does on its ability accurately to predict risks and to price premiums.[21]

Because the insurance industry is so dependent on successful investment, it is, like any investment industry, extremely sensitive to changes in the business cycle. Like Wall Street, the banking industry, pension funds, and other financial enterprises, the insurance industry is subject to sharp upturns and downturns in profitability as the economy swings from boom to bust. But because certain monopolistic pricing practices are legally permitted in the insurance industry, it responds to changes in the business cycle in a unique fashion. When times are good, insurers compete intensely with one another for market share, attempting to attract the maximum number of premium dollars to invest for those high returns. This competition drives premium prices down, sometimes to artificially low levels, which insurers rationalize with the prospect of handsome offsetting investment returns. When, however, the economy turns sour and return on investment plummets, insurers that may have deliberately underpriced their product during boom times fall back on their ability to engage in legalized price collusion, raise premium rates sharply, and thus attempt to restore profitability. During these bad times the insurers always find it convenient to blame, not their own previous investments or marketing strategy, but the courts and tort doctrine, for the need to raise premiums.[22]

According to the trial lawyers and some consumer groups, this is exactly the scenario that occurred over the period running from the late 1970s into the early 1980s. During the 1970s, when interest rates were high and property values were escalating, insurers (which, because of state laws regulating their investments, usually invest more heavily in bonds, commercial paper, and real estate than in equity markets) enjoyed high returns on their investments. Consequently, they competed for investment dollars by holding premiums artificially low, figuring that high investment returns would more than make up for any underwriting losses. But in the early 1980s, when the industry was hit by what was then the sharpest recession since the end of World War II, interest rates and property values suddenly tumbled, and insurers were caught in a profit squeeze of their own making.[23] To get out of it, they used their monopolistic pricing, and their ability to manipulate rate-setting procedures, to orchestrate sharp increases in liability premiums in order to offset their disappointing investment results.[24] Blaming the tort system for the increases became a convenient means of putting these rate increases through and covering for the shortsighted marketing strategies of the previous decade.

In the trial-lawyer view, correction of the problems of the 1980s thus requires no change in tort law. Rather, what is needed from this perspective is a fundamental change in the way insurance markets are regulated. Thus, trial lawyers, joined by some consumer groups, have called for elimination of the insurer exemption from federal antitrust laws, more aggressive rate and investment regulation by state insurance commissioners, and possibly some national regulation of insurance practices.[25]

As mentioned above, certain unique characteristics of the insurance industry make it virtually impossible to choose between these two competing scenarios—or indeed to construct a third. Because there is no centralized regulatory structure for insurance in the United States, there is also no central governmental source of comprehensive "objective" information about the functioning and fortunes of the insurance industry to which we can turn. Moreover, the methods of rate setting used by insurers, and the limited nature of public data-disclosure requirements applicable to them, make it impossible to come to any "realistic" projection of the costs of liability during recent years. These problems are compounded by the complicated processes by which direct marketers of insurance allocate portions of their risk to various reinsurers (a process that is virtually invisible to the consuming public),[26] and by insurer tendencies to lump various kinds of costs together in their financial reporting, so that actual payouts on tort lawsuits are extremely difficult to discern. Consequently, it is both impossible and probably fruitless to try to determine which of the two groups with the most at stake in the debate is "right" about what happened. Instead, one needs to take a broader view of the issue, a view that seeks to evaluate, not the particular premium crunch of the early 1980s, but general changes in liability rates over a longer period of time.

A Longer View of the Crisis: Other Explanatory Factors

Even assuming that the sharp increases in liability premiums during the early 1980s were partly aberrational, one simply cannot escape the fact that liability rates have risen significantly over the past twenty or thirty years.[27] Because of the cyclical sensitivity of the insurance industry, increases have undoubtedly been sharper in some periods than others; but the overall trend has been up, and the growth in premiums during that period has significantly outpaced inflation.[28] Nor can one deny that liability insurance has become either prohibitive or even unavailable in some sectors, while in other sectors it has recently become a big enough factor to influence and even sometimes drive certain important business decisions.[29] Since these developments have all occurred during the same period when the insurance rationale enjoyed its greatest role in shaping tort doctrine, it is at least plausible that there is a cause-and-effect relation.

There are, however, important reasons for doubting or at least qualifying this causal assertion. Other simultaneous developments that have also affected liability, and hence liability insurance, must be factored into analysis. When they are, it becomes impossible to assign to the insurance rationale the dominant, or even perhaps a leading, role in producing current liability premium costs. A complete list of these other factors may not be possible, but at least the following eight phenomena have surely contributed to the recent growth in insurance premiums: improved access to legal services by injured victims; better quality of legal services, especially for plaintiffs; procedural reforms in the courts facilitating recovery in deserving cases; increased jury sophistication; improved medical and scientific technology; rapid increases in the costs of medical treatment; general increases in national wealth; and the impact of a few extraordinary "toxic tort" disasters.

Access to Legal Services

During the past thirty years, the ability of a potential personal injury plaintiff to find a qualified lawyer has markedly improved for a host of reasons. Both the absolute and proportional numbers of lawyers in the country have increased dramatically: there are simply a lot more lawyers to go around.[30] This means, of course, that there are also a lot more lawyers *going* around, seeking potential clients.[31] During the same period, judicial interpretations of the First Amendment have significantly reduced limitations on lawyer advertising, thus enhancing the likelihood that lawyers will reach potential plaintiffs and persuade them to bring their claims.[32] The efforts of individual lawyers and firms, moreover, have been supplemented by development of bar-sponsored lawyer referral services in many large communities.

At the same time that the number of available lawyers and their ability to reach clients have been expanding, there has been a significant change in professional attitudes toward so-called personal injury lawyering. During the past twenty or thirty years, the plaintiffs' bar has gained considerably in the level of professional regard it receives. Moreover, the contingent fee has become during this period a firmly accepted, effective method of financing a lawsuit.[33]

The cumulative effect of these changes (more lawyers, more accessibility to potential clients, more lawyers seeking personal injury work) has been significantly to enhance the probability that "deserving" plaintiffs—that is, victims of personal injury who stand a good chance of establishing another party's liability and collecting substantial damages—will obtain vigorous and effective legal representation. Although one cannot say for sure, there is at least some reason to suspect that this was not the case in earlier decades. In earlier periods, many "deserving" plaintiffs may well have been unable to find capable counsel or may have been unable to afford the work of such counsel as they were able to locate.

These changes probably have not had that much of an effect on the defense side of the bar. Corporate defendants and their insurers have long enjoyed ready access to lawyers of high quality. But the changes on the plaintiffs' side have been immense. They have greatly increased the likelihood that an injured victim will end up as a plaintiff in a tort suit and that the plaintiff in a tort suit will end up making a recovery.

Quality of Legal Services

During the same period, the quality of legal services has also greatly improved, in ways that have increased the likelihood that a victim-plaintiff will end up with a successful outcome to his or her suit. During this period, organizations like the American Trial Lawyers Association have developed a broad array of programs to improve the knowledge and skills of the plaintiffs' bar. Other organizations, like the National Institute for Trial Advocacy have developed programs offering skills training for practicing trial lawyers. Law schools, bar associations, and other groups have instituted programs of continuing legal education. And within the law school curriculum itself, clinical education has received new emphasis.[34]

In practice, lawyers have used the technology of this "information age" to create techniques for pooling information on similar lawsuits, locating effective expert witnesses, sharing information on jury awards, and the like.[35] These efforts have met with particular success in the tort domain, since so many lawsuits involve the same or similar facts—for example, airplane crashes, toxic substances, failed products, hotel fires, and so forth. The factual similarities of the cases, together with improved access to clients, have also enabled a larger number of plaintiffs' trial lawyers to develop particular specialties, where they can hone their skills and knowledge to a sharp edge.

The cumulative effect of these changes has been to increase the competence and sophistication of many segments of the trial bar. There have been notable critics of trial lawyer competence; perhaps the most prominent among them has been former chief justice Warren Burger.[36] But their comments probably reflect more an environment of raised expectations than they do a true decline in lawyer abilities. The simple fact is that lawyers receive a lot more practical training in trial skills, both in law school and after, than they did twenty or thirty years ago.

Improvement in lawyer competence, like increases in the number of lawyers, is, at the outset, a neutral phenomenon, one that does not obviously favor one side of the typical tort case over the other. Defense lawyers can receive practical training in their craft, can share information, and can develop specialties every bit as well as plaintiffs' lawyers. But once again, closer examination reveals a probable pro-plaintiff effect. For decades, insurers and corporate/institutional defendants, through their constant involvement in the defense of tort-law suits, have been able to perform many of the information-pooling and idea-sharing functions that have only recently become available to the plaintiffs' bar. Moreover, as large purchasers of lawyer services, insurers and their corporate clients long have been able to command some of the most highly trained, experienced, and sophisticated legal talent in the nation. Thus, recent advances in skills training and information among trial lawyers probably have had considerably greater positive impact on the quality of legal services available to plaintiffs than they have had for defendants. There have been improvements on both sides, but they have been much sharper, in terms of relative impact, on the plaintiffs' side.

The cumulative effect of these developments has been significantly to increase the prospect that an injured victim will become a plaintiff; that the plaintiff will be successful in his or her suit; and that, if successful, he or she will get a larger damage award or settlement. Even if legal doctrine had remained static during the period (though it has not), these changes alone would have raised the practical "cost" of liability for defendants and their insurers at a pace faster than inflation. Moreover, if, as some have suggested, there has been a "litigation explosion" during the past thirty years,[37] so that a relatively greater proportion of injured victims are motivated to sue, the increase in relative liability cost would be still further augmented.

Procedural Reforms

The improving quality of the plaintiffs' bar has been considerably assisted by developments in civil procedure that have made it easier for plaintiffs' lawyers to win cases. During the second half of the twentieth century, many state court systems have followed the lead of the federal courts by liberalizing pleading and discovery rules in civil actions.[38] These developments have significantly improved plaintiffs' lawyers' access to the information they typically need to mount successful lawsuits, as well as their ability eventually to get that evidence before juries. By increasing the costs of litigation, they have also increased pressures on defendants and their insurers to settle lawsuits before trial.

Other procedural developments have assisted plaintiffs' lawyers in particular kinds of tort cases. The development of the class action, in particular, has facilitated plaintiff recoveries in toxic tort and mass disaster cases.[39] These actions have also been assisted by development of techniques for case consolidation and coordination of discovery.

Related to these procedural developments are some changes in the rules—and more important the practice—of evidence. Perhaps most significant in this regard is the now widespread use of and reliance on expert testimony. Use of experts can vastly expand the range of potential theories of liability, and credible expert witnesses can lend added support to claims for large damage awards.[40] Matters such as lost future wages, the economic effect of a disabling injury, or the costs of future therapy, which were once left largely to unguided juror discretion, are now the subject of explicit numerical projections by experts in the economics of injury.

One other aspect of trial practice that deserves mention is the apparently increasing tendency of trial judges to assume an active role in settlement of cases.[41] Many judges, worried about issues of case management, have assumed a pretrial role as mediator of disputes. Others have experimented with various techniques of alternative dispute resolution. This judicial involvement in case settlement has in turn increased settlement pressure on defendants.[42] No doubt judges pursue this role in as neutral a fashion as possible. But any judicial intervention in the settlement process at all, by increasing settlement pressure, is likely to improve the prospect that plaintiffs will be compensated, thus having a probable net effect of increasing liability costs.

These procedural developments are by no means peculiar to tort cases. But they have nonetheless transformed the way tort actions are tried and settled. Especially when coupled with the advancing sophistication of the trial bar, they have opened up new avenues for successful prosecution of tort claims. Once again, even if tort doctrine had been static during the last twenty or thirty years, these procedural developments probably would have independently operated to increase the costs of liability.

Juries

It has long been an axiom of tort practice that juries tend to sympathize with plaintiffs over defendants. In recent years, this tendency may have been enhanced by increased juror sophistication about tort actions in general and, more specifically, about damage awards. Because of media attention to tort trials and judgments, including such popular television dramatizations as *L.A. Law,* jurors are more likely to be aware of the potential for large damage awards. Because they are aware that other juries, in other cases, have granted large sums of money to successful plaintiffs, they are less likely to be inhibited from doing so themselves.[43] Indeed, with national media attention to the tort system, past regional differences in juror attitude—which may have depressed recoveries in poorer areas or communities where self-reliance was a cultural norm—though still present, may be breaking down.

In addition, innovations in juror selection techniques may enable some lawyers—at least in a few "big-ticket" cases—to enhance juror tendencies toward sympathetic verdicts and large damage awards. Lawyers have obtained the services of psychologists in structuring "profiles" of sympathetic and unsympathetic jurors and then have used voir dire, plus the practice of peremptory strikes to eliminate potentially hostile jurors, and to shape the jury in ways likely to augment its inclination to favor the plaintiff. Lawyers also occasionally use "shadow" juries, from whom they can obtain feedback on their performance, to test the effect of their presentations and guide the development of trial tactics. Most cases are not worth enough to support the expense associated with efforts such as these, but widespread dissemination of information about these techniques has probably improved the sophistication of juror selection generally.

Although juries have often been singled out as "culprits" in the liability insurance crisis, one should not press these observations about jury roles too far. Empirical studies fail to show the sort of lopsided pro-plaintiff jury bias that many trial lawyers and others imagine.[44] And, of course, the juror selection techniques available to plaintiffs' lawyers are available to defense lawyers as well. Nevertheless, there is probably a fair degree of truth to the notion that a jury today is much more intrepid about awarding a large verdict than a jury thirty years ago would have been about a comparable (inflation-adjusted) award.

The factors considered thus far have all been part of the litigation process, and hence, in a sense, part of the tort system. They are, however, features of the process that extend beyond the domains of tort law to include all kinds of litigation. They are rooted in a new vision of trial practice in which parties have full access to a wide range of tools for discovering and establishing the facts needed to prove their case, that has its modern source in the development and implementation of the Federal Rules of Civil Procedure. Both the fact and timing of their development, as well as their continued operation, are at least in part independent of tort doctrine, so that their effect on liability costs would have occurred even without doctrinal change fueled by the insurance rationale. And unless we are prepared to turn our back on the Federal Rules' ideal of trial by fully discovered and professionally advocated fact, the pro-plaintiff impact of these changes is likely to continue into the future even if liability rules themselves are changed.

Medical Technology

In addition to these features of the litigation process, other changes in society have also affected liability costs. Chief among them are advances in medicine and technology.[45]

Advances in American medical technology during the past generation have been extraordinary. They have significantly increased the range and sophistication of medical diagnosis and treatment for all kinds of disorders. Unfortunately, they have also dramatically increased, at levels far in excess of inflation, the cost of even relatively routine medical treatment. Indeed, these increases have recently contributed to another emerging insurance "crisis"—involving health insurance and the delivery of health care—that has captured national attention and that figures prominently in the legislative agenda of the Clinton administration.

Some might claim that the increasing cost of health care is actually itself the result of doctrinal change in tort law. According to this view, doctors, fearing potential liability, engage in so-called defensive medicine, which includes many procedures that the doctors themselves would not order, absent the threat of a malpractice suit if things go wrong.[46] That may be true to some extent. Medical malpractice liability has grown substantially over the past thirty years, and if there is any merit at all to the safety rationale for tort liability, one would expect an increased liability exposure to create incentives for safer medical practice. But the fact remains that the remarkable advances of medical technology, including medical research to develop new diagnoses and treatments, new equipment, new pharmaceuticals, new medical facilities, and the medical training on how to use these technical wonders, are all enormously expensive. A portion of that expense might be attributed to defensive medical tactics, but much of it would be incurred anyway as part of our nation's extraordinary commitment over the past half century to advancing the frontiers of medical knowledge and skill.

The rising cost of medical treatment has had a direct impact on liability costs. When tort victims sue, typically among the larger specific claims they make are claims for medical expenses incurred in the diagnosis and treatment of their personal injury.[47] Thus, the increased costs they have paid to receive the benefits of modern American medicine are often transferred to defendants and their insurers in the form of tort judgments and settlements. Moreover, to the extent that juries use the amount of specific damages as a guide in determining awards for pain and suffering (a practice that trial lore suggests is fairly common), the increases in specific claims for medical treatment can have a double impact. Thus, as medical costs have risen, so have the costs of liability.

Advances in medical research have also added immensely to our knowledge of the causal factors behind certain disorders. In many instances, research has isolated causal factors that can be traced to the products or activities of particular corporations or industries, thus increasing their potential tort liability exposure, sometimes astronomically. Leading examples of this interaction between law and medicine include some of the most significant arenas of tort liability in our generation: for example, asbestos, DES, and injuries from intrauterine devices such as the Dalkon shield. Others, such as environmental harms and hazardous waste, have opened up whole new provinces of civil liability. Thus, medical research has facilitated recovery for injuries that, without advances in medical knowledge, might never have made it into the tort system.

National Wealth

Another important factor contributing to the cost of liability has been the national increase in real wealth experienced over the past thirty years. During that period, real wealth and average incomes have outpaced inflation: the nation has grown richer.[48] Probably the chief factor in this increase in wealth is the increase in real wages earned by many employees. Of course, if a wage earner's salary increases faster than inflation, then so should compensation for loss of that salary when the wage earner is injured through a defendant's tortious behavior. And this factor, too, might have a double impact if juries use economic loss as a guide for calculating pain and suffering.

Changes in national wealth may have a more general and indirect impact on liability costs as well. A society in which wealth is growing is likely to be more sympathetic to compensation for those who have been injured—it is easier to share a portion of a growing pie than a shrinking pie. And to the extent that jurors themselves are familiar with or aspire to a higher standard of living, they probably are more sympathetic to claims for the larger amounts of damages that will afford an equivalent standard of living to injured plaintiffs.

Toxic Tort Disasters

Finally, one must factor into analysis the distorting effect of a few major tort law "disasters" that have made disproportionate contribution to the cost of liability in last two decades.[49] Probably the most remarkable among these is the tragic saga of asbestos. According to some accounts, the dangers associated with asbestos have been known, at least to some manufacturers and perhaps their insurers, for decades. Nevertheless, despite knowledge that might arguably satisfy even fairly rigid definitions of negligence, manufacturers took very few, if any, steps to avert potential liability, and their insurers dramatically underestimated the scope of their exposure.[50] When independent medical research in the early 1970s finally demonstrated the link between asbestos exposure and certain very serious, debilitating, and often fatal diseases, the result was a still-growing tidal wave of tort actions against manufacturers and users of asbestos products.[51] These cases have already produced judgments and settlements in the hundreds of millions of dollars, and some observers estimate that the defendants and their insurers ultimately will face billions more in liability.[52] Liability costs have already forced several once-thriving firms into bankruptcy, and others are likely to follow.[53]

Although the most immediate casualties of the asbestos liability tidal wave have been manufacturers, since the mid-1980s it has become increasingly clear that insurers also face a huge exposure.[54] But the extremely modest insurance premiums they charged the manufacturers for past coverage and investment income from those premiums will not begin to cover the ultimate costs. Thus, if insurers (including some major carriers) who underwrote asbestos liability in the past are to remain solvent in the future, they must find a way of spreading that cost to their other insureds, probably in the form of radically higher future liability insurance premiums.[55] Of course, asbestos is only one, albeit the worst, example of these liability "disasters." The emerging field of "toxic torts" is riddled with other situations where defendants and their insurers dramatically underestimated their potential exposure to liability.

In these instances, insurers simply have failed to perform their function. They have failed to predict the magnitude of exposure, and thus they have failed to spread losses in advance by charging appropriate premiums. The insurers would argue, however, that the failure was caused by changes in liability rules—and indeed some of the important doctrinal changes mentioned in Part II have greatly facilitated recovery in asbestos and similar cases. But the evidence also suggests that the insurers' mistakes in these cases may have as much, if not more, to do with an extraordinary failure to predict the frequency and severity of probable injury—the accident rate, not the liability rate. To the extent that is true, liability costs resulting from these disasters represent an unusual drain on insurer resources from a mistake that underwriters (one hopes) are unlikely to make again. If so, they amount to an extraordinary, one-time addition to premium increases.

To identify these other causes of disproportionate recent increases in the cost of liability is not, of course, to disprove the existence of *any* causal contribution by changes in liability rules. Indeed, that would prove too much. If there is any force to the insurance rationale at all, it follows that the adoption of such a rationale *should* have an expansive effect on liability, imposing it where, without the rationale, it would not have been imposed. Indeed, the same can be said of any rationale for the extension of liability, including safety. If we believe that the tort regime that existed prior to the 1960s, with its bevy of immunities (such as charitable and governmental immunity), defenses (such as contributory negligence and assumption of risk), no-duty rules (such as those applying to occupiers of land), restrictive notions of causation, and overly moralistic conceptions of fault, artificially depressed the level of liability for many producers, then we would expect the elimination of these barriers to compensation to correspond with a significant increase in the liability burden. Thus, *some* increase in liability, and hence in the cost of liability insurance, must be viewed as a natural, expected, and even potentially desirable outcome of the development of modern tort doctrine. The questions are how much of an increase is necessary and whether the perceived benefits of the doctrinal change are worth that price.

What consideration of these other factors does accomplish is to reduce the *magnitude* of the effect on recent liability costs and insurance premiums that can be confidently attributed to tort doctrine and the insurance rationale. Although it is true that we do not know exactly how much, a significant portion of the recent increases in liability insurance premiums must be attributed to the other causal factors mentioned above. If that is true, and if there is any merit at all to the business-cycle explanation offered by the trial lawyers, then the effect on liability costs of the adoption of the insurance rationale starts to look considerably more modest than many proponents of tort reform suppose.

The net effect of entertaining these other considerations is to reduce the perceived impact of tort doctrine in general and the insurance rationale in particular from a "crisis" to a more manageable dilemma. A general rise in liability costs should have been an expected result from the tort developments of the last three decades. The more precipitous increase that actually occurred was produced, at least in part, by social factors distinct from the insurance rationale, many of which are unlikely to recur. Moreover, because of the cyclical nature of the insurance industry, even these effects were probably exaggerated by the relatively sharp economic fluctuations that occurred in the last decade—a decade, it should be noted, that produced severe dislocations in other financial industries, such as securities firms, savings and loan institutions, and banks, for which changes in tort liability surely were not the cause.[56]

Consequently, careful evaluation of recent trends fails to support the prospect of unstoppable, wildly spiraling upward pressure on insurance rates. Instead, a more likely prediction is a gradual increase in liability costs over time, albeit one that proceeds by business-cycle fits and starts. Eventually, as the point of maximum implementation of the insurance rationale approaches, these costs should start to level out. We must still debate the desirability of these increasing costs. But the evidence does not suggest that a true "crisis point" has been reached.

NINE

The Insurance Rationale Reconsidered

Even though the hikes in liability premiums during the last decade do not establish a true crisis, this still seems to be an appropriate time to give thorough reconsideration to the insurance rationale. Several factors support this conclusion. This is probably the first point in our nation's history when we have accumulated sufficient experience with practical application of the insurance rationale to observe, even partially, its effect. Only since the widespread development of products liability law in the 1970s can it be said that the American tort system has given anything like a substantial embrace to the insurance rationale. Interestingly, this is also the first point at which the rationale has been subject to mature theoretical challenge. Further, although economic and social factors outside the tort system made it possible to imagine, during the 1960s and 1970s, that the insurance rationale was a relatively "costless" social policy, we now know that almost certainly is not true. And finally, given the intense campaign to change tort law—one that has even had its impact on the national legislative agenda—the social policies behind liability have become a live political issue, forcing us to determine where we stand. Only by reassessment of the insurance rationale can we formulate a thoughtful and coherent response to insurer and corporate-funded lobbying for tort reform.

Since there are now two sides to the debate, that reassessment can perhaps best proceed by attempting to evaluate the contemporary validity of the arguments for and against the insurance rationale. To what extent are the critics right in finding fault with the insurance rationale as a criterion of tort liability? To what extent are the latter-day disciples of the realists right in pressing for acceptance and even expansion of the insurance rationale? Since the critics have held most of the initiative in the last decade, perhaps it is best to begin with their assertions.

The Contemporary Insurance Critique

Forced Insurance

As described above, the critics argue that imposition of tort liability under an insurance rationale forces consumers to purchase insurance they do not want.[1] In evaluating this argument, one should note that, at bottom, it depends heavily on a preference for freedom of choice over assured compensation as a systemic value. In this view, the consumer should be able to choose the amount of insurance protection he or she wants, and we should be willing to tolerate some victims going uncompensated in order to extend that freedom of choice. As such, this argument represents simply a preference of one value over another. Since the values themselves cannot be converted to any common scale, a preference for one over another is neither "right" nor "wrong," though it may tell us a great deal about who we are. One can do little more than note the preference and register agreement or disagreement with it.

Nevertheless, certain observations may guide our decision whether to agree or disagree. First, there is considerable evidence in the United States of a democratic preference for compensation over choice in many settings.[2] Society often forces us, by legislative fiat, to buy insurance in order to protect ourselves and/or others from catastrophe. Examples abound in, near, and outside the tort system, including bank deposit insurance, flood insurance for people who dwell along the shore or in low-lying flood plains, compulsory motor vehicle insurance, workers' compensation, unemployment insurance, social security, and a variety of compulsory medical insurance programs.[3] They also include various kinds of tax-funded government programs to compensate victims of injury, such as disaster relief programs, government-funded bailout of failed financial institutions, veterans' and disability benefits, and legislative extensions of unemployment benefits during steep economic recessions. Essentially, in these programs the government charges us a tax "premium" in exchange for assured access to the program's benefits if we fall victim to the harm the program in question was designed to alleviate. Indeed, it seems fair to say that funding systems of assured compensation for victims of harm has become one of the primary functions of the modern democratic welfare state. Thus, one should not blithely assume that this nation, however steeped in the principles of individual liberty, is fully committed to the notion of free choice with regard to protection from injury or catastrophe.

Second, the forced-insurance argument, by positing the undesirability of third-party insurance structured as a cost of business, ultimately seeks a return to the ideology of the late nineteenth century. Played to its logical end, this position leads to the conclusion that defendants ought not to be able to insure against *any* losses from liability—or at least, if they do, they ought to be prohibited from passing the cost on to consumers—because by this definition *any* such insurance ends up being "forced," from the consumers' perspective, when its cost is attached to the price of a product or service. The only way to ensure that consumers have full power of choice over their insurance destiny would be to outlaw third-party insurance entirely. Consequently, any advocate who is willing to tolerate liability insurance at some point is also willing to tolerate some level of "forced insurance" for consumers. The question becomes at what point, and why, not whether.

Third, the forced-insurance argument theoretically operates only where the insurance rationale pushes liability beyond the limits of the safety rationale. Where the safety rationale suffices to justify liability, accident avoidance, not insurance, is the objective of the system and the theoretically predicted response. In theory, defendants will insure only where efficient cost avoidance is impossible. Given judicial reluctance to use the insurance rationale as a freestanding justification for liability, the forced-insurance phenomenon occurs, if at all, in only a relative handful of cases at the outer edges of tort liability. In all others, the defendant either made a bad business decision (preferring insurance to an available but unused cheaper cost-avoidance alternative) or simply covered for uncertainty about the degree of risk associated with a particular activity. In neither of these instances can the phenomenon of liability insurance, or its cost, be attributed to the compensation objective behind the insurance rationale.

The forced-insurance argument also contains some significant assumptions, at least a few of which may be of doubtful validity. Perhaps the most prominent of these is the assumption that consumers have sharply different levels of risk preference with respect to the products or services that they buy.[4] At some level, differences in risk preference almost surely exist. Some of us, for example, choose to buy automobiles loaded with safety devices, whereas others buy models that are sportier or cheaper, but also more dangerous. One reason this happens may well be that we place different values on the risk of being injured in an automobile accident.

But the degree of variance in our risk preferences, in relation to variance in product or service safety, is important. If the variance occurs only with respect to differences in risk that a tort system with the insurance rationale in place would tolerate, then those variances should be of no particular concern. For example, Justice Traynor's concurrence in *Escola* posited that we all expect products we buy to be reasonably safe for their intended use. That could be true, yet still leave room for substantial variation in risk preference *above that floor*. If so, a liability rule that "forced" insurance at the shared level of risk preference would in fact make no serious inroads in our freedom of choice about risk.

Also, one has to be very careful not to read as a difference in risk preference what is actually a difference in information about risk. Many consumers probably systematically *underestimate* risk associated with the products or services they buy, and others probably *overestimate* the same risks. They do this, not because they have different preferences regarding the risks in question, but rather because they are making different predictions of the degree of risk itself. And the chief explanation for the variance in their predictions is that they are all exercising judgment without sufficient facts.

To return to the example of the automobile, one decision consumers have had to make in recent years is whether to purchase automobiles equipped with air bags, which protect against head injuries in cases of head-on collision. But how many of us really know what our risk of being involved in such a collision really is? It seems plausible that many who choose not to purchase an air bag do so because they believe (without much information to support that belief) that the risk is small, whereas others purchase the air bag because they believe (with no better source of information) that the risk is large. If so, one could not confidently conclude that their different choices proceeded from different risk preferences, as opposed to different (and largely untutored) assumptions about the level of risk itself.

Indeed, the latter observation highlights another assumption undergirding the risk-preference argument: that consumers having different risk preferences have adequate information to gauge those preferences with respect to particular products or services. Sometimes this may be true—for example, I probably have a pretty good idea about most of the dangers that lurk in a toothbrush or a bar of soap, although even these common household objects probably present some medical risks of which I am unaware. But in other cases, both the identity of the danger and its likelihood are virtually unknown, even to someone who makes his livelihood out of studying risk—the risks of injury from the emanations of the computer screen on which I first drafted these words come quickly to mind as an example.[5] Unless we can be confident that consumers are well acquainted with all risks associated with a particular product or service, we cannot presume that risk preferences are accurately registered in the market.

Yet a third, probably flawed assumption is that individuals' risk *choices* accurately reflect their true risk *preferences*. As proponents of the insurance rationale have often observed, people have a psychological tendency, even where they know of risks, to underestimate the probability of the risk happening to *them*. Part of what gets most of us through life is that we overestimate the likelihood of good things happening (state lotteries and private gaming halls thrive on that empirical fact) and underestimate the likelihood of bad things happening. Thus, the tort system cannot count on us to be rational actors with respect to our own risk preferences.[6]

Finally, still another assumption of the forced-insurance argument is that individuals who wish to insure against the hazards of injury caused by others could find an alternative to the insurance they are now allegedly forced to buy. As is more fully developed in the next section, there are reasons to doubt that an adequate first-party alternative to third-party liability insurance is in fact available. Even if we subscribed to the forced-insurance argument, before acting on our belief we would have to have some assurance that such a first-party alternative was available for those who desired protection.

The dubious character of some of these assumptions suggests that the forced-insurance argument is seriously flawed—or perhaps more to the point—that it is more rhetorical than real. Ultimately, this argument breaks down into an assault on the importance of compensation for injury, rather than an honest attempt to achieve that compensation by a different, more voluntary route.

First-Party Versus Third-Party Insurance

If they care about compensation at all, those who assert the forced-insurance argument also argue in favor of a first-party, instead of a third-party, regime of accident insurance. In this they are joined by other critics who, though willing to impose obligatory insurance in some cases, are nonetheless opposed to liability insurance as an inefficient vehicle for compensation. The key to the first-party argument is the belief that first-party insurance, by avoiding the steep transfer costs of tort litigation, will achieve substantial administrative savings that will bring the total cost of accident compensation down without sacrificing the goal of effective compensation for injury.[7]

In theory, the argument has considerable initial appeal. As anyone having even passing familiarity with tort litigation knows, the transfer costs associated with accident compensation by that route are huge. If they could be avoided, the system could, in theory at least, deliver a much higher portion of the insurance premium dollar into the hands of the victim in the form of compensation. And if we could manage to pull that off, victims, corporations, institutions, *and* insurers would be better off; only the lawyers would complain.

Additionally, first-party insurance could greatly facilitate the speed of compensation.[8] That is of significant value in itself, especially when one considers that in some court systems tort litigation can take years before victims' claims are brought to judgment. And if we share the concerns of the forced-insurance advocates, first-party insurance could be structured to allow consumers some level of choice in the amount of protection furnished.

In practice, American experimentation with first-party insurance as an alternative to third-party liability insurance has not been very successful.[9] The "no-fault" automobile insurance movement that enjoyed considerable popularity in the 1970s was essentially an attempt, in the sphere of automobile accidents, to replace a regime of third-party liability insurance with a first-party alternative. Beginning with Massachusetts in 1971, several states enacted legislation that required motorists to purchase so-called no-fault insurance. In the case of an accident, each motorist would look to his or her own insurance policy for coverage of resulting injury or property damage, without regard to the other driver's fault. Tort actions against the other driver(s) involved in the accident would not be permitted in most instances. For a few years, no-fault insurance was extremely popular, and several other states adopted their own no-fault systems. The .movement toward no-fault auto insurance quickly ran out of gas, however, and it came to a virtual halt in the 1980s, principally because the promised cost savings failed to materialize; in fact, in some states the no-fault approach appeared to drive insurance costs up instead of down.[10] Although an elective version of automotive no-fault insurance is experiencing a modest revival of sorts in the early 1990s,[11] the lackluster historical experience with first-party alternatives in the automotive field requires us to take the claims of first-party advocates with at least a grain of salt.

One should be cautious about drawing any broad conclusions from the automobile no-fault experiment, however. The programs that were actually instituted in most states were really hybrids that used first-party insurance for some auto accidents but retained the third-party liability system for the more serious (and costly) cases.[12] Consequently, they failed to attain the theoretical advantage of eliminating the transfer costs of litigation, which is the heart and soul of the first-party thesis. Many injured motorists who would have been likely to sue before the no-fault system was inaugurated remained equally able and therefore likely to sue after the new system was in place. In the few instances where a much purer form of first-party insurance has been tried, the results have been more successful.[13]

There are, however, some serious problems with the first-party thesis. At least as a proposal for immediate reform, it shares with the forced-insurance argument the assumption that a satisfactory first-party alternative is available. This assumption, though not entirely without foundation, requires careful examination.

There are certainly some kinds of first-party insurance widely available today that protect against the costs of accidents. Accident insurance itself provides protection against certain specific forms of injury and/or death. Life insurance protects against accidents that result in death. Health insurance covers medical expenses that may be incurred in the treatment of accidents. Disability insurance covers losses in employment compensation that may result from a disabling accident. Some forms of auto insurance provide first-party coverage for injury to persons or property resulting from vehicular accidents. Moreover, these kinds of insurance are readily available. Most Americans probably either have or could purchase most of these kinds of insurance.

But this is piecemeal coverage, not comprehensive coverage. As such, it carries significant difficulties of its own that call into question its adequacy as an alternative. Only by a careful dovetailing of policy coverages, which is arguably beyond the abilities or inclinations of most consumers, could one, by selective purchase of multiple lines of insurance, obtain anything close to comprehensive protection from accidental injury caused through the activities of others. Moreover, it is probably inevitable that such a Byzantine method of obtaining protection would entail significant policy overlaps—duplicative protection that would add to the cost and deplete the efficiency of this form of protection. Further inefficiency would be introduced by the separate marketing of these different kinds of insurance protection and by the separate claims administration of the various policies one would have to purchase. One should bear in mind that just as litigation costs eat up premium dollars, so do sales commissions and insurer overhead. We should be careful lest we end up simply transferring the lawyer's "take" from the existing system to the insurance agent and/or claims adjuster under a clumsy, multiple-line first-party alternative.

Perhaps even more important, existing first-party alternatives leave significant gaps in coverage relative to third-party liability insurance. In dollar amounts, probably the largest of those gaps involves protection for pain and suffering. Recovery for pain and suffering is one of the most substantial elements of tort damage recoveries. So far as I am aware, with perhaps the limited exception of some kinds of accident insurance, where lump-sum benefits seem to be scaled to some degree according to the severity of injuries, *no* existing first-party line includes protection for this element. Similarly, other kinds of damage recognized in the tort system—loss of consortium comes to mind—would go uncompensated in a system dependent on existing types of first-party coverage.

Whether this is a serious deficiency or not depends on whether the reduction in compensation can be justified by some offsetting benefit to the victim, such as speed or certainty of compensation.[14] It also depends on how one feels about the validity of the elements of coverage that a first-party system dependent on existing forms of insurance would omit. Thus, not surprisingly, some commentators who prefer a first-party approach also minimize the real significance of pain and suffering as an item of damages. Since pain and suffering is a bogus element of damages anyway, they argue, omitting it from the scale of first-party recoveries does no real harm.[15]

This argument goes too far. To be sure, pain and suffering is one of the more unpredictable elements in the traditional tort damage calculus. But unpredictability is not tantamount to invalidity. The tort system compensates many losses that do not have a strict dollar-and-cents character to them and thus are difficult to quantify, such as emotional distress, psychological trauma, invasion of privacy, loss of reputation, even loss of consortium. Pain and suffering is no less a legitimate factor than these. Moreover, it may well have an economic impact, albeit one that can be difficult to quantify. People who experience pain can lose their concentration, their creativity, their productivity, even their nerve, all of which can interfere with their ability to engage successfully in various productive life activities. In any event, the institution of first-party insurance seems an awfully roundabout way of limiting recoveries for pain and suffering. If pain and suffering really is an illegitimate form of recovery, the age-old principle of Ockham's razor would suggest that we deal with the problem directly, by reforming damages law, rather than indirectly, by changing liability rules.

Except for its transfer-cost avoidance potential, the first-party thesis also fails to make a case for consumers as "better" insurers of accidents. The lack of a single, comprehensive package of personal insurance against injury by third parties defeats any claim that consumers enjoy an advantage of accessibility over producers. And while the likelihood that consumers will purchase the kinds of first-party insurance that are available is no doubt substantially greater than it was forty years ago, first-party protection for the ravages of injury is by no means universal. Many millions of individuals in our society do not possess adequate amounts of health insurance—probably the most basic of the first-party lines—and upwardly spiraling costs in that line are currently forcing further contractions in coverage. Indeed, the gaps in coverage have widened to the point where some form of governmentally mandated national health insurance may emerge as the only realistic option. Other kinds of coverage (life and disability insurance come to mind) are either completely unavailable or prohibitively expensive for individuals who are either ill or infirm. Moreover, first-party protection for economic loss from injury—after pain and suffering, probably the largest ingredient of the typical tort judgment—is very spotty indeed. For example, most people do not purchase disability insurance even when it is available to them.

As a consequence, if we were to shift to a first-party system that depended on existing insurance arrangements, large numbers of accident victims would lose large amounts, perhaps even all, of the coverage they now have from third-party sources. Those individuals experiencing the sharpest gaps in protection, moreover, would include the poor, the elderly, the ill, and the unemployed—the people in society least likely to have other assets they could turn to in order to absorb the impact of catastrophic loss.

Another important danger of relying on first-party insurance is the lack of information consumers have about the risks they run. Consumers can be better insurers only if they (or the underwriters whose policies they purchase) can predict with some accuracy what their risk of accident is likely to be, and only if they can be effectively sorted into different classifications bearing different degrees of risk. Neither seems likely at current levels of information.[16] As I observed above, most of us have virtually no idea how much risk we run from the mix of products and services we buy. Nor would our insurers have any idea how to predict in advance the riskiness of our behavior and activities, relative to that of other consumers in the marketplace. Even if they could, it is doubtful that insurers would have sufficient economic motivation to do so, since the process of collecting and analyzing the data necessary to make such predictions would be enormously expensive.[17]

Indeed, the lack of information for calibrating the riskiness of consumer behavior points up another difficulty with the first-party alternative. With only a few exceptions, existing forms of first-party insurance fail to segregate the risk of accident from other forms of risk.[18] Most of the lines of insurance mentioned above cover a multitude of risks beyond the risk of injuries from the activities of others. Health insurance, for example, covers hospital and doctor bills for all forms of illness or injury, regardless of the cause. Moreover, most of these forms of first-party insurance, which are usually sold in some form of group coverage, fail to make any but the crudest of classifications on the basis of relative risk. They might segregate a few particularly risky actors into separate categories—the skydivers and hang gliders among us, for example—but they usually do not differentiate degrees of risk among more normal users of products and services. Consequently, first-party loss spreading is likely to be a relatively blunt instrument, one that does not segregate and classify according to degrees of risk, but rather lumps nearly all consumers together in a single risk category. If these existing lines were adapted for use as a first-party alternative, it is unlikely that rates would (or perhaps even could) be set according the risk of injury associated with the products or services used by a particular insured.

Such a shotgun approach to insurance would obfuscate, if not completely sever, the link between the cost of insurance and the riskiness of particular conduct. In doing so, it might well, in the pursuit of a litigation-avoiding form of compensation, defeat the goal of deterring unsafe conduct. The "moral hazard" critics of third-party insurance bewail would reappear with a vengeance.[19] Consumers, unable to perceive any relation between insurance costs and conduct, would lose any direct or clear economic incentive to gauge the safety of their behavior or of the products and services they used.[20]

Finally, consumers lack bargaining power with insurers.[21] Accordingly, they are much less able than large corporations and institutions to demand needed changes in coverage, to insist on adjustment of standard policies to fit their particular needs (even if they know what those are), or to shop for coverage among competing underwriters. This lack of bargaining capacity raises a specter of insurer overreaching that could (as it may have done in the case of auto no-fault) devour the savings that eliminating the costs of litigation might otherwise have brought about.

The first-party approach also raises difficult questions about how to pursue safety. The main benefit of first-party insurance comes from its theoretical ability to eliminate the costs of litigation. But if the no-fault auto insurance experience shows anything, it is that savings of transfer costs will not accrue unless options for litigation are sharply curtailed, if not eliminated completely. If we do that, however, corporations and others who produce dangerous products or engage in dangerous activities will be effectively immunized by a strict first-party system from the consequences of their actions, thus losing *their* incentive to invest in efficient cost-avoidance techniques. As Guido Calabresi observed during the auto-compensation-plan debate of the 1960s, by finding a more direct mechanism for compensation, we may run the risk of sacrificing the ability of the system to deter socially unacceptable unsafe conduct.[22]

Of course, we could deal with these problems by erecting some kind of a hybrid system, one that depends on first-party insurance as the primary source of compensation but allows some litigation for recovery against third parties to achieve deterrence, perhaps through some enhanced doctrine of insurer subrogation. But such a system, like auto no-fault systems that permit tort suits for injuries above a certain threshold, risks sacrifice of the initial theoretical benefits of first-party insurance. There will still be litigation; there will still be transfer costs; there will still be corporate and institutional uncertainty about the scope of potential liability for enterprise activities; and there will still be a need for corporations and institutions to maintain third-party liability insurance. The system might end up looking remarkably like the one we have now, with overlapping first- and third-party insurance, liability rules that attempt to balance compensation between these two sources, and a great deal of expensive bickering by both sides about who has the responsibility to pay in individual cases.

Yet another alternative for restoring a measure of deterrence is the one advanced by Stephen Sugarman.[23] We could replace the general deterrence system of tort law with a more specific, governmentally administered system of fines for dangerous conduct.[24] Just as the Environmental Protection Agency fines producers who put dangerous pollutants into our air and water, a government-run "Public Safety Agency," or the like, could fine producers (or others) who engage in risky injurious conduct. There are at least two major difficulties with this solution, however. The first is the obvious cost of setting up yet another government bureaucracy to manage our affairs, with all the attendant inefficiencies and expenses we have come to know so well. The other difficulty is that the agency would inevitably be responsible for a huge range of human conduct, and it would have to invest a great deal of money and energy into figuring out the right amounts of deterrence for each dangerous activity, as well as spending further resources in detecting and prosecuting violators. Once these considerations are taken into account, it is difficult to forecast with any confidence that such an option would produce any significant transaction-cost savings over our present system, clumsy and costly as it is.

The point of these observations is not to reject the first-party alternative outright but to suggest that it is by no means a panacea and that it brings problems of its own that will require careful and sophisticated planning to avoid. In particular, it seems reasonably clear that *existing* forms of first-party insurance are not a particularly good vehicle for instituting reform. Rather, if a first-party alternative is to be pursued, it should be accompanied by the development of some new form of accident insurance that operates independently of existing first-party coverages and that attempts, from the consumer perspective, to cover risks—especially medical costs, lost wages and other economic loss, and whatever level of noneconomic compensation for pain and suffering we are prepared to acknowledge as legitimate—that are the same as or similar to those now handled by third-party liability insurance. It should also include careful thought about how to deter unsafe conduct without incurring the same levels of administrative expense we now encounter, and perhaps it should include more aggressive regulation of insurer marketing and claims administration to protect against inefficiency and overreaching. In other words, a move to first-party insurance for accidents would entail a major social undertaking and a huge commitment of governmental resources.

Unpredictability

This argument asserts that pursuit of the insurance rationale has rendered insurance markets unstable by interfering with insurers' ability to predict risks.[25] The argument is undoubtedly correct in its assertion that tort developments over the past thirty years have engendered a significant measure of unpredictability. This has been a dynamic period in which the contours of tort doctrine have changed rapidly. Any such change is bound to disturb the equilibrium between past and future necessary to accurate actuarial prediction of liability risks. Insurers, of course, use "confidence factors"—a lay observer would probably call them "fudge factors"—in an attempt to adjust for this disruption, but the effect is to switch the underwriting process from statistical empiricism to educated guesswork. This inevitably increases the risks of variability and error in those predictions.

The critics are also surely right to suggest that this unpredictability has had a deleterious effect on insurance markets in recent years. Once again, the tragic tale of asbestos graphically demonstrates the degree to which underwriters' predictions gone awry can wreak havoc on insurance markets.[26] The critics are less clearly correct when they assert that the unpredictability evident in the system is caused by judicial adoption of the insurance rationale and that continued acceptance of the insurance rationale in its current form will lead to perpetual uncertainty.

Unpredictability in the tort compensation system stems from at least four principal sources: unclear doctrine; doctrine that, however clear, affords immense discretion to fact finders to produce divergent results in similar cases; constantly changing doctrine; and dynamic changes in the social environment that alter the effect of clear and stable doctrine. In the last thirty years, American tort law has experienced all four of these phenomena in unprecedented degrees. But the links between these sources of unpredictability and the insurance rationale are either attenuated or unlikely to continue into the future.

There is nothing inherent in the insurance rationale that produces unclear legal rules. Determining liability by finding the best insurer (the standard that unqualified pursuit of the insurance rationale would lead to) is no less certain a method of setting legal rules than assessing liability by finding the cheapest cost avoider.[27] Both contain a measure of uncertainty because they require case-by-case assessments using a balancing process. As a result, both approaches end up investing substantial discretion in fact finders, who are capable of reaching highly divergent conclusions on similar sets of facts. This is a real source of uncertainty, but it is a kind of uncertainty the tort system has never escaped. If it is enough to make insurance markets unravel, then there is simply no hope for liability insurance under any readily imaginable doctrinal regime.

Indeed, if critics were correct in asserting that the insurance rationale pushes toward "absolute" liability, the insurance rationale ironically would emerge as much the clearer determinant of liability. There is no more *clear* legal rule than one that imposes liability for all the consequences of one's actions. It eliminates all but the amount of the victim's damages and some fairly rarified questions of causation as sources of uncertainty. Nor would a return to a world dominated by what Holmes called the "featureless generality" of the negligence standard produce any greater doctrinal clarity. One could, of course, argue that the negligence standard, however uncertain in individual circumstances, is "clear" because its effects are familiar, but that argument confuses clarity with stability. Familiar uncertainty seems "clear" to us, not because it is, but because through a long process of trial and error we have learned how to adjust for its vicissitudes.

There is also no reason, however, to believe that liability predicated on the ability to insure yields inherently unstable legal doctrine. It probably did contribute some instability to the system in the recent past, since its partial adoption required substantial revision of existing tort doctrine. To the extent that revision was unforeseen by underwriters, who assumed a static, rather than a dynamic, legal environment in their projections, adoption of the insurance rationale may have produced unanticipated increases in loss experience. But there is no reason to think that condition is necessarily permanent. The same phenomenon would occur in any period in which changing policies were reflected by changing legal doctrine. Yet once the new policy was fully articulated in a new set of legal rules, stability would be restored. Doctrine would stabilize at new levels of liability, underwriter prediction would catch up, and loss experience would become as fully predictable as before.

There is nothing in the insurance rationale that would prohibit the attainment of such stability at new liability levels. Once "best insurers" are determined for various recurring kinds of injury, once the places in the system where we are willing to rely on best-insurer status as a factor in fixing liability are established, once the degree of that reliance is set, and once legal rules that impede effective cost spreading without serving adequate countervailing policies are eliminated—in other words, once the process of adopting the insurance rationale and fitting it into our scale of tort compensation policies is complete—the period of instability should end.

Furthermore, to the extent that there has been unpredictability in liability insurance markets during the past two or three decades, much of it must be assigned to the relatively extraneous social factors mentioned in the previous chapter. If *these* are the causes of unacceptable levels of unpredictability, altering legal rules for assessing tort liability is both an inefficient and probably an ineffective method of addressing them. It would be much better if the extraneous causes of unpredictability were addressed directly, rather than by the roundabout process of trying to adjust unrelated or only indirectly related legal rules in an effort somehow to account for their effects.

Taken together, these observations yield an important conclusion about the unpredictability thesis. What this argument addresses is not a problem engendered by the insurance doctrine per se but rather a problem engendered by *any* rapid change in tort doctrine, whatever its source. From this perspective, the main thing we need to do to achieve predictability is to stabilize legal rules at some liability level and then to let insurers develop sufficient familiarity with their loss experience under those rules to predict their exposure accurately. Moreover, the need for predictability tells us nothing about what *level* of predictable exposure is optimally desirable. The unpredictability argument, in other words, is an argument about the *pace* of change, not about its direction or the forces that drive it.

Unpredictability in the direction of greater exposure hurts the profitability of insurers, whereas unpredictability in the direction of reduced exposure produces windfalls for them. Thus, it is not too surprising that insurers should complain of unpredictability only in periods of expanding protection for victims. But from the public perspective, neither form of unpredictability is particularly desirable, since both produce economic dislocation and inefficiency. Accordingly, the key lesson of the unpredictability argument is that in any insurance-backed system of tort compensation, the need for accurate predictions of risk by underwriters militates in favor of evolutionary, rather than revolutionary, change in the substance of legal doctrines. The need to insure the predictability of risk should leaven the vigor with which we pursue any new policies we choose to implement, whatever their content. It does not, however, contribute much to our discussion of what the content of those policies should be.

Adverse Selection

The adverse selection theme argues that use of the insurance rationale interferes with effective risk classification, causing "good" risks to leave the insurance market, thus preventing insurers from engaging in effective loss spreading. As with many other criticisms of the insurance rationale, evaluation of this argument requires careful attention to some of its underlying assumptions.

Preliminarily, this argument necessarily assumes that corporate actors are able to predict risks with a reasonable degree of accuracy. Otherwise, it would be impossible for "good" risks to tell that they are "good." The adverse selection thesis is, accordingly, at war with the unpredictability thesis discussed above, which asserts the opposite. It is perhaps some evidence of the rhetorical flavor of the debate over tort reform that at least some critics simultaneously advocate both the unpredictability and the adverse selection arguments, apparently without realizing the internal conflict in their fundamental empirical assumptions.

Of equal interest is the fact that the adverse selection argument presumes significant variation of risk among competitors who are producing essentially the same products or services. It is impossible for "good risks" to sort themselves out of the insurance pool unless there are, in fact, relatively "good" risks out there. And the "good" risks cannot be "good" unless they can produce the same quality goods or services, at competitive prices, yet more safely than their "bad" (that is, more risky) competitors. This assumption further depends on the critical subsidiary assumption that these "good" risks are "good" because they are making cost-efficient investments in safety that others in the same business are failing to make. Or, to put the point the other way, the "bad" risks out there are "bad" because they are not investing in optimal levels of safety. This, in turn, means that the higher levels of liability experienced by the "bad" risks are fully justified under the traditional safety rationale for tort liability. Learned Hand's famous *Carroll Towing* formula[28] would impose liability on them for their decision to forgo efficient safety measures.

Once these critical assumptions are recognized, the adverse selection theme turns out to have little, if anything, to do with the insurance rationale.

If there is in fact adverse selection going on, it is a phenomenon fully attributable to the *safety* rationale for tort liability, *not* the insurance rationale. Indeed, if we eliminated the insurance rationale tomorrow but kept a fully implemented safety rationale, the conditions that produce adverse selection would remain a feature of our tort system. Thus, it appears that adverse selection, if it is a problem, is not really a problem that can be placed at the doorstep of the insurance rationale, but rather one that stems from the decision to use a safety-oriented socioeconomic cost-benefit calculus for measuring liability.

Moreover, to the extent adverse selection is a problem, it arises not from the structure of our tort system, but rather from the structure of the system of private liability insurance that happens to accompany it. From a tort perspective, society really does not care if the better cost spreader (who in practice is probably also, as noted above, the cheaper cost avoider) spreads the loss through participation in a commercial insurance pool or by self-insurance[29] or by any other method. All we care is that the spreading occur by some reasonably effective means. The more cost-efficient the method is for the individual actor, the more we should like it. If self-insurance is a cheaper form of cost spreading for some actors, we should applaud their choice of that mechanism, even if insurers (who would have preferred the actor to buy their higher-priced protection) complain.

The decision by good risks to drop out of the insurance pool and self-insure will raise costs of spreading for "bad" risks, making their goods or services more expensive. But since they are bad risks only because of their suboptimal investment in safety, their increased insurance costs ought (in a reasonably competitive environment) to enhance the bad risks' motivation to seek out more cost-efficient safety investments. This, in turn, will reduce their accident costs, making them look more like the good risks, thus bringing their insurance costs back down and ultimately reducing the good risks' incentive to opt out of the insurance pool. In other words, at least in theory, adverse selection should be at most a temporary problem; the system should be capable of self-correction.

The only problem of consequence to the tort system arises if adverse selection becomes so severe that some parties who are reasonably safe actors (that is, good risks), but who lack the size and sophistication to self-insure, are also unable to procure affordable insurance because they remain stuck in a pool populated principally by more dangerous (that is, bad-risk) actors. There is some evidence that this may have happened in a few places during the late 1970s and early 1980s. Perhaps most notable were instances where doctors and other medical professionals decided to "go bare" (that is, drop insurance coverage) because they found the cost of medical malpractice insurance prohibitive.[30] But it is interesting to note that the most prominent occurrences of this type involved categories of tort law, such as medical malpractice, where courts have been relatively resistant to the insurance rationale, thus suggesting that the adverse selection problem may have other causes. Perhaps the most obvious potential other cause is the inability (or unwillingness) of insurers to adopt satisfactory techniques of risk classification—a problem that would be better addressed by reforming insurance than by reforming tort law.

In any event, there are strong reasons in theory to believe that the phenomenon of adverse selection is unaffected by the insurance rationale. This can be seen by a close examination of the principal argument that the insurance rationale's critics have used in an effort to link the two.

But before looking at this argument, it may be helpful to review a few basic principles of insurance that explain why adverse selection is a problem. Basically, any voluntary insurance system depends upon a balance between two conflicting goals: risk spreading and risk classification. Risk spreading is, of course, the central function of insurance. Risk classification, on the other hand, actually works against the risk-spreading function; but it is necessary in order to make insurance economically attractive to insureds.[31]

Insurance spreads risks in two ways: across time for individual actors, who pay a steady stream of premiums to guard against the materialization of risk at some single unspecified time in the future; and across a group of actors, who agree to "pool" their premiums and their risks in order to create the reserves needed to compensate individual events of loss, and to facilitate actuarial risk management. This pooling of risks occurs when individual risks are grouped together and charged the same premium regardless of variations in their actual and/or predicted loss experience.

In a system of perfect risk spreading, individual variations in riskiness are ignored, and all actors are grouped together in the same pool. By this means, the good risks in the pool subsidize the bad risks. The good risks pay the same premium, and they receive the same theoretical level of protection. But due to their lower loss experience, they end up receiving a lower portion of the loss compensation that the insurer pays out. They are thus less of a drain on the insurance fund reserves, even though they contribute equally to them.

We are all familiar with this tendency of insurance to force the good risks to subsidize the bad. Thus, for example, in life insurance, healthy people who live a long time subsidize unhealthy ones who die young: they pay more in premiums for the same level of death benefits. For pensions and annuities, the opposite effect occurs: the short-lived subsidize the long-lived. The same sort of subsidization occurs with liability insurance. Safe actors, who do not cause as many injuries and are not sued as often, subsidize unsafe actors, who do cause injuries and frequently end up being liable for sizable damage awards.

Since risk spreading is the ultimate purpose of insurance, the tendency of insurers is to lump actors together in this way regardless of risk. This saves the insurer the time and expense of determining variations in risk among the members of the group. It also permits aggregation of substantial resources (through regular collection of premiums from the relatively large number of insureds in a given pool), and it facilitates actuarial predictions of loss. But because the good risks, if they know who they are, do not like having to pay extra to accomplish protection of the bad risks, they are motivated to seek an alternative form of protection that reflects their relatively reduced risk by pooling them only with equally good risks and charging them lower premiums for the same protection.

If insurance is compulsory, pooling all actors together regardless of relative risk is no problem, because the less risky actors, who are subsidizing the more risky ones, have no choice but to participate in the same insurance pool. It is thus not surprising to find that many forms of legally mandated social insurance include all participants in a single pool: witness, for example, the vast amounts of money all Americans are paying to compensate failed savings and loan institutions and their depositors through the mechanisms of federal deposit insurance and the federally created Resolution Trust Corporation. But if insurance is voluntary, the tendency to lump unlike risks together creates an incentive for the good risks in the pool to seek a cheaper method of protecting against loss. They "drop out" of the insurance pool, either by self-insuring, if they have the financial capacity to do so, or by finding another insurer who is willing to group them only with other actors who face similarly reduced levels of risk, and thus to extend them the same level of protection for a lower premium.

In a voluntary system of insurance, the pooling together of good and bad risks thus inevitably gives rise to the phenomenon of adverse selection. The severity of this phenomenon depends on the degree of variance between the good and bad risks. If the variance is sharp, so that the good risks could save a lot of money by insuring elsewhere, they will leave the pool, so that only the bad risks remain. This raises the average level of risk for the entire pool and hence increases the cost of covering that risk. The effect is to drive the cost of insurance up. This, in turn, forces more relatively good risks out of the pool, and so on, until, in theory at least, only the worst risks are left.

But for them, the cost of insuring may now approach the costs of their accidents, so that they too may well find no advantage in remaining in the pool. Thus, the insurance system "unravels."

To guard against this phenomenon, insurers try to engage in some degree of risk classification. That is, they segregate higher-risk and lower-risk insureds into separate pools and charge a differential premium based on the different levels of risk in each pool. We are all familiar with this phenomenon as well. Smokers pay higher premiums for life insurance than nonsmokers. Drivers who have caused accidents recently pay higher premiums on their automobile insurance than drivers whose records are clean. And so forth.

Although the practice of risk classification seems to run counter to the risk spreading purposes of insurance, it serves important functions of its own. From the insurer's perspective, risk classification serves the purpose of making insurance financially attractive to the better risks. From tort law's perspective, it retains, even in an insurance-backed system of loss compensation, some degree of incentive for safer behavior. It allows the safer actors to reap the benefits of their safe conduct by paying lower premiums for their liability insurance coverage.

Thus, risk spreading and risk classification are both fundamental features of our private insurance system, and it is the job of insurers to find a proper balance between them. In reaching that balance, a third important factor comes into play. For the risk-spreading function of insurance to work, the pool must represent a fairly diverse field of risk. The same risk cannot materialize for all parties at the same time and with the same severity, or else the insurer will be unable to maintain adequate reserves.

This point can be illustrated by an example. Imagine three hypothetical insurers: the first sells "volcano damage insurance" only to homeowners in a single Philippine village below Mt. Pinatubo just before it erupts; the second sells "volcano damage insurance" during the same period to residents of volcanic areas all over the world, including some villages near Mt. Pinatubo; and the third sells general homeowners' insurance all over the world, insurance that includes volcano damage as one form of coverage. The first of these companies is probably wiped out by the disaster that ensues when Mt. Pinatubo erupts, because all its insureds share the same risk, at the same level, and the risk materializes for all of them at the same time. The second company may experience a sharp drain on its reserves as a result of Mt. Pinatubo's eruption, but it may be able to survive because its insureds are relatively risk diverse—they represent the combined risk of many different volcanoes in different areas erupting at many different times and inflicting varying degrees of damage. Since the other volcanoes do not erupt at the same time as Mt. Pinatubo, the company is able to use premiums it collected from residents in other areas (and the investment income from those premiums) to compensate insureds in the Philippines for their losses, although the company may well have to raise premiums for all its insureds in order to rebuild its reserves in anticipation of the next volcanic eruption somewhere else in the world. For the third company, compensation to policyholders around Mt. Pinatubo probably has still less effect, since the risk of volcanic eruption represents only a relatively small portion of the risks reflected in its pool of insureds. Because of the substantial diversity of its risk pool, this company may well be able to compensate victims of Mt. Pinatubo's eruption without raising its premiums much at all. To put the matter in colloquial terms, in the insurance business it is important not to carry all one's insured eggs in a single risky basket.

This basic proposition takes on added significance in an insurance system that uses a relatively high level of classification to break insureds out into different pools, with different risk levels and different premium rates. As classification increases, the insurance pools become smaller. As the pools become smaller, the danger that insureds who share the same risk will have it materialize at the same time becomes greater. Thus, it becomes increasingly important that the population within any particular classification be risk diverse.

With these three basic propositions in mind—risk spreading, risk classification as an antidote to adverse selection, and the desirability of a risk-diverse insurance pool—we can return to the question, How does resort to the insurance rationale allegedly aggravate the danger of adverse selection in liability insurance? According to the critics, use of the insurance rationale interferes with the diversification of risks within the insurance pool by introducing a new form of risk—"socio-legal risk"[32]—that all participants in the tort system share in common. Because the insureds share this risk, they assertedly lose much of their risk diversity. As a result, insurers can diversify risks in the pool only by increasing its size and lumping good and bad risks together—that is, by eliminating significant risk classification. Doing so, however, only creates an incentive for the good risks to leave the pool, and the resulting adverse selection produces the vicious unraveling spiral described above.

The problem with this argument is its first step, the assertion that the insurance rationale generates a significant shared socio-legal risk that eliminates risk diversity among the typical purchasers of third-party liability insurance. The critics offer no clear definition of socio-legal risk. On careful examination, the concept turns out to be a chimera.

Three possible definitions of socio-legal risk come to mind: the risk that the insured's products or services will cause accidents; the risk that the tort system will impose liability for the costs of those accidents; and the risk that a judge or jury prone to compensation will "overcompensate" the plaintiff, resulting in "excess" liability for the defendant. The question we must ask about these three possible definitions is whether any of them represents a nondiverse risk—that is, one that is likely to occur for all insureds within a given liability insurance classification, is likely to materialize for all of them at roughly the same time, and is likely to be visited on each with the same degree of severity. In all three instances the answer is negative.

The first of the three possible definitions of socio-legal risk can be fairly quickly dispatched. The risk that an insured's products or services will cause accidents varies significantly with the diverse productive activities of modern enterprise. It would be foolhardy to imagine that producing asbestos creates the same risk as, say, producing toasters or toothbrushes. Within a particular product or service line, even though risks may be similar in character, they materialize at different times and with different degrees of severity. For example, if a lawn mower manufacturer sells lawn mowers with a defective blade, some of those blades may never fail, others may fail in ways that produce only slight injury, and some may cause extreme injury. Some may fail on the first use, some on the one hundredth use, some on the ten thousandth use. Some may fail this year, others in two or three years, others in ten years. Variations among consumers and in their use of the product introduce their own diversity into the risk equation. Moreover, it seems clear that the risk of accident operates independently of the insurance rationale, which comes into play, if at all, only *after* the accident has occurred and a lawsuit has been brought to trial.

This brings us to the second possibility, that socio-legal risk is the risk of having liability imposed once a case is brought to trial. To put it another way, this is the risk that an *accident,* once it occurs, will produce a *loss* that the defendant's liability insurer will be required to compensate.

It is probably true in one sense that this is a factor all actors share. On an actuarial basis, any legal system theoretically yields a unique statistical prediction of liability from the fact of accident. Moreover, it is probably true that a system committed to the insurance rationale produces a higher predicted risk of liability from accident than a system that rejects that rationale.

Thus, the presence or absence of the rationale does contribute something to this "shared" risk.

But to draw these conclusions hardly ends analysis. We must next ask whether this risk is "shared" in the same sense that the risk of damage from Mt. Pinatubo might be shared by all the residents of a single Philippine village—that it will occur at the same time with the same severity for each insured. The answer is that it is not shared in this sense, for several reasons.

Initially, we arrived at the conclusion that all actors possess a "shared" risk only by the process of statistical averaging. This does not mean that the risk is in fact *the same* in all events. For example, as trial lawyers well know, the risk of liability and the cost of liability in a *particular* case depend on a wide range of relatively distinctive variables, including at a minimum such factors as the quality of the lawyering on both sides, the strength and presence of the witnesses, evidentiary rulings from the court, and the composition of the jury. These factors alone probably introduce significant variance around the statistical mean, so that even for comparable injuries from comparable products or services, there is in fact fairly substantial variance in the likelihood and cost of liability for individual accidents.

Other diversifying factors arise when we consider the possibility of different risk-management strategies by different producers. Two manufacturers of the same product, experiencing the same kind of accident, may adopt entirely different strategies. One may adopt a policy of early settlement; another may litigate each claim to the end. The result is significantly different outcomes in similar situations.

As a consequence, the level of liability risk defendants face, even for accidents from the same product or service, is actually quite diverse. Indeed, critics who complain about unpredictability actually stake much of their claim on the notion that such diversity of outcomes for comparable cases not only exists but has significantly increased in recent years.

In addition, even if the risk of liability were constant, the amount and timing of loss have nothing in common. There is no reason that diverse enterprises producing diverse goods and services and selling them to diverse consumers who use them in diverse ways will be sued and assessed with liability at the same time, or in the same amounts each time their product or service produces injury. If socio-legal risk in this form is shared, evidently it is not shared in ways that interfere with effective cost spreading.

Finally, since the risk of accident itself is diverse, the risk of liability from accident retains all that diversity. Even if the risk of liability were absolute (and what empirical evidence we have suggests it is far from being so), the diversity among insureds in the risk of accident itself would be more than sufficient to allow for reasonable levels of risk classification.

The latter point can perhaps be best illustrated by imagining a system in which liability for injuries to others were automatic. Would insurance be possible? The answer is almost certainly that it would be. There would still be variations of risk among various productive activities, and there would be diversity in the timing and severity of the risks that actually materialized. These variations would permit insurers to engage in effective cost spreading, both temporally and across actors within a particular insurance pool.

Indeed, in many other forms of insurance, loss from a covered event is virtually certain, yet insurers are still able to find means of adequately diversifying their risk classifications. Life insurance may be the best example. Death of an insured is almost certain to bring about compensation. With rare exceptions, a life insurer that refuses to pay can be sued and held liable for the insured loss. Thus, one could, I suppose, term "death" a "socio-biologico-legal risk" that is "shared" by all persons who purchase life insurance. Yet the variety of risk factors in the *cause* of death, and the differences in *timing* of death by individual insureds, are more than sufficient to support a satisfactory balance between risk spreading and risk classification, even in the face of this shared risk. The same would be true in a system of third-party liability insurance, even if absolute liability were enforced.

The third possibility is that socio-legal risk is the risk of the "runaway" jury, the likelihood that the plaintiff will be significantly overcompensated. Once again, to get to the point of labeling this a "shared" risk, one has to engage in statistical averaging. Yet unless one is willing to posit that *all* juries vastly overcompensate, it is likely that a true runaway jury is a purely random occurrence. Its random character virtually guarantees that it will not happen to all insureds simultaneously.

Even if there were some content to the notion of a nondiverse socio-legal risk, argument predicated on this factor ignores other important considerations that facilitate risk diversification. One major factor is the modern reality of intracorporate product and service differentiation. It is rare, in today's modern enterprise, for a liability insurance policy to cover but a single product or service, with a single accident and a single degree of socio-legal risk. Most businesses and institutions today produce a wide range of products and engage in a wide range of different operations, all of which contribute to the overall risk of insuring that particular business or institution against liability. Presumably, the premium charge to insure such an entity under a comprehensive general liability policy (the kind most businesses usually purchase) is derived by factoring these various risks together. Thus, even if the entity stood alone in its own insurance "pool," the diversity of its own activities would allow for some diversification of risk.

The same phenomenon is apparent within particular industrial groups. Thanks to the advent of the corporate conglomerate, one cannot assume that particular products or services are performed by businesses that have the same, or even a very similar, product or service mix. One lawn mower manufacturer, for example, might be a subsidiary or a division of a firm that also manufactures automobiles; another, of a firm that makes power tools; another, of a firm that runs hotels; another, of a firm that sells greeting cards; and so forth. Since most liability insurance is sold in comprehensive packages by *firm* rather than by product or service, any pooling together of such diverse entities will inevitably produce significant risk differentiation.

It bears repeating that the problem of adverse selection ultimately flows, not from the tort system or its rules, but from the structure of our private liability insurance markets. The way to address the problem, at least initially, is not by tinkering with liability rules but by reforming the structure of those insurance markets themselves. If current methods of classifying risks are producing unacceptable levels of adverse selection, the most immediate answer is to experiment with alternative forms of classification. For example, one technique insurers sometimes use to combat adverse selection is "experience rating," a process in which good risks may receive an after-the-fact premium reduction based on their favorable loss experience. Moreover, there is nothing to prevent insurers from setting up classifications that deliberately pool similarly risky insureds who sell completely different products and services. There is no evidence that liability insurers have experimented with devices such as these to relieve the perceived effects of adverse selection. Until they have, there is no cause to consider more-radical and indirect solutions, such as reforming tort rules.

If a private market system is unable to combat adverse selection and we are uncertain that actors will adequately self-insure, we must also remember that there remains the alternative of some form of compulsory liability insurance. The cost of resorting to such an alternative is loss of freedom and of the self-correcting forces of the market, as well as the administrative cost of setting up a bureaucratic system to deliver it, so we should not turn to such an alternative lightly. But as noted above, in other areas where private alternatives have failed, we have been willing to step in with compulsory social insurance. It remains an option to be considered here as well.

Finally, we must bear in mind that adverse selection, to the extent it really happens, simply mirrors the structure of the market. Under a regime of rampant adverse selection, the worst-case scenario is this: the good risks drop out of the insurance pool and self-insure; the bad risks are unable to purchase the insurance they need at now-higher prices; they thus are forced to "go bare" and are ultimately wiped out by an uninsured liability payout. For the individual actor, that is a horrible outcome. But for a society committed to a competitive market economy, such outcomes, at some level, must be expected. We *want* competition over safety. And the result of economic competition is always that there are both economic winners and economic losers. We certainly cannot ignore the dislocative impact of business failure on society, nor would we want such a result to occur with great frequency. But as we learned in the case of asbestos, we do have a mechanism —bankruptcy law—for handling actors whose inadequate investments in safety make them bad risks and get them into economic trouble. At some point, then, the proper response to the problem of adverse selection may lie, not in reform of tort law, but in closer attention to the way that liability claims are handled in bankruptcy proceedings. In any event, until there is greater evidence of corporate failure *caused* by adverse selection,[33] there is little reason to accord the adverse selection theme much weight, let alone to link it in any significant way with the insurance rationale.

Moral Hazard

The moral hazard critique rests on the idea that use of the insurance rationale promotes both a "why worry?" attitude on the part of consumers, who lose their incentive toward safe use of products or services they buy, as well as a "why bother?" attitude by producers, who come to regard investments in safety as pointless because they fail to prevent liability.[34] My research has failed to disclose any empirical data supporting either of these assertions, both of which should be subject to relatively easy empirical verification.[35] On the producer side, moreover, there is significant anecdotal evidence to the contrary, since many producers have demonstrated an acute interest in product safety and a remarkable ability to react quickly to previously unforeseen risks. One outstanding example is the swift development by food and drug producers of tamper-proof packaging after the occurrence of several highly publicized product-tampering incidents.[36] Beyond that, neither argument withstands careful theoretical analysis.

The argument about consumers neglects three important realities of our present system of loss compensation. First, the moral hazard argument necessarily presumes that many, if not most, consumers, are willing to risk *personal injury* because of assured compensation—that they are, in other words, either willing to trade their personal health for compensation they might receive in case of injury or at least value health and money on a par.[37] This is a doubtful assumption. Moral hazard can be a significant problem where property damage is the source of compensation. But that problem should be significantly reduced when consumers must face the prospect of losing an arm or a leg, or suffering a long hospital stay, or the like, in order to be compensated.

Second, in a third-party system, a substantial portion of a victim's tort compensation is lost to transfer costs. The typical personal injury plaintiff stands to lose one-third or more of his or her tort judgment to lawyers' fees and costs.[38] Although these costs are the bane of the system in other respects, they ought to deflect concerns about consumer moral hazard. Indeed, they work something of the same effect for third-party liability that coinsurance does in first-party insurance: by making the beneficiary of insurance pay part of the cost (through fees and litigation costs), they inhibit the incidence of a "why worry?" attitude.

Some critics of the system might dispute this observation by contending that juries are aware of the need to pay legal fees and that they "pad" their awards to deserving plaintiffs, especially those awards for pain and suffering, to account for this reality.[39] If so, the deserving plaintiff can count on full recovery and may be tempted into the moral hazard. If that is true, the system certainly engages in an elaborate charade, since juries receive no instructions equating pain and suffering, or any other element of damages, with lawyers' fees, and any evidence of the need to pay those fees or their amount would be inadmissible at trial. Unless we are prepared to make the assumption that juries routinely and callously disregard judicial instructions (in which case the entire debate about what liability rules to set loses much of its point, since whatever we tell them, juries will probably do something different), we have to assume that many, perhaps even most, deserving plaintiffs emerge from tort suits less than fully compensated.

Third, in a third-party liability system, payments to victims are significantly delayed by the time it takes to press a legal claim to judgment or settlement. In hotly contested cases or ones brought in overloaded state courts, the time delay can be years. There are strong reasons to believe that most actors do not want to risk potential short term privation while they await the outcome of a lawsuit. In many instances, this desire to speed the pace of compensation motivates many plaintiffs to compromise their claims and accept considerably less than full compensation in settlement. This delay factor and its influence on ultimate recovery sharply deter any significant consumer moral hazard from developing.

On the producer side, the moral hazard argument is really just another version of the economic stagnation argument dealt with below, albeit one that posits the stagnation of safety technology. Yet even with insurance, producer interest in efficient cost-avoidance measures ought to remain. So long as there is a reasonable amount of risk classification, investments in safety that reduce the number of accidents should lower liability exposure and thus reduce premiums.[40] This would be true even in a system of absolute liability. And as the costs of insurance rise, the attractions of safety technology increase. Indeed, given the sharp rise in insurance costs over the last two decades, it might make more sense to raise concerns about *over*investment in safety than to complain about the risks of moral hazard.

Producer moral hazard might become a problem in a system devoid of significant risk classification. If producers could not reduce their insurance premiums by safer behavior, then they might lose the motivation to invest in safety, particularly if insurance costs represented the lion's share of the costs of accidents they experienced. But as we observed above in the context of adverse selection, the insurance industry has long experience with a variety of techniques to reduce this tendency, which ought to be applicable to third-party liability insurance. The most obvious is risk classification itself. Others include experience rating, coinsurance, and large initial deductibles that force the insured partially to self-insure.[41] Until these possibilities are exhausted, the case for altering liability rules to avoid moral hazard remains weak.

Moreover, one cannot ignore, in addition to insurance premiums, other costs of accidents that are also affected by producer safety. These include administrative expenses incurred in handling legal claims, possibly fees for legal defense (although those may be partly or wholly covered by insurance), and loss of business good will.[42] A producer can realize savings in these areas from investments in safety, even if insurance premiums fail to reflect variations in degree of risk.

These considerations do not completely obviate the risk of producer moral hazard, but they do suggest that, as with adverse selection, there are more immediate, effective techniques for managing this phenomenon than a thoroughgoing restructuring of tort liability rules. Until these more modest measures have been fully implemented, the case for tort reform as an antidote to moral hazard is at best premature.

It is perhaps of equal importance to observe that the problem of moral hazard by no means disappears if we switch from third-party to first-party insurance. Moral hazard remains an issue if victims have the obligation to insure themselves against injuries caused by others. Under such a regime there is an increased risk of producer moral hazard, since producers might be tempted to engage in riskier behavior, secure in the knowledge that victims will be compensated through their own insurance and the costs will not be transferred. And victims who possess insurance, if they in fact value health and money equally or are willing to trade the former for the latter, will have an even greater incentive to behave carelessly, since in a first-party system the obstacles to moral hazard presented by delay and transfer costs, in theory at least, are significantly reduced. As with third-party insurance, adequate risk classification, deductibles, coinsurance, and the like, could be employed to reduce these dangers. But there is no evidence to suggest that these techniques are any easier or more likely to be effective with victims than with producers.

Regressive Taxation

This argument asserts that cost spreading by producers, augmented by judicial embrace of the insurance rationale, is passed on to consumers in the form of higher prices and effectively operates as a kind of regressive tax, forcing the poor to subsidize the rich.[43] This argument rests on several important empirical assumptions: (1) that the accident rate is essentially the same for rich and poor; (2) that the rich, by virtue of their greater economic loss, receive higher compensation than the poor for the same injury; (3) that insurance costs are directly passed on to consumers; (4) that rich and poor consume the same goods and services; and (5) that they consume these goods and services in the same amounts. If all these assumptions held, there might be some accuracy to this argument. As it is, there is some evidence supporting the second and third assumptions,[44] although in theory at least, some elements of recovery (such as medical expenses and pain and suffering) ought not to vary significantly according to wealth. But the other assumptions have not been verified, and when carefully examined they seem rather doubtful.

It seems unlikely, for example, that the poor and the rich purchase the same goods and services. Luxury items, surely, are much more frequently purchased by the rich, who can afford them, than by the poor, who cannot. And even regarding various "necessities," the seemingly endless capacity of modern enterprise to engage in product differentiation is likely to bring about substantially different product and service mixes between the poor and the rich. The equally well-known phenomenon of product substitution[45] is likely further to sharpen the difference, since the poor seek out cheaper substitutes for products and services they "need" but find it difficult to afford.

Consider, for example, transportation—close to a necessity in our modern, highly mobile world. For long trips, the exceedingly rich may fly in their own private jets; the very rich may charter a jet; the rich may fly on public airlines in first class; the middle class may fly tourist; the poor may take a public bus or not go at all. For transportation at home, the very rich may choose a private limousine with all the amenities; the rich may settle for a general-production luxury sport sedan; the middle class may purchase a late-model standard sedan; and the poor may either drive a much older used car or take public transportation. What is true of air and auto travel is probably true in all aspects of the travel budget. Although it may well represent a smaller portion of their income, the rich are likely to spend much more on travel than the poor, with the rest of us falling on a continuum in between.

Consequently, even if we assume that companies providing various forms of travel goods or services completely pass on their insurance costs in the form of higher prices for their goods or services, it is by no means obvious that the poor pay a disproportionate share of these added costs. Indeed, without the hard empirical data we need to make a firm judgment, it is more likely that the rich bear a proportionally greater share of the liability insurance costs. Companies that cater solely to the travel of the wealthy (such as manufacturers of luxury private jets) have no means of allocating their insurance costs to the poor. Other producers appealing to a broader spectrum of travelers by offering a variety of wealth-differentiated products or services also are not likely to allocate a disproportionate insurance burden to the poor. For example, if these producers allocate their insurance costs as a flat percentage of the costs of the goods or services they provide, the rich, by purchasing more (in dollar terms) of these goods and services, will pay a greater portion of the insurance. On the other hand, if producers choose to allocate varying percentages of their insurance costs to the different products and services they offer (perhaps based on actual liability experience with each good or service, perhaps on some more arbitrary scale), they will have at least some incentive to allocate proportionally more of those costs to the goods and services purchased by the rich. This is true partly because (by our initial assumption) these goods and services create a greater liability burden when the rich are injured by them, so that they simply cost more to produce. In addition, the ability of the rich to purchase the item in question is probably less price-sensitive. If the price goes up, consumption by the wealthy is less likely to go down.

It also is probable, with respect to many goods and services, that demand is *not* constant regardless of wealth. The rich surely spend more, not only on luxury items but on the standard staples of life. Shelter is a human necessity.

But wealthy people may live in costly mansions, while the poor may live in relatively cheap inner-city row houses or apartments in run-down neighborhoods, and some of the extremely poor may be forced to resort to the "substitute" of homelessness. Clothing is a necessity, but wealthy people buy new wardrobes of expensive designer clothing every year, while the poor make do with fewer and cheaper items of apparel, and they may wear them until they are threadbare. So also with food. Wealthy people may often dine at expensive restaurants; the poor may eat out at fast-food restaurants or consume modest fare at home. And so forth. As liability insurance costs are allocated to these goods, the rich regularly end up paying a greater portion of the tab.

Even the assumption that the accident rate is identical for rich and poor may be subject to some doubt. The accidents we experience are at least partly a function of (1) the relative safety of the goods and services we use, (2) the relative safety of our daily activities, and (3) our knowledge of safety risks and how to avoid them. There are reasons to believe that all three of these factors may allow the wealthy to lead safer lives.

Wealthy persons, when they choose goods and services, are able to afford those with costly additional safety features. For example, the wealthy can afford to purchase late model automobiles with antilock brakes, air bags, side-body crash protection, crumple zones, and other technologically advanced (and expensive) safety options. The poor may not be able to afford all this high-tech protection, so they may have to buy cars without all these safety amenities.

Similarly, wealthy people can afford to forgo certain dangerous activities that the poor may not. For example, wealthy people tend to choose relatively low-risk occupations, such as practicing law or medicine, managing securities portfolios, or serving as business executives, whereas poorer individuals are more likely to work in high-risk positions. At home, the wealthy person can afford to hire someone else to perform such relatively dangerous home-maintenance tasks as mowing the lawn or repairing a leaky roof. A poorer person may have to do the lawn mowing and roof repair him- or herself, at personal risk. A wealthy person out on the streets at night might pay for the relative safety of a taxi, whereas a poor person, to save money, might risk the dangers of walking or taking public transit.

Of course, not every dangerous activity sorts out this way. The wealthy might also choose some dangerous leisure activities that the poor could not afford. Skydiving, boating, and downhill skiing come to mind as examples. But these seem to be the exceptions rather than the rule. Probably one of the reasons most of us aspire to greater wealth is the commonsense perception that with it comes greater security—not just financial security if something does go wrong, but also the security of greater personal health. Part of the reason wealth gives us this security is that wealthy individuals can choose to avoid dangerous activities that would otherwise entail an enhanced risk of injury.

Finally, wealthy individuals, by virtue of the better education that their money can afford, may well know of and avoid risks that the poor, lacking equal access to information, may unwittingly experience. The field of public health abounds with examples of health risks that are more prevalent in poor communities, at least partly because of lack of information.

The purpose of these observations is not to prove that the poor in fact lead more dangerous lives. Rather, it is an attempt to show that we really do not know for sure whether accident rates do or do not vary according to wealth, and that if we had to guess, we would have strong reasons to believe that accident rates for the rich and the poor are *not* identical.

Consequently, at least three of the five empirical assumptions listed above seem to be of doubtful validity.[46] As a result, the regressive tax argument that depends upon them becomes a doubtful foundation for tort reform. It simply does not make sense to predicate social policy on factual assumptions that are both unverified and counterintuitive.

There is another, still more fundamental difficulty with the regressive tax argument. It insinuates that a tort recovery involves a positive redistribution of wealth to the recipient. At the moment the transfer takes place, that may seem to be true. But if we lengthen our perspective enough to include the moment of injury, the picture changes dramatically. Instead of gaining wealth, the tort plaintiff is recovering wealth previously lost. From the victim's perspective, even with full compensation the net is zero. Thus, as long as the system is only *compensating* victims for their existing losses, over the long term we are not in fact redistributing wealth.

To put the matter in the jargon of tax, it is as though there were *two* taxes, not just one—an "injury tax" (demanding payment in kind) and a "compensation tax." If the latter tax is regressive, the former is, by the same set of assumptions, progressive. That is, under the assumptions listed above, the rich sustain a disproportionate share of the losses occasioned by accident. Since the "compensation tax" is imposed solely to fund what we might term "refunds" to those who were previously subjected to the "injury tax," the progressive and regressive aspects of the two imaginary taxes cancel each other out. Thus, the tort system ends up making no significant wealth redistribution.

It is probably not particularly helpful to describe tort law as though it were tax law. There is a distinct rhetorical flavor to all arguments about the tort system that use the language of taxation. Who is getting "taxed" and who is getting "subsidized" depends a great deal on one's choice of a starting point for analysis. Historically, for example, one of the arguments supporting the expansion of liability has been the assertion that, without compensation, the victims of injury have been forced to subsidize enterprise—that they have been "taxed" of their health and property in order to make goods and services cheaper for the rest of us.[47] Critics of expanded tort liability arrive at the opposite conclusion—that consumers are being "taxed" to subsidize victims—by nothing more than the simple expedient of moving the time frame for discussion from the point of injury to the point of compensation.[48]

Perhaps the best way to get rid of the rhetoric is to eliminate the tax metaphor and to view the issue, less metaphorically, in insurance terms instead. From this perspective we have a group of individuals (the consumers of a given product or service, whether rich, poor, or in between) who, by virtue of their common behavior, face a common risk of injury. Because, by assumption, the cost of insuring against that risk is fully passed on through producer pricing, they pay the premium for insurance coverage of that risk. They thus become the pool to which the risk is spread. Although we have assumed (however doubtfully) that they all experience injury with the same frequency, some of them (by the set of assumptions above, the rich) are relatively "bad" risks because, if they are injured, they suffer greater loss; others (by the same assumptions, the poor) are relatively "good" risks because their injuries produce proportionately smaller loss. In the process of cost spreading, this difference in the relative riskiness of the two groups is ignored, as the premiums for the entire group are based on the average payout.

If the starting assumptions hold true, this way of looking at the issue does suggest that the poor may be "subsidizing" the rich, but it is a very different sort of subsidy from the wealth redistribution that we associate with progressive or regressive taxation. The poor "subsidize" the rich under these assumptions only in the sense that they pay the same premium for the same protection but receive a smaller portion of the total payout. But that kind of "subsidy" inheres in virtually *any* cost-spreading scheme. As we observed in the discussion of adverse selection above, it is, indeed, the essential function of insurance to pool risks in precisely this way.

The fact that this sort of subsidization is virtually inescapable in insurance leads to an important inference: switching from one method of insuring loss compensation to another is unlikely to eliminate it. Thus, if the same starting assumptions are retained and we examine a first-party, rather than a third-party, scheme, we are likely to find exactly the same kind of "subsidization" going on. Unless the poor and the rich are separately classified under such a scheme, the poor still end up paying the same amount in premiums for a lower total payout. If the current structure of first-party insurance in other spheres is any guide, risk classification on the basis of wealth seems no more likely under a first-party, than under a third-party, regime.

Of course, under a first-party system, the poor could reduce their subsidization of the rich by purchasing less insurance—by engaging, that is, in adverse selection through "self- insurance." However, the poor lack the financial capacity and information resources really to insure themselves against loss—that is, to predict their future losses and set up a reserve fund to cover them. When we use the term "self-insurance" here, it is just a euphemism for noninsurance. But if that is the point of the regressive tax argument, it breaks down into another version of the forced-insurance argument, discussed above. And it is a peculiarly unattractive version at that. Under this argument, we should retreat from full third-party insurance so that the segment of society most in need of protection—the poor—will be "free" to give it up. We know that what will happen in fact is that they will simply suffer uncompensated injury.

Ultimately, the regressive tax argument, if it has any validity at all, pushes one, not away from the insurance rationale, but toward a system of social insurance, in which any regressive features of payout can be offset by funding through true progressive taxation.[49] If insurance protection were extended through a government program, it would be easy to address any regressive features by the simple expedient of charging the rich a higher tax rate to pay for the program. But at this point it bears repeating that we lack any solid empirical evidence to move us in such a direction. Unless and until the unverified and counterintuitive assumptions of the regressive taxation are demonstrated, there is no reason to let the argument influence decisions about the structure of either tort doctrine or insurance arrangements.

Economic Stagnation

This argument asserts that the high costs of liability produced by the insurance rationale are deterring technological advances because corporations are so concerned about the liability risks of new products that they are unwilling to market them.[50] This argument is hardly new. It has been a favorite theme of those favoring limits on liability since Holmes's day. Indeed, the argument appears, in slightly different terms, as a centerpiece of Holmes's defense of the negligence standard in *The Common Law,*[51] where he criticized strict liability for its tendency to deter the sort of "individual activity" from which "the public generally profits." Presumably, Holmes primarily had productive economic activity in mind.

In recent years, there have been a few documented instances of such an effect. One example occurred during the swine flu epidemic of the mid-1970s. The United States wanted to institute a national vaccination program for swine flu, but pharmaceutical firms refused to produce and distribute the vaccine unless they were effectively guaranteed immunity from liability.[52] Based on experience with decisions such as the *Reyes* case, discussed in Part II, the pharmaceutical manufacturers feared that a mass immunization program using a drug that had not been extensively tested might lead to widespread liability. Congress had to provide statutory protection, by allowing all suits to proceed against the United States government rather than the manufacturers, before the manufacturers were willing to begin supplying the vaccine.[53] It turned out that the vaccine did create some unfortunate risks, including the tendency in some cases to cause Guillain-Barre syndrome, a form of paralysis that can sometimes be fatal. The United States ended up bearing substantial liability costs.[54]

The swine flu episode illustrates an interesting but little noticed aspect of the economic stagnation argument. It turns out that it is not really so much an argument about the *development* of technology as it is about the *marketing* of existing technology. In the swine flu situation, for example, the vaccine already existed. The technology was there. The problem was that manufacturers were concerned (correctly, as it happened) about the safety of mass distribution. This is no mere coincidence. In fact, the economic stagnation argument always presumes a sufficient level of technological development for manufacturers to predict, at least in rough terms, the degree of risk associated with a new product or service. Without a fairly significant level of technological mastery, producers would have no idea whether the liability risks of marketing were sufficiently great to deter further investment.

This refinement of the argument has an important ramification. If we are talking about decisions regarding marketing of existing technology rather than decisions about investment in research and development, there is no immediate reason to conclude that the existence of tort liability is deterring the growth of knowledge. Moreover, if technology, in the form of a new product, already exists and we have sufficient information roughly to predict the level of risk associated with the product, we should be able to balance social burdens and benefits of imposing liability *with respect to that particular product,* and thus to decide on a product-by-product basis whether any relief from the existing regime of tort liability is warranted.

Existing tort doctrine already attempts to accommodate such a balancing process. In the field of product liability, most jurisdictions employ some version of the risk-utility test for determining defects in product design,[55] and Restatement Section 402A places limits on liability for so-called unavoidably unsafe products.[56] Both of these doctrines involve a weighing of the costs of liability against the social benefits of the product in question. Even with these provisions, there may be some cases, as in the instance of swine flu, where the process of social balancing will lead to the conclusion that a new product should be even further immunized from existing tort liability. If so, we can do that through product-specific legislative immunity—perhaps, as in the swine flu situation, through providing a first-party or social-insurance alternative to tort compensation.

Thus, the economic stagnation argument may support some limited reform of existing tort law. But it does not support *wholesale* restructuring of tort liability. Indeed, such a response would suffer from serious overbreadth. The rapid proliferation of new products and services in our economy is ample evidence that stagnation due to tort liability is the exception, not the rule. In most instances, the risks of tort liability do not prevent enterprises from bringing new technology into the market. Changing liability rules for products that are already on the market or for those that would be marketed anyway would produce a social cost, in the form of reduced compensation for injury, without producing any offsetting benefit in the form of new marketing initiatives. The stagnation argument is necessarily an argument for special cases, not general reforms.

Even in deciding the special cases, we must bear in mind that changing liability rules for the safety risks of new products does not in fact eliminate the risks themselves. The question we are facing is who should bear the risk. Unless the government is willing to assume and spread the risk, as it did in the instance of the swine flu vaccine, the choices are the victim (and anyone to whom the victim can spread the loss) or the manufacturer (and anyone to whom the manufacturer can spread the loss). Shifting liability away from the manufacturer inevitably shifts it toward the victim. It makes the victim (and his or her cost-spreading pool) the bearer of the risk and, to the extent of that risk, the indirect insurer of the marketing initiative. Given that some victims are likely to be uninsured and others underinsured, what we have to ask is whether the social benefits of the marketing initiative in question justify imposing on a select group of victims the social and personal costs of uncompensated injury. In a society where the value of compensation for injury is esteemed, that is a choice we should never make lightly.

Summary

The preceding discussion of the insurance rationale's contemporary critique yields several conclusions. Probably the most important is that the arguments against the insurance rationale do not, either separately or together, really justify its abandonment. They suffer from a combination of unjustified or undocumented assumptions and theoretical flaws that render them an unsound platform from which to launch a broadscale movement of reform.

We cannot dismiss these criticisms entirely, however, since they do suggest some important areas of concern about the existing system. I believe they support the following conclusions.

First, there is a need for greater stability in tort doctrine than we have experienced in the last thirty years. An insurance-backed system of injury compensation cannot flourish unless the insureds' exposure to loss can be predicted with some accuracy. To do so requires a relatively stable set of liability rules.

Second, there is a need to do something to trim the high transfer costs of third-party liability, although we do not presently have an adequate basis for moving toward a first-party alternative. There may be segments of the field of accident compensation where first-party alternatives appear more desirable, but changes in the design of first-party insurance products and reforms in the structure of insurance markets are necessary before a move to first-party insurance is likely to produce success. The auto no-fault experiment of the 1970s suggests that developing a cost-effective first-party alternative could prove to be a long and hard labor. In the meantime, reducing the costs of tort litigation should be a leading priority.

Third, we need to watch the adverse selection problem to make sure it does not get out of hand. But at the same time, we must recognize that some degree of adverse selection is actually desirable from tort law's perspective because it puts pressure on bad risks to increase their investment in safety. We must also recognize that the primary techniques for controlling adverse selection lie in the structure of insurance arrangements, not the structure of tort doctrine.

Fourth, we need to do more empirical research on the problem of regressivity. If it is more severe than common sense would lead us to think, we need to consider social insurance alternatives that would allow us to counteract the regressive features of compensation through funding by a true progressive tax.

Fifth, there may be some special cases in which individually tailored immunities can promote the marketing of needed technological developments. But we have to tread carefully before making victims, as bearers of the costs of their own injuries, serve as indirect subsidizers of technological advance. Where we extend such immunities, we should seriously consider providing a social insurance alternative.

Reforms that significantly address one or more of these five concerns merit consideration. Reforms that do not must be supported by arguments unrelated to the contemporary critique of the insurance rationale.

The Traditional Rationale

Even if the current critique of the insurance rationale is overstated, it remains to be seen if the original rationale itself has continuing vitality. That can be evaluated by reassessing the themes supporting it.

Access to Insurance

This theme stresses the advantages of typical corporate and institutional defendants in obtaining insurance against the costs of accidents.[57] Those advantages are significantly less pronounced today than they were fifty years ago. Nevertheless, there are still strong reasons to believe that corporate and institutional actors possess superior access to the types of insurance that respond best to the needs of the tort system.

The empirical foundation of the access argument has been weakened to a degree by the widespread access most individuals now have to health and accident insurance. Most individuals either have or can readily obtain (usually in group plans offered by employers) insurance against the immediate medical costs that accidents impose. Whether they can easily insure against other kinds of loss, such as lost wages and pain and suffering, remains doubtful. Nonetheless, because we now have fairly comprehensive health insurance, as well as such social "safety nets" as unemployment compensation, the risk of personal financial catastrophe through uncompensated loss, which fueled the writings of Fleming James and his contemporaries,[58] is considerably reduced today. It is simply no longer accurate to assume, at least in many cases, that an accident will leave the individual victim destitute, without any financial recourse whatsoever. As a consequence, arguments in favor of the insurance rationale must be based on *relative* access, not the "all *versus* nothing" proposition assumed by earlier scholarly writings and some judicial opinions.

It should be noted, however, that there remain significant and persistent gaps in victim coverage. In particular, significant gaps in health coverage exist, for example, for the unemployed, the self-employed, those between jobs, students, and those who work for employers too small to maintain group plans. Because of the way our health insurance markets are structured, these individuals are likely to experience tremendous difficulties obtaining adequate insurance. As a result, the number of individuals who lack basic coverage may well run into the tens of millions. In the economic recession of the early 1990s, these gaps in health coverage became more prominent, and they have done much to precipitate the current debate about health-care reform. One cannot blithely assume that potential tort victims will have ready access to the basic forms of coverage they need for protection from unexpected injury.[59]

On the theoretical branch of the access rationale, there is still some good reason to prefer producer-insurers over consumer-insurers, however. Producers more closely typify rational actors whose response to the imposition of accident costs can be predicted and channeled for social benefit. They also have distinct advantages in their ability to gather and process information needed to construct effective programs of risk management. They have some advantages in terms of their ability to shop for coverage and to bargain with insurers over the terms of coverage. And they have advantages over consumers in many situations in their ability to make rational choices between cost spreading and cost avoidance. They are also better able, given the current structure of insurance markets, to obtain comprehensive coverage for all the types of costs we typically associate with an accident.

Thus, although the access argument has suffered some reduction in its persuasive force, it continues to support a moderate preference for spreading the costs of accidents through third-party liability. One should note, however, that the force of this argument is further reduced as one moves from large corporate or institutional actors—such as Fortune 500 corporations, major nonprofit organizations, or large municipalities—to smaller ones, such as small proprietorships and small towns. At the extreme end of the continuum (for example, an individual tradesperson running a service business out of his or her home) the access distinctions between producers and consumers pale considerably, although they do not completely vanish. One weakness of the tort doctrine that has grown up around the insurance rationale is that it fails to distinguish in any meaningful way between large and small corporate or institutional actors in terms of their ability to procure adequate liability insurance.

Likelihood of Purchasing Insurance

As with access, arguments based on the relative likelihood that typical corporate and institutional defendants will insure retain a reduced validity.[60] Although the steep insurance-premium hikes of the 1980s increased the occurrence of enterprises "going bare," it is still considered a customary, prudent business practice to insure against tort liability. Except for large corporate actors or institutional actors who have sufficient financial resources to self-insure, most producers of goods and services still customarily obtain insurance against liability. They may have to pay a much larger deductibles than in previous years, and the costs of insurance may have forced them to cap the maximum amount of coverage at a lower level; but they still carry liability insurance. Thus, it is still reasonable to assume that most corporate and institutional defendants in fact spread a substantial portion of the costs of liability through the mechanism of insurance.

On the other side of the equation, as already noted, the likelihood that individuals also insure against at least some of the costs of accidents has increased. But there are still millions of individuals who may not be adequately insured. Moreover, there are probably significant gaps in most individuals' insurance portfolios—especially with respect to economic loss and pain and suffering. Nevertheless, when the increased likelihood of individual insurance is coupled with the limits on producer coverage mentioned above, the result is a less dramatic disparity in the likelihood of cost spreading with regard to plaintiffs versus defendants than was probably the case forty or fifty years ago. The argument for imposing liability on likelihood grounds thus carries less force today, although it still lends some support to the insurance rationale.

Cost Effectiveness

One of the more dramatic miscalculations made by early proponents of the insurance rationale was the assertion, sometimes articulated but more often implicit, that corporate and institutional actors could insure against liability at a relatively low cost.[61] As we have already seen, costs have risen dramatically from what were once probably artificially low levels to fairly high levels, much higher than the halcyon expectations of the early insurance rationale advocates. We must face the reality that compensating the injured carries with it a fairly high price tag and that shifting the cost of that compensation to third parties does not reduce it. If anything, because of transfer expenses, shifting the burden through liability introduces a high level of "friction" in the system.

Historically, much of the appeal of the insurance rationale seems to have rested on its promise that spreading could be accomplished at relatively low cost. The failure of that promise, more than anything, lends impetus to the call for extensive reform. If the absolute costs of accidents are high enough, they may force us to rethink our approach to controlling and distributing them. In particular, we may have to think about ways of containing accident costs other than through third-party liability. Or we may have to think of ways of spreading them other than private third-party insurance. The high costs may even force us to set upper limits on the amounts of compensation, by any mechanism, that we can collectively afford to extend to those who have been injured by the acts of others.

Nevertheless, we must bear in mind that except for transfer-cost savings, *leaving the costs on the victims does not reduce or eliminate them.* The costs are still there. They are just being borne (and, at least to some extent, distributed) by a different group.

Accident costs. We have to be fairly careful about what conclusions we draw from the observation that implementation of the insurance rationale seems to have carried a fairly high price tag. The costs may well be high simply because the costs of accidents are in fact greater than we expected. The limitations on duty, artificially low standards of care, defenses, and immunities that pervaded tort law before the advent of the insurance rationale may have camouflaged those costs in the past, so that only in recent decades have they come into full relief. Barriers to effective recovery that held liability costs in check in previous generations have been eliminated. And late-twentieth-century advances in technology may have brought with them a more dangerous world (as well as a world whose dangers and their causes are better understood) with more injuries, which in turn produce higher liability costs.

If accident costs themselves are higher than expected, that fact alone does not support a move toward tort reform, because tort reform measures do not change accident costs; they only affect who is responsible for paying for them. Unless one can make a firm claim that assignment of accident costs elsewhere will create a positive incentive for safety, shifting those costs from the party who now bears them to another party will not in any real sense eliminate them. The cost of an accident borne by a plaintiff rather than a defendant is *still* the cost of an accident. Eliminating third-party liability for these costs will not make them go away; it will simply make them take a different, less visible form.

Unless there are other values that we can serve by such a change, moving to a system that hides the costs of accidents would not be a particularly desirable response to the discovery that they are substantial. If we are to make sensible decisions about how to manage the costs of accidents, it is helpful to have a clear idea what those costs are, both in terms of their absolute magnitude and in terms of their probable social impact. To some degree, at least, the present system permits us to do that.

Transfer costs. There are, in addition to the costs of accidents themselves, the costs of transfer.[62] The high costs of transfer are easily the worst failure of our existing liability system. The dangers they pose are nothing new. Tort theorists long have been aware of those costs as a leading blemish on the tort system's countenance. Nonetheless, it is probably fair to conclude that these costs also have risen beyond original expectations, so that they are today much higher than the original proponents of the insurance rationale anticipated.

Doing something to reduce transfer costs thus emerges as an important avenue for potential tort reform. But it is important to note that concern about reducing transfer costs operates largely independently of one's acceptance or rejection of the insurance rationale itself. Proponents of the insurance rationale, no less than its opponents, ought to favor reducing transfer costs, because doing so leaves a larger fund available for compensation and enhances the efficiency of third-party cost-spreading mechanisms. Thus, concern over the high cost of transferring responsibility for accidents does not lead directly to suspicion about the insurance rationale. Rather, it leads to an evaluation of alternative means for implementing that rationale that can reduce the financial drain of lawyers' fees and other costs associated with litigation.

The high costs of transfer may be attributed, at least in part, to judicial and legislative failures to complete their embrace of the insurance rationale. The primary source of transfer costs is, of course, litigation. The primary cause of civil litigation is uncertainty about the parties' respective legal rights and obligations. During the past thirty years, one source of uncertainty has been the rapid change in tort doctrine, which of course was partly fueled by courts' gradual acceptance of the insurance rationale but which would cease once the rationale was fully implemented. But a continuing high level of uncertainty stems from the courts' cautious retention of a variety of defenses, immunities, and other doctrines that either run counter to the insurance rationale or are grounded in policies that press the liability framework in different directions. The availability of these defenses, and uncertainty about their scope, have given defendants (who naturally seek to avoid liability) something about which to litigate. This in turn has frustrated out-of-court settlement, which is a third-party liability system's principal means of transfer-cost reduction.

Thus, just as failure to make a complete switch to first-party insurance frustrated the transfer-cost savings potential of automobile no-fault insurance, failure completely to adopt the insurance rationale has unnecessarily clouded its transfer-cost picture. We do not know how much litigation there would be if courts fully implemented the insurance rationale. What we do know is that a hybrid system, which shrouds liability in the uncertainty of a panoply of fact-specific liability theories and defenses, increases transfer costs.

This point is dramatically illustrated by the contrast between the typical tort case and the typical workers' compensation claim. Under workers' compensation, the field of injury compensation where the insurance rationale has achieved the greatest acceptance, only a relatively few limited defenses are available, and the facts concerning them are usually fairly easily established. Moreover, the amount of compensation for a meritorious case may well be predetermined. As a consequence, although the law is by no means devoid of litigation-producing complexity,[63] it is simpler and more straightforward than, say, the field of product liability. Consequently, the vast majority of workers' compensation claims are settled without litigation. The system's relative simplicity facilitates a reduction in transfer costs, without sacrificing the objectives of the insurance rationale.

Whatever our ultimate conclusion about the insurance rationale may be, it thus appears that one goal of any system that includes a significant component of third-party liability is simplicity. Plaintiffs and defendants need clear directives indicating whether a particular case falls into the category of liability or not. Where possible, liability itself should be set in a categorical fashion, rather than by a series of refined jury determinations of fact that give the parties an opportunity to litigate and waste transfer-cost dollars. And where we can simplify calculations of damages, we should do that as well. A system that depends on many layers of alternative liability theories and defenses more or less guarantees high transfer costs. A system that makes liability *vel non* as indisputable as possible at the outset, in contrast, portends the significant advantage of substantial transfer-cost savings.

Accidents as a Cost of Business

This argument, to the extent it is not simply a restatement of the insurance rationale itself, posits that making accident costs a cost of business promotes cost internalization and hence a more efficient level of accident-cost avoidance.[64] There has been considerable scholarly debate over the validity of this notion. Legal economists, in particular, have extensively debated the question whether strict liability or negligence produces superior cost internalization.[65] It is not my purpose here to rehearse the arguments for and against the idea of liability-cost internalization under these alternative standards that have been so ably pressed elsewhere. Rather, what needs to be done here is to consider whether producers or consumers are *relatively* better at whatever level of cost internalization the assessment of accident costs precipitates, and whether judgments about relative cost-internalization capacities in fact support the adoption of the insurance rationale.

Whether producers or consumers are better at internalizing costs depends on who has more control over safety risks. If safety risks are beyond a particular actor's control, then assessment of that party for accident costs is unlikely to produce any significant internalization unless, as Calabresi puts it, that actor is able to find and "bribe" the party who in fact can avoid the accident.[66] Thus the question boils down to a determination whether producers or consumers are the ones with greater control—either directly or through negotiation with others—over safety risks associated with some particular product or activity.[67]

Wholesale generalization on this issue may well be impossible. With respect to most consumer products, for example, it is apparent that producers have superior control over some risks, whereas consumers have superior control over others. Consider the lawn mower, a perennial source of product liability litigation. A lawn mower manufacturer probably has superior control over risks such as those associated with defects in a mower's blade, engine, and rotor assembly, whereas a consumer has greater control over risks such as those associated with various kinds of use—such as, to borrow a famous apocryphal example, the risks of trying to use the mower to cut hedges. To decide who has greater control over the aggregate of all risks associated with lawn mower manufacture and use, however, we would have to undertake the laborious task of identifying every conceivable risk; considering the options of each party for controlling that risk; determining, risk by risk, whose options were superior; then pooling all the results for individual risks into one grand calculation. It is immediately apparent that we are unlikely to undertake that task for even a single product or service, let alone for the myriad products, services, and activities that the tort system encompasses.

Alternatively, we could try to identify some structural characteristics of producers and/or consumers that *suggest,* even if they do not guarantee, superior risk control. This approach is probably what supports the cost-of-business argument that has been advanced to support strict product liability. Advocates of such liability believe (as Justice Traynor did in *Escola*) that product manufacturers have more control over the totality of risks associated with their products, and therefore that they have a better chance of internalizing the costs of compensating for injuries those products cause.

Is this belief justified? In the case of products, manufacturers have significant structural advantages in controlling safety risks associated with manufacture, design, and distribution of the product. Consumers, on the other hand, have some important structural advantages in controlling use. Although consumers have most immediate control over use of the product, however, manufacturers are not without some elements of control in that sphere as well. They can create directions for proper use, warnings against certain forms of dangerous use, and design elements that prevent or frustrate certain kinds of dangers associated with use. They can also monitor use of the product to identify and address unanticipated risks that materialize once the product is on the market. Consumers, in contrast, have relatively few means for controlling risks of manufacture and design, and they may even lack requisite knowledge to guard against some dangers associated with use of the product.[68]

Thus, as to products at least, structural considerations point (somewhat indeterminately) at producers as superior in the area of risk control. But even this very modest generalization is speculative, founded more on intuition than empirical fact. At current information levels, we can do no more than guess who has superior risk-control ability, and we are unlikely (because of the sheer cost of doing so) to acquire sufficient additional information to make any more solid determination.

There is, however, another way of looking at the cost internalization issue. As Calabresi and Hirschoff have argued, if we do not know who can actually avoid costs more cheaply, we can try to determine who is better positioned to make intelligent cost-avoidance decisions.[69] This is usually the party with the most information about risks, the best information-gathering capacity, the greatest likelihood of making rational cost-benefit calculations regarding risk, and the best ability to use market forces to transfer accident costs to the most efficient cost avoider or else to spread them where avoidance is not prudent. Assigning liability to such a party maximizes the prospect that accident costs will ultimately be distributed in ways that optimize cost avoidance. In other words, even if we do not know who is better at cost internalization with respect to a particular product or service, we can look for the party who is best able to find out about cost internalization and best able to structure transactions to achieve whatever level of internalization is possible.

For this inquiry, the structural advantages of corporate and institutional actors, and their insurers, become more salient. They are natural repositories of information about the risks associated with their own goods and services, and they have at their behest techniques such as product differentiation, pricing strategies, warranties, service contracts, warnings, and the like, in addition to insurance, which may be used to allocate costs either toward production or toward the consumer in order to maximize internalization opportunities.[70]

This vision of the cost-of-business argument is very different from the one most evident in writings by advocates of the insurance rationale. It also bears a surprisingly attenuated relation to the insurance rationale itself. Effective cost internalization is more immediately supported by the safety rationale for tort liability. Producer advantages in making cost internalization decisions, to the extent they exist, would support imposition of liability on producers rather than consumers even if the values of cost spreading were eliminated from the mix of controlling policy goals.

The only place where cost internalization and the insurance rationale intersect is in the arena of uncertainty. If we are certain about who is better at internalizing costs or (alternatively) about who is better at making cost internalization decisions, we can justify imposing the costs of accidents on that party in the name of safety, regardless of risk-spreading considerations. But what if we are in doubt? In that event, there is an argument for resolving that doubt in favor of the party who is the better insurer, so that, if our original belief in the party's internalization capabilities turns out to be unfounded, we can at least reap the secondary benefits of risk spreading. Only to the extent that risk spreading is a hedge against uncertainty does the cost internalization argument lend any significant support to the insurance rationale.

Risk Management

This argument maintains that corporate/institutional actors and their insurers have superior risk management abilities, which justify imposing liability on them.[71] In general, this argument is little more than a variation of the cost internalization theme discussed above. But it does add one unique wrinkle, since it emphasizes the special role that *insurers* may play on behalf of their insureds in establishing effective risk-management programs.

Insurers have been notable for their safety leadership in certain fields, such as industrial accidents and automotive safety. Because of their unique ability to gather and process information about accidents and accident costs—something they must do in order to perform successful risk classification and accurate premium pricing—they seem well positioned to render their insureds invaluable aid in identifying and eliminating controllable risks. Thus, on a theoretical level, this argument seems to carry a certain validity. Unfortunately, there is relatively little evidence that this sort of risk-management assistance has occurred in practice beyond two or three select zones.

The reasons insurers have been less than vigorous in helping corporate/institutional insureds to reduce liability risks of their products and operations are not immediately clear. One possibility is that, until recently, liability insurance was so thoroughly underpriced that corporate and institutional insureds simply had no motivation to call for such aid. Another possibility is that energies that might have been spent on the joint enterprise of better accident cost control have been invested elsewhere, such as in trying to maximize returns on investments, defending against potential tort liability, or lobbying for tort reform. Another possibility is that these advantages do not materialize unless it is clear that insurers, as a group, have to bear nearly all the accident costs in question. That seems to be true in such areas as workplace injury (where there is fully insured strict employer liability) and automotive injury (where there is either no-fault or a negligence-based allocation between roughly equally insured motorists), where insurer emphasis on safety has had its highest profile. In any event, the theoretical ability of insurers to contribute to risk management has not, in the main, materialized in practice.

Equity

This argument asserts that it is inequitable to extend the protection of third-party liability to certain classes of victim, such as workers, but not to others, such as consumers.[72] Whatever its rhetorical appeal, this argument in fact carries very little weight.

Equity, of course, requires that similarly situated groups or individuals be treated in similar ways. There is no reason all tort plaintiffs or all tort defendants should be treated uniformly, if in fact there are differences among them in the way the policy goals of tort law play out. Thus, the implicit assumption of the equity argument is that injured victims inside and outside the workplace are similarly situated with respect to the operative goals of tort liability, in particular the insurance rationale. But the risk environments of workers and consumers seem sufficiently different that any generalization from the workers' compensation approach would require independent reasoning beyond mere considerations of equity. In particular, employer control over risks in the workplace environment is far superior to the control that corporate and institutional producers of goods and services generally enjoy.

Moreover, the equity argument, like the unpredictability argument discussed above, does not point in any particular direction. One could just as well achieve "equity" by eliminating workers' compensation and treating injured workers under general principles of tort law as by modifying general principles of tort law to resemble the handling of workers' compensation. Which approach to take requires consideration of values other than the desire for equal treatment itself.

The workers' compensation model remains attractive. It is far from perfect, but at its core it seems to work reasonably well—especially in contrast to other tort law environments. It represents a reasonable accommodation between the insurance rationale and other, competing goals of the tort system. Although by no means the sole cause, it seems to have contributed to significant advances in industrial safety. And as noted above, it has at least partially avoided some of the chief ills of general third-party liability, such as uncertainty and high transfer costs.

Nevertheless, generalization from the workers' compensation model to the much more complex environment of nonindustrial accidents must proceed cautiously, if at all. The industrial environment is highly structured, and subject to extensive employer control. The domain of general tort law is highly unstructured, and no party has full control over major risk factors. There is no reason blithely to assume that what works in one environment will also work in the other.

Furthermore, proposals for revamping tort law to resemble the model of workers' compensation, however attractive they may seem in theory, must inevitably take into account political realities. Like proposals for no-fault insurance, wholesale adaptation of workers' compensation to other kinds of injury would involve a substantial commitment of political resources. Given the reality of legislative gridlock in many states over the much more modest agenda of changes in the structure of workers' compensation itself, the prospects for expanding the scope of the model seem doubtful.

Inevitable Risk

This argument asserts that the presence of "inevitable risk" in modern society justifies resort to the insurance rationale as a basis for liability.[73] In absolute terms, of course, the only truly "inevitable" risks are natural disasters and other "acts of God" that, by long-standing social consensus, lie outside the ambit of tort liability. Nevertheless, there are obviously many risks that are theoretically avoidable but that society is unwilling to bear the cost of avoiding.[74] We could, for example, avoid some traffic fatalities by lowering the national speed limit to twenty-five miles per hour, but as a society we would be unwilling to incur the huge economic cost of doing so. Presumably, such theoretically avoidable but practically necessary risks are the "inevitable risks" to which this argument principally relates.

There does seem to be a germ of truth to the idea that, for such risks, it is easier to tolerate them if we know the victims will be compensated. And it does make sense to spread the cost of compensating such risks on a fairly broad plane. Since we have deliberately incurred the risks in order to benefit society, there is an element of fairness in requiring the groups or individuals within society who received that benefit to pay the freight. If the victims of such "inevitable accidents" could be clearly identified in advance and the connection between their injury and the public weal definitively established before the injury occurred, we would feel strong pressures to compensate them, much as we do for those who have been injured in the course of military service for our common defense.

The problem lies in distinguishing "inevitable" accidents from "avoidable" accidents—that is, accidents that could be avoided without any harm to the public interest. For accidents in this latter category, society at large owes no general debt of compensation. If we do choose to compensate in that context, it must be for other reasons, such as our desire to promote optimum levels of safety.[75] Moreover, as to avoidable accidents, there remains the possibility that the victims themselves could have been efficient cost avoiders; in that event, far from wanting to compensate, we might have positive reasons for refusing to do so. Thus, the inevitable-risk argument applies only to one category of victims, and misapplication of the rationale to victims in another category could interfere with important social objectives.

Unfortunately, however, we lack any tools for making the necessary distinction between categories of victim. We cannot make that judgment in advance. And even after the fact, whether a particular accident was "avoidable" or "inevitable" in the senses used here usually remains a highly debatable issue. One could imagine a system that asked juries to try to sort out victims of "inevitable" accident and compensate them on a different basis, but jury discretion on such an issue would necessarily remain largely unguided, and consistency of results would be difficult to maintain.

There is an additional difficulty in linking the notion of compensation for inevitable accident with the assessment of particular defendants for liability. In a modern echo of Oliver Wendell Holmes, one might well argue that if society wants to compensate victims in return for the social good their injuries permit, then the proper mechanism would be distribution of governmental largesse specifically directed to that end, not the imposition of tort liability on defendants who are, at best, but weak proxies for the commonwealth. With respect to municipal or governmental defendants, this argument obviously does not carry great force, since the defendant and the commonwealth are one. But for corporate defendants, the assertion that they should not be forced to pay society's debts carries a surface appeal.

Further reflection, however, cuts against this argument. In the case of a corporate actor, the benefit society receives from the actor's injuring activity is likely to be secured through enjoyment of the goods or services the actor produces. The segment of society that most immediately derives the benefits comprises those individuals who actually use the products or services in question. These are the corporate actor's customers. If the corporate actor is saddled with liability and insures against it, the cost of that insurance is added to the cost of the relevant goods or services and is paid by the customers. Thus, imposing liability in order to compensate inevitable accidents actually should result in spreading the cost of that liability to the very group in society for whose benefit the risk was incurred. Indeed, this approach is arguably more precise—arguably "fairer"—than a governmental social program directed to the same object. It lets the individuals who want the good or service despite its accident costs to buy them at a price that reflects those costs, while the rest of us can avoid paying the injury compensation freight by simply excluding the product or service in question from our shopping list.

Ultimately, how much the inevitable-accident argument adds depends in large measure on how many accidents one believes fit the criterion of inevitability. The early proponents of the insurance rationale seem to have believed that the portion of accidents in modern society that could be termed "inevitable" was relatively large. If one shares that view, one is thereby impelled to the belief that assurance of compensation for victims of such accidents is an important norm. In view of our inability to sort the victims of inevitable accident out, one is then drawn to the proposition that victims may be entitled to a certain "benefit of the doubt" that their injury was "inevitable" and hence entitled to compensation absent powerful evidence that shifting the loss would have a negative social impact. If, on the other hand, one regards most accidents as "avoidable," so that inevitable accidents, even in the qualified social sense used here, are rare, one is more likely to conclude that special provisions to assure compensation for the inevitably injured are unnecessary.

Unfortunately, neither side of the debate over the insurance rationale offers any useful technique for measuring or determining the "inevitability" of accidents. Instead, both sides rely on either flat assertions or unspoken assumptions about the degree of inevitability. Consequently, at current levels of information there is no objective way of measuring the force of this argument.

Summary

Assessment of the traditional arguments in support of the insurance rationale significantly narrows our focus in judging its worth. Of the seven arguments for the rationale considered here, two—the equity and risk-management arguments—carry relatively little force. The former relies on an analogy to workers' compensation that at best needs further exploration and at worst may well be flawed; the latter asserts a potential for insurer involvement in safety that is theoretically possible but in practice largely unrealized. A third argument, inevitable risk, depends on judgments about the magnitude of a phenomenon concerning which we have very little information and no accepted techniques for measurement.

A fourth factor, cost, yields a more complicated picture. Cost attributable to accidents themselves cuts neither way, although the information we have about it is surely sobering. Cost attributable to the friction of transferring loss actually cuts against the insurance rationale, albeit in a fairly qualified way. Far from saving transfer costs, adoption of the insurance rationale seems to have aggravated them. This conclusion is undercut in part by the observation that *full* embrace of the insurance rationale has almost never happened and that courts' retention of doctrines and defenses at war with the rationale have complicated adjudicatory processes in ways that tend to keep transfer costs high. But it would take more temerity than I have to assert against the weight of the historic record that adoption of the insurance rationale would tend to keep transfer costs low.

A fifth argument, cost of business, though perhaps the linchpin of the insurance rationale during much of its development, is surprisingly disappointing. To survive at all, it must be reformulated into an argument about relative decision-making capacities, and in that guise it turns out to have much more to do with safety than with insurance. To the extent it supports liability based on insurance, it does so only as a hedge against uncertainty about the ability or likelihood of parties making rational decisions about safety investments.

Still, in that very watered-down form, the cost-of-business rationale does provide some support. Uncertainty about cost internalization is a very real phenomenon, and in view of the costs of acquiring information about safety, it is unlikely to go away. As long as we continue to experience such uncertainty, it does make some sense to place the risk of that uncertainty on parties who are better able, if not to eliminate it, at least to spread its cost.

Only two of the arguments in favor of the insurance rationale—access and likelihood—have anything resembling the force in favor of the rationale that its scholarly proponents have envisioned. Today, even the force of these arguments is qualified by the reality that victims as well as injurers can and do obtain insurance against their misfortunes. Victim insurance in its present form is imperfect, incomplete, unwieldy, and far from universal, and the task of developing better first-party alternatives would require a daunting commitment of political resources. Thus, there are still reasons to believe that injurers may be *better* insurers. But this comparative judgment is nowhere near as stark and clear today as it was forty or fifty years ago.

TEN

The Insurance Rationale and the Future of Tort Reform

What, then, should be the modern contours of the insurance rationale? In part, the preceding discussion confirms that there is neither a clear nor a demonstrably "right" answer to that question. The answer we give depends in large measure on the relative importance we assign to the social value of compensation as a goal of tort liability. It also depends on a host of guesses and assumptions we have to make, without the benefit of much information, about an extremely wide range of social phenomena associated with injury, the characteristics of injurers and victims, and the ways in which they react to the administration of liability rules. Nor can these phenomena be treated in isolation from our assessments regarding the impact of other social forces that, by acting on the process of tort litigation, also influence the effect and direction of tort liability rules.

Yet, it is both too easy and not very helpful simply to throw up our hands and proclaim that we cannot draw any firm conclusion. The reality is that we *must* draw some conclusion, however tentative. If we decide to leave the law where it is, that decision, in effect, reflects an implicit judgment that the insurance rationale has a moderately significant role to play. This follows from the fact that the rationale, at least to some degree, stands behind the development of existing liability rules. If we decide to change the law, we cannot thoughtfully do so without paying some regard to the role of insurance and reflecting in our decision a judgment about how we want that role to play out.

Whatever the law does, the reality in practice is that, in effect, liability rules are insurance-backed and insurance-driven. As long as there is any tort law at all, businesses and other entities that engage in injury-causing activities will find it prudent to carry substantial amounts of liability insurance.

As long as the contingent fee remains part of our system, plaintiffs' lawyers will be willing to advocate victims' cases only where there is an apparent source of recovery—usually an insurance fund of one sort or another. Where such a fund is present, those same lawyers can be counted on to press, with creativity, energy, and perseverance, whatever theories of recovery the law will allow. Enterprises and other insured institutions will thus continue to be the primary targets of most tort suits. In those suits juries will either learn about insurance or, if that information is suppressed, imagine its existence, and they will factor that real or speculative consideration into their judgment. Ignoring at a theoretical level what is so palpable and forceful at a practical level makes no sense.

Beyond these practical considerations, it seems unrealistic to cast aside the goal of compensation through cost spreading as an important element in the mix of values that support imposing tort liability. Compensating victims of one kind or another is one of the major undertakings of government in our society. We devote considerable energy to that undertaking. We spend a great deal of money for it. We pay taxes to support it. And in doing so we either wittingly or unwittingly embrace the validity of cost spreading as a mechanism for combatting the undesirable effects of personal loss or disadvantage. It would seem strange for a society that finds the value of compensation through cost spreading so appealing in other domains to deny its significance in a legal system that deals explicitly and almost exclusively with injury. If the victims of tortious injury were grouped together as victims of some single mass disaster, we would surely recognize the legitimacy of their claims for compensation, as we have for the victims of Hurricane Andrew and the 1993 Mississippi and Missouri River floods. That the victims in the tort system usually suffer their injuries in small groups or alone, or that their injury comes from an act of enterprise rather than an "act of God," should not materially alter our collective judgment concerning the social value of compensating their loss.

Thus, unless the mix of social values that we share changes in some unforeseeably radical fashion, it makes sense to think about fashioning liability rules to accomplish an insurance compensation function. That is not of course the sole, or even the primary, goal of tort law. If it conflicts with other goals of equal rank, we must strike a balance between them. If it conflicts with other goals of higher rank, we must decide whether to sacrifice assured compensation in order to achieve those higher goals. But where compensation through insurance does not demonstrably conflict with other competing goals, it is consistent with our general social fabric deliberately to shape liability rules to achieve it.

Much of the current critique of the insurance rationale does not really challenge the propriety of cost spreading as a *potential* goal for tort liability. Rather, the critics have attempted to prove that the rationale is hopelessly in conflict with other goals, especially safety; that it is an unworkable criterion for liability that ultimately produces more harm than good; that it is too costly; or that it is distinctly inferior to other modes of compensating loss, most notably first-party insurance. The extended discussion in Chapter Nine shows that these arguments for the most part lack persuasive force. They may, to some extent, influence how vigorously we are prepared to apply the rationale; but they do not, either singly or collectively, make a very strong case for backing away from the insurance rationale or jettisoning it altogether. This is particularly true in view of the courts' long-standing tradition of employing the insurance rationale with caution, as a distinctly secondary focus for adjudication—a rationale in a perpetual supporting role.

Further, the arguments in favor of the insurance rationale continue to have some power. There is still enough validity to the access and likelihood themes, in particular, to justify the inference that corporate and institutional actors are probably better at effective cost spreading than individuals. And with some reformulation, the cost-of-business theme yields support for the notion that these same actors are probably better at managing uncertainty about efficient cost avoidance. Thus, as Justice Traynor understood,[1] using insurance as a complement to the safety rationale helps us to resolve our doubts about how to secure safety, and it enables us to control for imperfections in our ability to make accurate safety determinations. It also helps us to make categorical judgments about liability that offer the potential for greater simplicity and predictability. Except in circumstances where we can say with confidence that corporate or institutional actors are *not* the cheapest cost avoiders, there is, as Holmes put it, some "clear benefit to be derived" from resolving uncertainties about cost avoidance in favor of those institutions' cost-spreading advantages.[2]

This reasoning would not support placing insurance *ahead* of safety in the scale of values to be achieved through tort liability. If we have a clear choice between spreading costs and developing effective incentives for avoiding them, the latter objective ought to prevail. But there is no persuasive evidence for the assertion that present legal doctrine inverts these values. Rather, the principal uses of insurance to date have been to eliminate partial or total immunities from the obligation to make cost avoidance decisions, to cover for imperfections and uncertainties about relative cost-avoidance capacities, or, in rare instances, to achieve compensation in situations where safety incentives would be futile because the courts are facing an instance of "inevitable risk." Rather than serve as a radical tool for massive transfer of wealth, the insurance rationale has served a more modest role as a mechanism for adjustment at the margins of our knowledge about safety and cost avoidance.

The growing phenomenon of first-party accident insurance, though not a particularly strong foundation for departure from the insurance rationale, should strengthen this deep-seated social preference for safety over insurance in those few situations where the values clearly conflict. It is easier to let the loss lie where it falls, in cases where we are confident that doing so will promote safety, if we know that the victim has not only some ability to avoid the accident but also some capacity to guard against it through first-party insurance. Indeed, more-aggressive experimentation with first-party options remains an attractive avenue for potential social reform, although constructing an effective first-party regime that preserves adequate producer incentives for safety may prove to be an extremely challenging task. What we must bear most in mind about first-party insurance, however, is the inadequacy of *existing* vehicles for achieving the benefits in transfer-cost saving that the first-party model theoretically offers.

Just as first-party options remain attractive, so does the noble social experiment of workers' compensation. The prospect of developing a third-party liability system that uses a combination of strict liability, simplified factual inquiry, limited damages, and alternative dispute resolution to assure compensation without expensive transfer costs continues to be attractive as a way to minimize the weaknesses of a third-party approach. The difficulties here are to find zones of human activity, beyond the workplace, where such an approach might work, and to construct a system that avoids some of the problems in execution that administration of workers' compensation has brought to light.

To the extent that we are motivated to tamper with existing insurance arrangements, we should also be motivated to reform existing modes of insurance regulation. Much could be said in favor of national regulation of this major financial industry. But even within the existing state-based regulatory system, at a minimum there should be (1) more-aggressive requirements for meaningful financial accounting and disclosure of useful data regarding loss experience; (2) more-effective regulatory oversight of rate-making decisions; (3) initiatives to improve risk-classification practices; (4) initiatives to create more comprehensive forms of first-party accident insurance; (5) assistance for those who are experiencing difficulty obtaining adequate coverage; and (6) oversight of claims handling and litigation management to control costs and speed recoveries.

There is abundant evidence that the insurance rationale should not be applied without attention to its cost. The unspoken assumption of earlier times that cost spreading is a relatively "costless" phenomenon clearly must be discarded. But it would be equal folly to indulge either the assumption that costs that are not transferred and spread have vanished or the assumption that costs borne by a victim have no social implications. What we must recognize is that injury *is* costly no matter where we place the burden, no matter to whom it is spread.

Nevertheless, in applying the insurance rationale, courts and legislatures must be cost-conscious. Compensation for injury drives up insurance premiums, which in turn drives up the costs of goods and services, thus putting them out of reach for some and depleting the general consumable wealth of all. This, too, is a form of social dislocation, albeit of a different sort than the dislocation that can result from a decision to make victims bear the loss. The higher the price tag of compensation, moreover, the more likely it is that shifting the cost to injurers will cause undesirable effects. Consequently, where compensation is allowed, we must pay closer attention to the measures we use for determining the *amount* of compensation; and we may even be forced to the conclusion that some victims must be only partly compensated in order to reserve funds for compensating others. Just as there are cases where total safety is too expensive for society, there may be cases where total compensation is too expensive for society. We need to begin exploring how to make that determination in a fashion that honestly takes the impact of injury on victims as well as injurers into account.

Furthermore, there is great need for closer attention to the transfer-cost problem. Transfer costs are by far the greatest weakness of the third-party liability system. Even without the insurance rationale, they would remain a problem, as long as we use compensatory liability as a vehicle for promoting safety. Consequently, courts and legislatures need to pay much greater attention to finding ways of reducing these costs effectively.

For courts, the primary focus in reducing transfer costs should be on devising and enforcing procedures that streamline trial processes and promote early settlement without impairing the courts' capacity to render fair and impartial adjudication. Equally important is the need for courts to delineate liability rules more clearly in order to minimize uncertainty. Where possible, they should also reduce the number of factual inquiries—the grist of the litigation mill—that affect liability determinations.

For legislatures, procedural reform is also a promising vehicle for controlling transfer costs. In an earlier era, legislatures needed to address the problems associated with trial by ambush; today, the greater problem is trial by siege—endless procedural maneuvering that adds directly to the transfer-cost bill. Direct limitations on procedural warfare specifically directed at tort cases may be advisable. In addition, more energy should be devoted to designing attractive options for alternative dispute resolution and creating positive incentives for their use. Regulating attorney practices and fees may also be necessary.

Nevertheless, legislatures should resist the temptation to use cutting off access to the courts as an artificial means of holding down transfer costs. For example, placing undue limits on the ability of attorneys to attract clients or to earn satisfactory fees from personal injury cases might seem expedient measures to control costs, but they would do so by arbitrarily cutting off recovery and by denying effective representation for some deserving victims. Similarly, evidentiary or discovery rules that prevent victims from securing the information they truly need to press their claims amount to willful ignorance, not honest accident cost control. As noted above, hiding the costs of accidents does not eliminate them; and there is no good case for placing the transfer-cost problem on the backs of poorer victims who, without the ability to share their recovery with attorneys, would be unable to attract legal services and press their claims. Rather, regulation should be focused on excesses. More important, it should be directed at eliminating legal maneuvers (on either side of the litigation) that add expense incommensurate with their contribution to reliable liability judgments.

Beyond cost, courts and legislatures must remain aware of the value of predictability. The insurance rationale itself is predicated on the assumption that defendants assessed with liability, and their insurers, are best positioned to spread the loss in an effective manner. The validity of the rationale depends directly on the validity of that assumption. But that loss-spreading advantage exists only if those parties are able to predict in advance the probable incidence and magnitude of the losses they are supposed to spread. This can, of course, be done by statistical inference from past experience, but only in a legal environment that is reasonably stable. Without the ability to make those predictions, any insurance system will founder.

The recent period of dynamic change in tort law unquestionably has strained the predictive abilities of liability insurers. Changes in tort rules have not interfered with insurers' abilities to predict *accidents,* but they have affected the ability of insurers to determine from the accident rate for a given product or activity the expected level of liability exposure. Such unpredictability, compounded by the ultimately subjective way in which liability insurance premiums are set, tends to precipitate extreme variability and even irrationality in insurance pricing. If carried on for too long, these phenomena could produce unwholesome effects that would ultimately defeat the insurance rationale's initial goal: provision, by reasonably efficient means, of an assured fund for accident compensation.

These considerations support the notion that, at least for the immediate future, some degree of stability in the development of tort liability rules would be welcome. Sudden sharp changes, in any direction, will place further strain on predictability, and this undesirable effect must be weighed in the balance against any claim for departure from current norms. Consequently, change in liability rules themselves should be modest, not massive, more in keeping with evolutionary growth of the law than with revolutionary change. Change, however, that simplifies determination of liability, so that it turns on relatively easily ascertained facts, could assist in speeding up litigation, promoting settlement, and avoiding large transfer costs—developments that would actually improve predictability.

One promising avenue for reform would be to enhance the directness with which insurance issues are addressed in the process of setting the structure and direction of tort doctrine. There may be a good justification for suppressing information about insurance, and about the insurance effects of liability, from juries—at least, that is the conventional wisdom. But there is no similar merit in hiding these factors from judges and legislatures when they are called on to chart the course of liability. Yet our tort doctrine remains full of formalisms and legalisms that send, at best, mixed and confusing signals about the insurance implications of doctrinal judgments. Frank discussion of the realities behind the rules is rare. Discussion informed by useful data is even rarer.

In setting a course for tort reform, courts and legislatures (and the advocates who appear before them) should be prepared to address directly the insurance implications of their doctrinal choices, and they should demand hard data on the empirical implications of their decisions. Questions such as Who is the better insurer? or How will the loss be spread, to whom, and at what cost? should be constant components of reasoning about tort law, not (as they so often are now) occasional afterthoughts. They should not replace equally pertinent questions such as Who can most cheaply avoid the loss? but they must be at the front rank of tort inquiries if we are to strive for comprehensive and effective solutions.

Courts and legislatures, once they begin asking those questions and assembling the data needed to answer them, should also structure liability rules to eliminate duplicative insurance and resulting overcompensation of victims. This is partly a matter of restructuring the collateral source rule, a development that is already well under way in many jurisdictions. It may also be a matter of reviving the insurance-law doctrine of subrogation and employing it in tort contexts in a manner explicitly designed to promote the insurance rationale.[3] Where, by virtue of subrogation, the compensation of the victim effectively drops out of the case and the question is which of two or more insurers should pay, the answer ought to depend at least in part—and perhaps in the main—on which insured party has superior cost-spreading capacities for the particular injury in question.

Finally, reform-minded courts and legislatures should learn to regard tort law as part of a much larger accident-prevention and accident-compensation system, one that embraces legislative and administrative as well as judicial schemes, and one that mixes compensation from private and public sources. Too often, the components of that system have functioned in a vacuum, almost as if ignorant of one another. Too often, whether a particular injury is treated under one regime or under another has been more an accident of history or politics than a product of rational choice. Integrating these various means of dealing with accident costs into a more unified whole would contribute much to the development of a more efficient and effective program of accident compensation and control.

The prescriptions for future tort reform outlined here are necessarily general. They are not by any means a comprehensive list of all the factors that ought to be taken into account in setting future directions for tort liability. Nor do they chart an unmistakable course to a single panacea. Yet they do provide a rough gauge of sorts by which particular reform proposals can be measured. Or, to put the matter in perhaps more accurate terms, they offer the beginnings of a rational vocabulary for evaluating the inevitably hot and rhetorical debate between proponents and opponents of particular reform measures. How individual proposals will affect the system, how they will intersect or conflict with other competing proposals, what the arguments for and against them will be, and what implicit value choices those proposals reflect can be ascertained by assessing them against issues and arguments that have been considered here. My goal has been to convert the arguments for and against change that often surface in an atmosphere charged with the rhetoric of crisis into a more mature, objective, and systematic process of deliberation.

Like every student of the tort system, I have my own agenda of preferred tort reform measures. After attending to the procedural and insurance-regulatory reforms mentioned above, I would devote substantial attention to the reform of damages determinations. For some recurring accidents or some particular elements of damage (such as medical diagnosis and treatment), it might be possible to follow the workers' compensation model and develop schedules of prescribed recovery (or perhaps a range of acceptable amounts with a prescribed ceiling and floor), a step that would promote predictability and reduce one source of litigation. For other situations, there should be greater effort to particularize the permissible elements of damages, to prescribe with particularity the types of required evidence, to give juries more explicit instructions on how damages should be calculated, and to give courts better means of oversight to ensure reasonable consistency among verdicts in comparable cases.

There may also be value in capping damage awards in some instances, or perhaps setting ceilings on particular elements of the award, such as pain and suffering. Damage caps proved to be a popular sort of reform measure during the 1980s. Courts and legislatures should be wary, however, of the risk that damage caps can arbitrarily cut off compensation in some of the more deserving cases. I believe that efforts are better spent in attempting to bring about greater consistency in the amount of recovery for particular forms of harm than in setting absolute upper limits on the total damage award. The latter is simply too blunt an instrument to accomplish much good.

There is also room for experimentation with the workers' compensation model. Wholesale adaptation of that approach may be unwise as well as politically inexpedient, but there are some instances where the model might work. For example, recurring disasters that happen in particular industries, such as airplane crashes or hotel fires, might be effectively handled through a strict liability third-party compensation scheme. Some toxic torts might be treated in a similar fashion. For example, in retrospect it probably would have made sense if, when the vast scope of potential liability for asbestos exposure first became known, legislatures had enacted a strict liability compensation scheme for victims of asbestos-related injury, a scheme structured in a manner similar to workers' compensation. Injuries to patients that are receiving hospital treatment might be yet another candidate for treatment along the workers' compensation model. In these situations, the likelihood of injury should be fairly predictable, producers enjoy major advantages in control over risk and capacity to insure, some level of injury is probably "inevitable," and spreading the cost of injury to all the beneficiaries of the activity in question seems to make particularly good sense. The trade-off between assured compensation and limited recovery that is the hallmark of the workers' compensation model seems, in each of these settings, to represent a reasonably fair accommodation between producer and victim interests. In using the workers' compensation model, however, legislatures should be wary of the problems that have arisen over time in workers' compensation itself, and they should design any new system with an eye toward minimizing those difficulties.

With respect to liability rules themselves, I would resist the temptation to fiddle, except in circumstances where it would be possible to simplify liability determinations. Artificial duty limitations and immunities should continue to be eliminated, especially in cases where defendants have a superior capacity to insure. Standards of care should be defined in terms that simplify factual inquiries as much as possible and thus minimize opportunities for dispute. Litigation-producing defenses should be eliminated, except in limited circumstances where they are clearly justified by the objective of promoting safety. But in the main, legislatures should defer to courts on these problems, which the courts can sort out in their evolutionary common-law fashion. Courts have never run away with the insurance rationale, and they can be counted on to keep it in bounds.

The purpose of this book, however, is not to advocate this or any other specific program of tort reform. What is ultimately more important than the particular agenda is the way that we frame and evaluate the debate over any new set of proposals. On this hangs our ability to separate the wheat from the chaff, to figure out which proposals make good social sense and which ones will only end up serving the parochial concerns of particular interest groups.

The politics of tort reform are such that the debate, in legislatures and in the courts, is likely to be joined in the first instance by partisans whose views are heavily colored by self-interest. That is, quite simply, inevitable. Billions of dollars in accident costs are at stake, and the fight over rights and obligations with respect to such a large fund will certainly be pressed by the interest groups having the most to win or lose. As Leon Green recognized long ago, tort law is simply public policy—that is, politics—in disguise.[4] The current battle over tort reform is no exception, and it includes all the exaggeration, hyperbole, undocumented assertions, and hidden assumptions that are the constant accompaniments of such a partisan and politically charged affray. But if we can master the principles that lie behind the politics, and if we can use them to put the rhetoric of crisis into perspective, we have at least some chance of directing this political tug-of-war toward socially beneficial ends.

NOTES

INTRODUCTION

1. Fowler Harper and Fleming James Jr., *The Law of Torts* (Boston: Little, Brown, 1956), 2:765.

2. Walter Isaacson, "Let the Buyers Beware: Consumer Advocates Retrench for Hard Times," *Time,* September 21, 1981, 22.

3. Kenneth S. Abraham, "Private Insurance, Social Insurance, and Tort Reform: Toward A New Vision of Compensation for Illness and Injury," *Columbia Law Review* 93 (1993): 75; Antoinette Paglia, "Taking the Tort out of Court—Administrative Adjudication of Liability Claims: Is It the Next Step?" *Southwestern University Law Review* 20 (1991): 41.

4. Jerry Phillips, "Attacks on the Legal System: Fallacy of Tort Reform Arguments," *Trial* 28 (February 1992): 106–10. See also Robert L. Habush, "The Insurance 'Crisis': Reality or Myth? A Plaintiff Lawyer's Perspective," *Denver University Law Review* 64 (1991): 641; Philip J. Hermann, "Million-Dollar Verdicts and Other Fantasies," *Wall Street Journal,* April 4, 1987, 30.

5. David Cummins, Scott E. Harrington, and Robert W. Klein, "Cycles and Crises," *Best's Review: Property-Casualty Insurance Edition* 92, no. 9 (1992): 15.

PART I

1. An overview of early scholarly work on tort theory is provided by Priest, "The Invention of Enterprise Liability: A Critical History of the Intellectual Foundations of Modern Tort Law," *Journal of Legal Studies* 14 (1985): 461. See also G. Edward White, *Tort Law in America: An Intellectual History* (New York: Oxford University Press, 1980), 147–53 ("Few features of the history of twentieth-century American law more clearly illustrate the triumph of reformist thought than the massive infiltration of liability insurance into the field of torts"). Nearly all modern tort theory traces its origins to the 1881 lectures of Oliver Wendell Holmes Jr. See Holmes, *The Common Law,* ed. Mark DeWolfe Howe (Cambridge: Harvard University Press, 1963), 198–201.

2. Holmes, *The Common Law;* Peter Huber, *Liability: The Legal Revolution and Its Consequences* (New York: Basic Books, 1988); idem, *Galileo's Revenge* (New York: Basic Books, 1991); George Priest, "The Current Insurance Crisis and Modern Tort Law," *Yale Law Journal* 96 (1987): 1521; idem, "Invention of Enterprise Liability"; idem, "Modern Tort Law and Its Reform," *Valparaiso University Law Review* 22 (1987): 1.

3. Francis Bohlen, "Fifty Years of Tort Law," *Harvard Law Review* 50 (1938):

725, 1225; Jeremiah Smith, "Sequel to Workmen's Compensation Acts," *Harvard Law Review* 27 (1914): 235, 344.

4. A. A. Ballantine, "Compensation Plan for Railway Accident Claims, *Harvard Law Review* 29 (1916): 705; William O. Douglas, "Vicarious Liability and Administration of Risk," *Yale Law Journal* 38 (1929): 584, 720; Albert Ehrenzweig, "Assurance Oblige: A Comparative Study," *Law and Contemporary Problems* 15 (1950): 445; idem, *Negligence Without Fault,* (Berkeley and Los Angeles: University of California Press, 1951): 4; idem, "Full-Aid Insurance for Traffic Victims: A Voluntary Compensation Plan," *California Law Review* 43 (1955): 1; Lester Feezer, "Capacity to Bear Loss as a Factor in the Decision of Certain Types of Tort Cases," *University of Pennsylvania Law Review* 78 (1930): 805; ibid. 79 (1931): 742; Charles O. Gregory, "Trespass to Negligence to Absolute Liability," *Virginia Law Review* 37 (1951): 359; Harper and James, *The Law of Torts;* Clarence Morris, "Hazardous Enterprise and Risk-Bearing Capacity," *Yale Law Journal* 61 (1952): 1172; Young B. Smith, "Frolic and Detour," *Columbia Law Review* 23 (1923): 444.

Of all the scholars who have written on the subject, the one most indelibly identified with the insurance rationale is Fleming James. James wrote extensively throughout the middle part of the twentieth century, nearly always employing the insurance rationale in his work. See, e.g., the following by James: "Legislative Loss Distribution" (book review), *University of Chicago Law Review* 4 (1936): 158; "Last Clear Chance: A Transitional Doctrine," *Yale Law Journal* 47 (1938): 704; "Contribution Among Joint Tortfeasors in the Field of Accident Litigation," *Utah Bar Bulletin* 9 (1939): 208; "Contribution Among Joint Tortfeasors: A Pragmatic Criticism," *Harvard Law Review* 54 (1941): 1156; "Accident Liability: Some Wartime Developments," *Yale Law Journal* 55 (1946): 365; "Accident Liability Reconsidered: The Impact of Insurance," *Yale Law Journal* 57 (1948): 549; "The Functions of Judge and Jury in Negligence Cases," *Louisiana Law Review* 11 (1950): 95; "The Impact of Insurance on the Law of Torts" (by Fleming James and John V. Thornton), *Law and Contemporary Problems* 15 (1950): 431; "Accident Proneness and Accident Law" (by Fleming James and J. J. Dickinson), *Harvard Law Review* 63 (1950): 769; "Qualities of the Reasonable Man in Negligence," *Missouri Law Review* 16 (1951): 1; "Proof of Breach in Negligence Cases," *Virginia Law Review* 37 (1951): 179; "Legal Cause," *Yale Law Journal* 60 (1951): 761; "Assumption of Risk," *Yale Law Journal* 61 (1952): 141; "Scope of Duty in Negligence Cases," *Northwestern University Law Review* 47 (1953): 778; "Contributory Negligence," *Yale Law Journal* 62 (1953): 691; "Tort Liability of Occupiers of Land," *Yale Law Journal* 63 (1953): 144; "Products Liability (Parts 1 and 2)," *Texas Law Review* 34 (1955): 44; "Full Aid Insurance for Traffic Victims" (book review), *California Law Review* 43 (1955): 559; "General Products: Should Manufacturers Be Liable Without Negligence?" *Tennessee Law Review* 24 (1957): 923; "Damages in Accident Cases," *Cornell Law Quarterly* 41 (1956): 582; "Some Reflections on the Bases of Strict Liability," *Louisiana Law Review* 18 (1958): 293; "The Columbia Study of Compensation: An Unanswered Challenge," *Columbia Law Review* 59 (1959): 408; "Book Review," *Utah Law Review* 1966 (1966): 297; "The Future of Negligence in Accident Law," *Virginia Law Review* 53 (1967): 911.

5. W. Page Keeton, "Products Liability—Some Observations About Allocation of Risks," *Michigan Law Review* 64 (1966): 1329; idem, "Manufacturer's Liability: The Meaning of 'Defect' in the Manufacture and Design of Products," *Syracuse Law Review* 20 (1969): 559; idem, "Products Liability: Inadequacy of Information," *Texas Law Review* 48 (1970): 398; idem, "The Meaning of Defect," *St. Mary's Law Journal* 5 (1973): 30; John Wade, "Strict Tort Liability of Manufacturers, *Southwestern Law Journal* 19 (1965): 5; idem, "On the Nature of Strict Tort Liability for Products," *Mississippi Law Journal* 44 (1973): 825.

6. Guido Calabresi, *The Costs of Accidents: A Legal and Economic Analysis* (New Haven: Yale University Press, 1970); idem, "Some Thoughts on Risk Distribution and the Law of Torts," *Yale Law Journal* 70 (1961): 499; idem, "The Decision for Accidents: An Approach to Non-Fault Allocation of Costs," *Harvard Law Review* 78 (1965): 713; idem, "Does the Fault System Optimally Control Primary Accident Costs?" *Law And Contemporary Problems* 33 (1963): 429; idem, "Transaction, Costs, Resource Allocation, and Liability Rules: A Comment," *Journal of Law and Economics* 11 (1968): 67; idem, "Views and Overviews," *University of Illinois Law Forum* (1967): 600; Calabresi and Jon Hirschoff, "Toward a Test for Strict Liability in Torts," *Yale Law Journal* 81 (1972): 1055.

7. E.g., Kenneth S. Abraham, *Distributing Risk: Insurance, Legal Theory, and Public Policy* (New Haven: Yale University Press, 1986); idem, "Cost Internalization, Insurance, and Toxic Tort Compensation Funds," *Virginia Journal of Natural Resources* 2 (1982): 123; idem, "Efficiency and Fairness in Insurance Risk Classification," *Virginia Law Review* 71 (1985): 403; idem, "Individual Action and Collective Responsibility: The Dilemma of Mass Tort Reform," *Virginia Law Review* 73 (1987): 845; idem, "Making Sense of the Liability Insurance Crisis," *Ohio State Law Journal* 48 (1987); idem, "Principle and Pragmatism in the Compensation Debate," *Oxford Journal of Legal Studies* 7 (1987): 302; Patricia M. Danzon, *Medical Malpractice Theory, Evidence, and Public Policy* (Cambridge: Harvard University Press, 1985); idem, "Tort Reform and the Role of Government in Private Insurance Markets," *Journal of Legal Studies* 13 (1984): 517; Richard Epstein, *Modern Products Liability Law: A Legal Revolution* (Westport, Conn.: Quorum Books, 1980); idem, "The Unintended Revolution in Products Liability Law," *Cardozo Law Review* 10 (1980): 2193; idem, "Products Liability as an Insurance Market," *Journal of Legal Studies* 14 (1985): 645; Huber, *Liability;* idem, "Junk Science in the Courtroom," *Valparaiso University Law Review* 26 (1992): 723; Richard Pierce, "Institutional Aspects of Tort Reform," *California Law Review* 73 (1985): 917; Priest, "Modern Tort Law and its Reform"; idem, "The Invention of Enterprise Liability"; idem, "Insurance Crisis"; idem, "A Theory of Consumer Product Warranty," *Yale Law Journal* 90 (1981): 1297; Robert Rabin, "Indeterminate Risk and Tort Reform: Comments on Calabresi and Klevorick," *Journal of Legal Studies* 14 (1985): 633; Alan Schwartz, "Products Liability, Corporate Structure, and Bankruptcy: Toxic Substances and the Remote Risk Relationship, *Journal of Legal Studies* 14 (1985): 689; Michael J. Trebilcock, "The Role of Insurance Considerations in the Choice of Efficient Civil Liability Rules, *Journal of Law, Economics, and Organization* 4 (1988): 243; idem, "The Social Insurance Dilemma of Modern North American Tort Law: A

Canadian Perspective on the Liability Insurance Crisis," *San Diego Law Review* 24 (1987): 929; W. Kip Viscusi, "Alternative Approaches to Valuing the Health Impacts of Accidents: Liability Law and Prospective Evaluations," *Law and Contemporary Problems* 46 (1983): 49; idem, "Structuring an Effective Occupational Disease Policy: Victim Compensation and Risk Regulation," *Yale Journal on Regulation* 2 (1984): 53; idem, "Consumer Behavior and the Safety Effects of Product Safety Regulation," *Journal of Law and Economics* 28 (1985): 527.

8. Robert E. Keeton and Jeffrey O'Connell, *Basic Protection for the Traffic Victim* (Boston: Little, Brown, 1965); Henson Moore and Jeffrey O'Connell, "Foreclosing Medical Malpractice Claims by Prompt Tender of Economic Loss," *Louisiana Law Review* 44 (1984): 1267; Jeffrey O'Connell, *Ending Insult to Injury: No-Fault Insurance for Products and Services* (Champaign: University of Illinois Press, 1975); idem, "Expanding No-Fault Automobile Insurance: Some Proposals," *Virginia Law Review* 59 (1973): 749; idem, "Alternatives to the Tort System for Personal Injury," *San Diego Law Review* 23 (1986): 17; idem, "Balanced Proposals for Products Liability Reform," *Ohio State Law Journal* 48 (1987): 317; idem, "A Model Bill Allowing Choice Between Auto Insurance Payable With and Without Regard to Fault," *Ohio State Law Journal* 51 (1990): 947; Stephen D. Sugarman, *Doing Away with Personal Injury Law* (New York: Quorum Books, 1989); idem, "Taking Advantage of the Torts Crisis," *Ohio State Law Journal* 48 (1987): 329, 353–58; idem, "Doing Away with Tort Law," *California Law Review* 73 (1985): 555.

CHAPTER ONE

1. Lawrence Friedman, *A History of American Law,* 2d ed. (New York: Simon & Schuster, 1985), 467; G. Edward White, *Tort Law in America: An Intellectual History* (New York: Oxford University Press, 1980), 3.

2. Charles O. Gregory, "From Trespass to Negligence to Strict Liability," *Virginia Law Review* 37 (1951): 359.

3. See Friedman, *A History of American Law*, 329–33.

4. For an early discussion exploring some of the problems encountered in constructing a moral theory of civil accident liability, see James Barr Ames, "Law and Morals," *Harvard Law Review* 22 (1908): 97.

5. Oliver Wendell Holmes Jr., *The Common Law,* ed. Mark DeWolfe Howe (Cambridge: Harvard University Press, 1963), 62–103.

6. Ibid., 77–78.

7. Ibid.

8. For example, Holmes rejects his imagined alternatives in part because "[t]he state does none of these things." Ibid, 77.

9. Ibid., 77.

10. Guido Calabresi, *The Costs of Accidents: A Legal and Economic Analysis* (New Haven: Yale University Press, 1970), 252; Ronald H. Coase, "The Problem of Social Cost," *Journal of Law and Economics* 3 (1960): 15; Richard A. Posner,

Economic Analysis of Law, 4th ed. (Boston: Little, Brown, 1992), 61–62, 95–96, 164.

11. Holmes would not incur the transfer costs of litigation "unless some clear benefit is to be derived from disturbing the *status quo*." Holmes, *The Common Law*, 77.

12. A cost-benefit, or balancing, approach is implicit in Holmes's juxtaposition of the "cumbrous and expensive machinery" of loss-shifting against his requirement that "some clear benefit . . . be derived." Ibid.

13. The possibility of an insurance rationale lies behind the following language: "The state might conceivably make itself a mutual insurance company against accidents, and distribute the burden of its citizens' mishaps among all its members. There might be a pension for paralytics, and state aid for those who suffered in person or estate from tempest or wild beasts." Ibid. Holmes did not describe how he thought the state might "make itself a mutual insurance company," although he did mention "pensions," implying a more direct form of aid. But the presence of this discussion in the context of a comparison between strict liability and negligence suggests that Holmes understood that a similar effect might be obtained through the structure of third-party liability.

14. Thus, Holmes concluded that victim compensation was not a sufficiently "clear benefit" to warrant the expense of "disturb[ing] the *status quo*." Ibid.

15. Apparently, the chief evidence for this conclusion is Holmes's time-bound empirical surmise that while the state "might" set itself up in various ways to provide compensation for various injuries, it "does none of these things," in accord with "the prevailing view." Ibid.

16. Holmes thus asserted that "[u]niversal insurance, if desired, can be better and more cheaply accomplished by private enterprise." Ibid. Although he did not differentiate between types of insurance, the reference seems to fit better with first-party insurance, where the purchaser of the insurance protects against his or her own accidental injury, than it does with third-party liability insurance, where the purchaser of the insurance protects against the risk of being held liable for compensation to others. Thus, Holmes may be the intellectual progenitor not only of modern law-and-economics cost-benefit reasoning about torts but also of the modern proponents of first-party "no-fault" insurance alternatives to the tort system. See *infra* Chapter Three, pages 40–41, 42–44.

17. Ibid.

18. Holmes's arguments regarding the state's cumbrous and expensive machinery (transfer costs), the preference for the safety goal, the preference for private over social insurance, and the general injustice of strict liability are clearly echoed in the tort reform movement of the late twentieth century, however. See, generally, George Priest, "Modern Tort Law and Its Reform," *Valparaiso University Law Review* 22 (1987): 1.

19. "The state *might* make itself a mutual insurance company against accidents . . . There *might* be a pension for paralytics, and state aid for those who suffered in person or estate from tempest or wild beast. . . . As between individuals it *might*

adopt the mutual insurance principle . . . and divide damages . . . or it *might* throw all loss upon the actor." Holmes, *The Common Law,* 77 (emphasis added).

20. Ibid., 78.

21. Ibid., 77.

22. Thus, when Holmes speaks of "pensions for paralytics" and "state aid" for victims of "tempests" or "wild beasts," he clearly recognizes an insurance effect to such compensation. By providing the benefits, the state, as "mutual insurance company," is performing a cost-spreading function. Holmes, *The Common Law,* 77.

23. Holmes argued that imposing liability to redistribute losses would "offend . . . the sense of justice" because it was not "justifiable" to enforce compensation "unless under the circumstances a prudent man would have foreseen the possibility of harm." Ibid., 77–78. Since he argued elsewhere in the lecture that the purpose of the "prudent man" standard was to secure a "certain average of [safe] conduct" that "is necessary to the general welfare" (ibid., 86), Holmes was setting compensation and safety against each other as competing and contradictory values. Only the latter (obtaining an average level of safety) did he regard as worth the cost of transferring losses from the victim to the injurer.

24. Ibid., 77–78.

25. "[T]he public generally profits by individual activity. As action cannot be avoided, *and tends to the public good,* there is obviously no policy in throwing the hazard of *what is at once desirable* and inevitable upon the actor." Ibid., 77 (emphasis added).

26. Ibid.

27. "[The state's] cumbrous and expensive machinery ought not to be set in motion unless some clear benefit is to be derived. . . . *State interference is an evil,* where it cannot be shown to be a good." Ibid., 77–78 (emphasis added).

28. This is apparent in his consideration of the state as "mutual insurance company," as against the alternative of "[u]niversal insurance . . . accomplished *by private insurance*." Ibid., 77 (emphasis added). He frankly viewed the latter as the "better" and "cheap[er]" alternative, although he made no effort to back up these claims.

29. Research has failed to uncover comparable consideration of any type of insurance rationale by any of Holmes's contemporaries.

30. William L. Prosser, *Handbook of the Law of Torts,* 4th ed. (St. Paul, Minn.: West Publishing Co., 1971), 526–27; Alpheus H. Snow, "Social Insurance," *University of Pennsylvania Law Review* 59 (1911): 283–84.

31. Friedman, *History of American Law,* 470–73; Prosser, *Handbook of the Law of Torts,* 526–29; Stefan A. Riesenfeld, "Forty Years of American Workmen's Compensation," *Minnesota Law Review* 35 (1951): 527.

32. Lamson v. American Ax & Tool Co., 58 N.E. 585 (Mass. 1900).

33. Ibid. at 585.

34. Ibid. at 585–86.

35. Richard Epstein, "The Historical Origins and Economic Structure of Workers' Compensation Law," *Georgia Law Review* 16 (1982): 775, 790.

36. In reaction to the study done by the New York Employers' Liability Commis-

sion on the effect of conditions in the workplace in 1910, organized labor took an active role in the promotion of compensation legislation. See Samuel Gompers, "The Price We Pay," *American Federationist* (part two) 17 (1910): 665. See also James Weinstein, "Big Business and the Origins of Workmen's Compensation," *Labor History* 8 (1967): 156 (emphasizing that workers' compensation statutes were passed with the support of many businesses and unions).

37. Prosser, *Handbook of the Law of Torts,* 530 (citing Francis Bohlen, "A Problem in the Drafting of Workmen's Compensation Acts," *Harvard Law Review* 25 [1912]: 401).

38. William L. Prosser, W. Page Keeton, et al., *Prosser and Keeton on Torts,* 5th ed. (St. Paul, Minn.: West Publishing Co., 1984), 573. See, generally, Fowler Harper and Fleming James Jr., *The Law of Torts* (Boston: Little, Brown, 1956), 2, § 11.2; Arthur Larson, *Law of Workmen's Compensation* (New York: Matthew Bender & Co., 1952), §§ 2.20, 5.20, 5.30.

39. See Arthur Larson, "The Nature and Origins of Workmen's Compensation," *Cornell Law Quarterly* 37 (1952): 206.

40. As previously noted, workers and employers in some industries did set up voluntary mutual aid societies to provide benefits for workers injured on the job. Compensation from these funds, however, was usually meager. For a discussion of the structural relation between the voluntary funds and subsequent workers' compensation legislation, see Epstein, "Historical Origins of Workers' Compensation."

41. See, e.g., Francis M. Burdick, "Is Law the Expression of Class Selfishness?" *Harvard Law Review* 25 (1914): 235, 371; Arthur Gray Powell, "Some Phases of the Law of Master and Servant: An Attempt at Rationalization," *Columbia Law Review* 10 (1910): 1; Eugene Wambaugh, "Workmen's Compensation Acts: Their Theory and Constitutionality," *Harvard Law Review* 25 (1911): 129; F. P. Walton, "Workmen's Compensation and the Theory of Professional Risk," *Columbia Law Review* 11 (1911): 36; Roscoe Pound, "The End of Law As Developed in Legal Rules and Doctrines," *Harvard Law Review* 27 (1914): 195, 233.

42. See Warren A. Seavey, "Negligence: Subjective or Objective?" *Harvard Law Review* 41 (1927): 1; Jeremiah Smith, "Sequel to Workmen's Compensation Acts," *Harvard Law Review* 27 (1914): 235; Henry T. Terry, "Negligence," *Harvard Law Review* 29 (1915): 40.

43. See, e.g., Harper and James, *The Law of Torts* 2, § 12.1 et. seq. (describing prevalence of negligence standard); Ames, "Law and Morals," 97 (stating that "the ethical standard of reasonable conduct has replaced the immoral standard of acting at one's peril"); Jeremiah Smith, "Tort and Absolute Liability," *Harvard Law Review* 30 (1917): 241, 319, 409; Percy H. Winfield, "The History of Negligence in the Law of Torts," *Law Quarterly Review* 42 (1926): 184, 195 (English law). Cf. R.F.V. Heuston, *Salmond on the Law of Torts,* 11th ed. (London: Sweet & Maxwell, 1953), 22 (criticizing the rule of *Rylands v. Fletcher,* L.R. 1 Ex. 265 [1866], which set strict liability rather than negligence as the standard for injuries to land, on the ground that "[n]o decision in the law of torts has done more to prevent the establishment of a simple, uniform, and intelligible system of civil responsibility").

44. See Eugene Wambaugh, "Workmen's Compensation Acts: Their Theory and

Their Constitutionality," *Harvard Law Review* 25 (1911): 129; Bohlen, "Problem in Drafting Workmen's Compensation," 328.

45. But cf. Fleming James Jr., "Accidental Liability: Some Wartime Developments," *Yale Law Journal* 55 (1946): 365 (noting that in the twenty-five years since first adoption of workers' compensation, some inroads into the hegemony of the fault principle had occurred).

46. One of the earliest judicial treatments of workers' compensation found it unconstitutional because it replaced fault liability with strict liability. Ives v. South Buffalo Railway Co., 94 N.E. 431 (N.Y. 1911).

47. Albert Ehrenzweig, *Negligence Without Fault,* (Berkeley and Los Angeles: University of California Press, 1951), 16–17; idem, "Assurance Oblige—A Comparative Study," *Law and Contemporary Problems* 15 (1950): 445–46; Gregory, "Trespass to Negligence," 385; Lester Feezer, "Capacity to Bear Loss as a Factor in the Decision of Certain Types of Tort Cases," *University of Pennsylvania Law Review* 78 (1930): 805; idem, "Social Justice in the Field of Torts," *Minnesota Law Review* 11 (1927): 313.

48. J. Smith, "Sequel to Workmen's Compensation," 235, 23 8–39 (arguing that implementation of a strict liability regime under workers' compensation "is in direct conflict with the fundamental rule of the modern common law as to the ordinary requisites of a tort"). For a thoughtful analysis of Smith's position, see Wex S. Malone, "Damage Suits and the Contagious Principle of Workmen's Compensation," *Louisiana Law Review* 12 (1952): 231.

CHAPTER TWO

1. See, e.g., Warren A. Seavey, "Negligence: Subjective or Objective?" *Harvard Law Review* 41 (1927): 1; idem, "Mr. Justice Cardozo and the Law of Torts," *Harvard Law Review* 52 (1939): 372, *Columbia Law Review* 39 (1939): 20, *Yale Law Journal* 48 (1939): 390; Henry T. Terry, "Negligence," *Harvard Law Review* 29 (1915): 40.

2. The common response was to make the old rules serve the developing industrial demands through development and expansion of the doctrines of respondeat superior and res ipsa loquitur. Albert Ehrenzweig, *Negligence Without Fault,* (Berkeley and Los Angeles: University of California Press, 1951), §§ 4, 19. See also Percy H. Winfield, "The History of Negligence in the Law of Torts," *Law Quarterly Review* 42 (1926): 184, 195; Leon Green, "The Duty Problem in Negligence Cases," *Columbia Law Review* 28 (1928): 1014; idem, "The Duty Problem in Negligence Cases: II," *Columbia Law Review* 29 (1929): 255. Charles O. Gregory, "From Trespass to Negligence to Strict Liability," *Virginia Law Review* 37 (1951): 359, provides a valuable and critical overview of judicial and scholarly efforts to preserve and "retool" negligence doctrine in response to modern developments.

3. See, e.g., Albert Ehrenzweig, "Assurance Oblige—A Comparative Study," *Law and Contemporary Problems* 15 (1950): 445; idem, *Negligence Without Fault,*

§§ 11–15; Fleming James Jr., "Accidental Liability: Some Wartime Developments," *Yale Law Journal* 55 (1946): 365–66.

4. For a general description of the Legal Realism movement as it developed in tort law, see G. Edward White, *Tort Law in America: An Intellectual History* (New York: Oxford University Press, 1980), ch. 3; see also Lawrence Friedman, *A History of American Law,* 2d ed. (New York: Simon & Schuster, 1985), 688–89.

5. E.g., Ehrenzweig, "Assurance Oblige"; idem, *Negligence Without Fault;* Lester Feezer, "Capacity to Bear Loss as a Factor in the Decision of Certain Types of Tort Cases," *University of Pennsylvania Law Review* 78 (1930); Green, "The Duty Problem in Negligence Cases," 1014; idem, "The Duty Problem in Negligence Cases: II," 255; Clarence Morris, "Hazardous Enterprises and Risk Bearing Capacity," *Yale Law Journal* 61 (1952): 1172; Fleming James Jr., "Last Clear Chance: A Transitional Doctrine," *Yale Law Journal* 47 (1938): 704; idem, "Wartime Developments," 365; idem, "Accident Liability Reconsidered: The Impact of Insurance," *Yale Law Journal* 57 (1948): 549.

6. Harry Shulman and Fleming James Jr., *Cases and Materials on the Law of Torts* (Chicago: Foundation Press, 1942), vii.

7. Morris, "Hazardous Enterprises," 1177. See also James, "Accident Liability Reconsidered," 550.

8. Ehrenzweig, *Negligence Without Fault,* 30; James, "Accident Liability Reconsidered," 561; Morris, "Hazardous Enterprises," 1176.

9. "The negligence rule has come to be used largely to impose liability for harm caused by the lawful activities of modern enterprise. 'The attempt is to compensate the plaintiff for one set of reasons, and to punish the defendant for an entirely different set of reasons, by the single act of making the defendant pay a sum of money to the plaintiff.'" Ehrenzweig, *Negligence Without Fault,* 39 (quoting Clarence Morris, "Rough Justice and Some Utopian Ideas," *Illinois Law Review* 24 [1930]: 730, 733.)

10. Ehrenzweig, *Negligence Without Fault,* 30; James, "Accident Liability Reconsidered," 561.

11. Ehrenzweig, *Negligence Without Fault,* 55–56; Fowler Harper and Fleming James Jr., *The Law of Torts* (Boston: Little, Brown, 1956), 2: 763 n. 7.

12. Gregory, "Trespass to Negligence," n. 34 and p. 383; Feezer, "Capacity to Bear Loss," 767.

13. This has sometimes been expressed in terms of the "diminishing marginal utility of money" theory. See Guido Calabresi, "Some Thoughts on Risk Distribution and the Law of Torts," *Yale Law Journal* 70 (1961): 517–19; Feezer, "Capacity to Bear Loss," 805, 809–10.

14. Harper and James, *The Law of Torts* 2:746: "[W]hile [the fault principle's] philosophical justification lies in morals, it does not seek to punish wrongdoers (save in exceptional cases where wrong is grievous) but to compensate its victims." But cf. R.F.V. Heuston, *Salmond on the Law of Torts,* 11th ed. (London: Sweet & Maxwell, 1953), 21: "The ultimate purpose of the law in imposing liability on those who do harm to others is to prevent such harm by punishing the doer of it. . . . Pecuniary compensation is not in itself an ultimate object or a sufficient justification of legal

liability. It is simply the instrument by which the law fulfills its purpose of penal coercion."

15. See Ehrenzweig, *Negligence Without Fault,* 47 et. seq. The new standard for liability became predicated upon the defendant's exposing the community to risk, rather than the defendant's causal fault. Ibid., 55.

16. Ehrenzweig, "Assurance Oblige," 452; James, "Wartime Developments," 371–72.

17. James, "Accident Liability Reconsidered," 564.

18. Fleming James Jr., "Qualities of the Reasonable Man in Negligence," *Missouri Law Review* 16 (1951): 18.

19. William O. Douglas, "Vicarious Liability and Administration of Risk I," *Yale Law Journal* 38 (1929): 584, 594, 603–4; idem, "Vicarious Liability and Administration of Risk II," *Yale Law Journal* 38 (1929): 720, 725–26; Green, "The Duty Problem in Negligence Cases: II," 270, 274, 276.

20. Ehrenzweig, *Negligence Without Fault,* 87; see also Calabresi, "Risk Distribution," 545–46.

21. James, "Accident Liability Reconsidered," 559–63.

22. Ibid., 557.

23. Fleming James Jr., "The Columbia Study of Compensation: An Unanswered Challenge," *Columbia Law Review* 59 (1959): 412; Symposium, *Columbia Law Review,* 32 (1932): 785. See George Priest, "The Invention of Enterprise Liability: A Critical History of the Intellectual Foundations of Modern Tort Law," *Journal of Legal Studies* 14 (1985): 497 (noting that advocates of insurance rationale paid great attention to motor vehicle liability but failed to anticipate development of strict product liability).

24. Albert Ehrenzweig, "Full-Aid Insurance for Traffic Victims: A Voluntary Compensation Plan" *California Law Review* 43 (1955): 15; Leon Green, *Traffic Victims: Tort Law and Insurance* (Evanston, Ill.: Northwestern University Press, 1958); Robert E. Keeton and Jeffrey O'Connell, *Basic Protection for the Traffic Victim* (Boston: Little, Brown, 1965).

25. See, e.g., Morris, "Hazardous Enterprises," 1179.

26. Prosser maintained that the risk-distribution arguments of strict liability theory were "makeweights" and that public safety was its principal rationale. William L. Prosser, "The Assault upon the Citadel: Strict Liability to the Consumer," *Yale Law Journal* 69 (1962): 1099, 1123; White, *Tort Law in America,* 177. See, generally, Howard C. Klemme, "The Enterprise Liability Theory of Torts," *University of Colorado Law Review* 47 (1976): 153.

27. Prosser, "Assault upon the Citadel," 1123 . See White, *Tort Law in America,* 178.

28. White, *Tort Law in America,* 77–78.

29. Harper and James, *The Law of Torts.*

30. Ibid. 2:762–63.

31. Calabresi, "Risk Distribution"; idem, "The Decision for Accidents: An Approach to Non-Fault Allocation of Costs," *Harvard Law Review* 78 (1965); idem, *The Costs of Accidents: A Legal and Economic Analysis* (New Haven: Yale Univer-

sity Press, 1970); Richard A. Posner, "A Theory of Negligence," *Journal of Legal Studies* 1 (1972): 29, 33–34. See Gary Schwartz, "Foreword: Tort Scholarship," *California Law Review* 73 (1985): 548.

32. Calabresi, "Risk Distribution"; idem, *The Costs of Accidents*, ch. 4.

33. Calabresi, *The Costs of Accidents*, 27–28.

34. Ibid., 164–65, 311–18.

35. Ibid., 274–85.

36. Page Keeton, "Product Liability and the Meaning of Defect," *St. Mary's Law Journal* 5 (1973): 30, 35; John Wade, "Strict Tort Liability of Manufacturers," *Southwestern Law Journal* 19 (1965): 5, 10–11; idem, "On the Nature of Strict Tort Liability for Products," *Mississippi Law Journal* 44 (1973): 834.

37. See, generally, Klemme, "Enterprise Liability Theory," 153 n. 11 (quoting J. Smith, "Sequel to Workmen's Compensation Acts," *Harvard Law Review* 27 [1914]: 235: "A community which accepts the principle of [a workmen's compensation statute] cannot be expected to find anything intrinsically unreasonable in the doctrine which seeks to throw upon the undertaker the full responsibility for harm arising from his enterprise, on the theory that the business should bear its losses in the first instance regardless of fault or proximate cause, and that ultimately, like any other overhead charge, they would fall on the consumer").

The term "enterprise liability," which originated in the work of Albert Ehrenzweig, is misleading because it appears to confine the theory of the insurance rationale to situations involving profit-oriented business activities. Such activities do occupy the core of the concept, but the insurance rationale is actually much broader, encompassing any entity that enjoys advantages in obtaining insurance against the risks of injury associated with its activities. Thus, the rationale extends to nonprofit charitable organizations, municipalities, drivers of motor vehicles, and even homeowners, all of whom, according to its reasoning, should be subject to liability in circumstances where they enjoy material advantages in their ability to insure against the risk of injury. It is principally for this reason that I have avoided using the term "enterprise liability" in this book, although it is probably too late in the day to change popular terminology.

38. James, "Accident Liability Reconsidered," 550.

39. Ehrenzweig, *Negligence Without Fault*, 55; James, "Accident Liability Reconsidered," 558.

40. Calabresi, *The Costs of Accidents*, 53–54; idem, "Risk Distribution," 500–507.

41. There is some evidence that more manufacturers are self-insuring. Neil Komesar, "Injuries and Institutions: Tort Reform, Tort Theory, and Beyond," *New York University Law Review* 65 (1990): 23, 39–40.

42. James, "Wartime Developments," 558.

43. Ibid.

44. Feezer, "Capacity to Bear Loss," 742.

45. See G. Edward White, "Tort Reform in the Twentieth Century: An Historical Review," *Villanova Law Review* 32 (1987): 1276–82.

46. James, "Wartime Developments," 365; idem, "Accident Liability Reconsidered," 559.

47. James, "Accident Liability Reconsidered," 552.

CHAPTER THREE

1. Calabresi, whose work has already been discussed, was one of the principal tort scholars to use an economic approach during the 1970s. The other key law-and-economics tort scholar during the 1970s was Richard A. Posner, and it is chiefly from his work that the law-and-economics critique of the insurance rationale stems. See, e.g., Richard A. Posner, "A Theory of Negligence," *Journal of Legal Studies* 1 (1972): 29; idem, *Economic Analysis of Law,* 4th ed. (Boston: Little, Brown, 1992), esp. 179; idem, "Strict Liability: A Comment," *Journal of Legal Studies* 2 (1973): 205; William Landes and Richard A. Posner, "The Positive Economic Theory of Tort Law," *Georgia Law Review* 15 (1981): 851, 851–57 (tracing the history of economic analysis of tort law).

Supporters of first-party insurance draw on ideas that have been developed and pressed with indefatigable detail by Jeffrey O'Connell. See *supra* Part I, note 8. See also idem, "A Proposal to Abolish Contributory and Comparative Fault, with Compensatory Savings by Also Abolishing the Collateral Source Rule," *University of Illinois Law Forum* 1979 (1979): 591; idem, *The Lawsuit Lottery: Only the Lawyers Win* (New York: Free Press, 1979).

2. E.g., George Priest, "The Current Insurance Crisis and Modern Tort Law," *Yale Law Journal* 96 (1987); Jeffrey O'Connell, "Alternatives to the Tort System for Personal Injury," *San Diego Law Review* 23 (1986); Peter Huber, *Liability: The Legal Revolution and Its Consequences* (New York: Basic Books, 1988).

3. See, generally, *infra* Part III, Chapter Eight.

4. Huber, *Liability,* 164 (modern rules of tort law do not deter risk but rather deter "behavior that gets people sued, which is not at all the same thing"); ibid., 185–88 (objectives of deterrence and compensation are inconsistent); George Priest, "Modern Tort Law and Its Reform," *Valparaiso University Law Review* 22 (1987): 1, 13, 20 (asserting that safety would be increased and accident rates reduced if liability required proof of a specific act that could practicably have been taken to prevent the harm; beyond that, liability becomes insurance for unpreventable risks); idem, "Insurance Crisis," 1537 ("Where damage measures are compensatory . . . there is a very definite ceiling to the accident prevention investments that any provider will make").

5. Priest, "Insurance Crisis," 1559; Stephen D. Sugarman, "Doing Away with Tort Law," *California Law Review* 73 (1985): 591–96; Robert E. Keeton and Jeffrey O'Connell, *Basic Protection for the Traffic Victim* (Boston: Little, Brown, 1965), 76–102.

6. Huber, *Liability,* 192 ("Legal rules, rooted in a spirit of compulsion, and applied emotionally case by case, are profoundly inimical to insurance"); Priest,

"Insurance Crisis," 1562–63; Emilio Venezian, "Insurer Capital Needs Under Parameter Uncertainty," *Journal of Risk and Insurance* 42 (1975): 19.

7. Ronald Coase, "The Problem of Social Cost," *Journal of Law and Economics* 3 (1960): 1; Landes and Posner, "Positive Economic Theory," 852–64.

8. "[D]uty . . . is a function of three variables: (1) The probability that . . . [a harm will occur] . . . ; (2) the gravity of the resulting injury, if [it] does; (3) the burden of adequate precautions. Possibly it serves to bring this notion into relief to state it in algebraic terms: if the probability be called P; the injury, L; and the burden, B; liability depends upon whether B is less than L multiplied by P: i.e., whether B < PL." United States v. Carroll Towing Co., 159 F.2d 169, 173 (2d Cir. 1947).

9. See Posner, "A Theory of Negligence," 32–34.

10. Huber, *Liability,* 153–71; Priest, "Modern Tort Law," 12 ("holding providers liable where they cannot prevent accidents diminishes the effectiveness of the law"). Priest argues, in particular, that producers need more-substantial incentives for safety investment than the marginal accident-cost reductions that are available under a strict liability regime: "The greatest incentive effect provided by the law derives from the prospect that complying fully with the applicable legal standards reduces legal liability *totally*. The absence of immediate gain from choosing the most advanced practicable design is very likely to influence the extent to which providers search for alternative designs, or try to develop alternatives based upon design methods or safety innovations in related, but not identical, product or service lines." Ibid., 13. See also ibid., 20–22 (where Priest looks for a middle ground between the modern doctrine of strict liability and traditional doctrines of negligence and fault); idem, "Products Liability Law and the Accident Rate," in *Liability: Perspectives and Policy,* ed. Robert E. Litan and Clifford Winston (Washington, D.C.: Brookings Institution, 1988); idem, "Insurance Crisis," 1537 (providers will simply pay damages when they are less expensive than prospective safety improvements; thus, extended liability beyond this break-even cost-benefit point has no effect on increased safety). The tort critics have expressed similar skepticism about the capacity of specific government safety rules to accomplish net safety gains. W. Kip Viscusi, "Consumer Behavior and the Safety Effects of Product Safety Regulation," *Journal of Law and Economics* 28 (1985): 527, 538, 553 (noting that failure to take into account an individual consumer's behavior leads to ineffective regulations; for example, the Consumer Product Safety Commission's requirement of safety caps on medicine to prevent childhood poisonings led to no reduction in the poisoning rate, presumably because of the "lulling effect" of the regulation on parents, which in turn led to greater carelessness in their supervision of medications).

11. Richard Epstein, "Products Liability as an Insurance Market," *Journal of Legal Studies* 14 (1985): 654–55.

12. Priest, "Modern Tort Law," 13 (criticizing doctrines imposing liability for "unreasonably dangerous products" and rejecting the state-of-the-art defense, claiming that "holding a manufacturer liable based on . . . retrospective liability is the equivalent of flunking a student in an algebra class because of his or her failure to use calculus").

13. Priest, "Modern Tort Law," 11–14 (asserting the consumer's influence in the rate of product accidents).

14. Epstein, "Products Liability as an Insurance Market," 645–669; idem, "Medical Malpractice, Imperfect Information, and the Contractual Foundation for Medical Services," *Law and Contemporary Problems* 49 (spring 1986): 201.

15. George Priest, "A Theory of Consumer Product Warranty," *Yale Law Journal* 90 (1981): 1297; see Steven P. Croley and John D. Hanson, "Rescuing the Revolution: The Revived Case for Enterprise Liability," *Michigan Law Review* 91 (1993): 791.

16. Priest, "Modern Tort Law," 24–25, 30, 31–33.

17. Huber, *Liability,* 73–83; Priest, "Modern Tort Law," 37.

18. Huber, *Liability,* 50–58, 63–70.

19. Priest, "Modern Tort Law," 13; Priest, "A Theory of Consumer Product Warranty," 1297; W. Kip Viscusi, *Consumer Product Safety Regulation* (Washington, D.C.: American Enterprise Institute for Public Policy Research, 1984); Sam Peltzman, "The Effects of Automobile Safety Regulations," *Journal of Politics and Economics* 83 (1975): 677; Jeffrey O'Connell, "Balanced Proposals for Product Liability Reform," *Ohio State Law Journal* 48 (1987): 320.

20. E.g., James B. Sales and Kenneth B. Cole Jr., "Punitive Damages: A Relic That Has Outlived Its Origins," *Vanderbilt Law Review* 37 (1984): 1117.

21. Huber, *Liability,* 70–78, 98–104; Priest, "Modern Tort Law," 33–36.

22. U.S. Department of Justice Tort Policy Working Group, *The Causes, Extent, and Policy Implication of the Current Crisis in Insurance Availability* (Washington, D.C., 1986) (henceforth cited as the DOJ Report); idem, *An Update on the Liability Crisis* (Washington, D.C., 1987).

23. American Law Institute Reporters' Study, *Enterprise Responsibility for Personal Injury* (Philadelphia: American Law Institute, 1991). Many of the critics whose work is discussed here participated as associate reporters or advisers in the preparation of this study, including Kenneth S. Abraham, W. Kip Viscusi, Jeffrey O'Connell, and George Priest. Guido Calabresi also served as an adviser.

24. Jeffrey O'Connell, *Ending Insult to Injury: No-Fault Insurance for Products and Services* (Champaign: University of Illinois Press, 1975) ; idem, "Expanding No-Fault Automobile Insurance: Some Proposals," *Virginia Law Review* 59 (1973); idem, "Alternatives to the Tort System for Personal Injury," *San Diego Law Review* 23 (1986); idem, "Balanced Proposals for Products Liability Reform," *Ohio State Law Journal* 48 (1987); Stephen D. Sugarman, *Doing Away with Personal Injury Law* (New York: Quorum Books, 1989); idem, "Taking Advantage of the Torts Crisis," *Ohio State Law Journal* 48 (1987); idem, "Doing Away with Tort Law." See also Jeffrey O'Connell and C. B. Kelley, *The Blame Game: Injuries, Insurance, and Injustice* (Lexington, Mass.: Lexington Books, 1987).

25. Jeffrey O'Connell, "A 'Neo-No-Fault' Contract in Lieu of Tort: Preaccident Guarantees of Postaccident Settlement Offers," *California Law Review* 73 (1985): 906–7.

26. O'Connell and Kelly, *The Blame Game,* 123; O'Connell, "Balanced Proposals for Product Liability Reform," 320–21.

27. Huber, *Liability,* 196; O'Connell, "Balanced Proposals for Product Liability Reform," 321; O'Connell, "Expanding No-Fault," 749–59.

28. W. Page Keeton, "The Case for No-Fault Insurance," *Mississippi Law Journal* 44 (1973): 1, 8–14; Jeffrey O'Connell and Robert H. Joost, "Giving Motorists a Choice Between Fault and No-Fault," *Virginia Law Review* 72 (1986): 61; O'Connell, "Balanced Proposals for Product Liability Reform," 322; idem, "Expanding No-Fault," 749–59.

29. O'Connell, "Balanced Proposals for Product Liability Reform," 322.

30. Fleming James Jr., "The Columbia Study of Compensation: An Unanswered Challenge," *Columbia Law Review* 59 (1959): 415.

31. For a classic exposition of the corrective-justice perspective, see John Fletcher, "Fairness and Utility in Tort Theory," *Harvard Law Review* 85 (1972): 537. See also Richard Epstein, "A Theory of Strict Liability," *Journal of Legal Studies* 2 (1973): 151.

32. E.g., Richard Abel "A Critique of American Tort Law," *British Journal of Law and Society* 8 (1981): 199 (updated and republished in *The Politics of Law,* ed. David Kairys [New York: Pantheon Books, 1992]); idem, "The Real Tort Crisis—Too Few Claims," *Ohio State Law Journal* 48 (1987): 443; idem, "Should Tort Law Protect Property Against Accidental Loss?" *San Diego Law Review* 23 (1986): 79.

33. E.g., Leslie Bender, "Frontier of Legal Thought III: Feminist (Re)Torts: Thoughts on the Liability Crisis, Mass Torts, Power, and Responsibilities," *Duke Law Journal* 1990 (1990): 851.

34. Huber, *Liability,* 3–5, 7; Priest, "Insurance Crisis," 1564–65; Patricia M. Danzon, *Medical Malpractice Theory, Evidence, and Public Policy* (Cambridge: Harvard University Press, 1985), 153.

35. Priest, "Insurance Crisis," 1545–47; Priest, "A Theory of Consumer Product Warranty," 1350; Huber, *Liability,* 19–32.

36. Huber, *Liability,* 3–5, 11; Priest, "Insurance Crisis," 1557–58; Larry M. Pollack, "Medical Maloccurrence Insurance (MMI): A First Party, No-Fault Insurance Proposal for Resolving the Medical Malpractice Controversy," *Tort and Insurance Law* 23 (1988): 552, 556 n. 18.

37. Priest, "Modern Tort Law," 16; Priest, "Insurance Crisis," 1547, 1559. This lack-of-demand argument may be lurking below Priest's assertion that as third-party liability premiums are tacked on to the price of products, demand for those products diminishes among certain consumers—presumably those to whom the insurance does not seem worth the price. See also Pollack, "Medical Maloccurrence Insurance," 556.

38. Huber, *Liability,* 167–69; Priest, "Insurance Crisis," 1557–58.

39. Priest, "Insurance Crisis," 1558, 1564–65.

40. See, generally, Huber, *Liability* (an argument for a return to contractually bargained-for compensation); Priest, "Modern Tort Law," 37–38; idem, "Compensation for Personal Injury in the United States, in Sweden, and Other Countries," in *International Colloquium on Compensation for Personal Injury,* ed. J. Hellner (Stockholm: Juristforlaget, 1988).

41. Priest, "Insurance Crisis," 1552.

42. Huber, *Liability,* 150–52, 193, 225; Priest, "Modern Tort Law," 18–19, 20; idem, "Compensation for Personal Injury"; Paul C. Weiler, *Medical Malpractice on Trial* (Cambridge: Harvard University Press, 1991), 62.

43. Unlike some no-fault proponents, Jeffrey O'Connell sometimes advocates third-party as well as first-party no-fault plans. E.g., O'Connell, "Balanced Proposals for Liability," 322–28 (proposing for product injuries an elective "no-fault" plan modeled after workers' compensation).

44. Jeffrey O'Connell, "A Proposal to Abolish Defendants' Payment of Pain and Suffering in Return for Payment of Claimants' Attorneys' Fees," *University of Illinois Law Review* 1981 (1981): 333, 337–39; idem, "A 'Neo-No-Fault' Contract," 898, 899; Stanley Ingber, "Rethinking Intangible Injuries: A Focus on Remedy," *California Law Review* 73 (1985): 772, 785.

45. Priest, "Modern Tort Law," 17; idem, "Insurance Crisis," 1554; Jeffrey O'Connell and Rita James Simon, "Payment for Pain and Suffering: Who Wants What, When, and Why?" *University of Illinois Law Forum* 1972 (1972): 1.

46. Sugarman, *Doing Away with Personal Injury Law,* 183 ("It is often argued that . . . pain and suffering damages serve as a practical matter to pay for the victim's lawyers"); O'Connell, *The Lawsuit Lottery;* Valerie P. Hans and Neil Vidmar, *Judging the Jury* (New York: Plenum Press, 1986); John Guinther, *The Jury in America* (New York: Roscoe Pound Foundation, 1988), 99; see also Louis L. Jaffe, "Damages for Personal Injury: The Impact of Insurance," *Law and Contemporary Problems* 18 (1953): 221 (juries receive minimal guidance from judges regarding assignment of damages).

47. Huber, *Liability,* 121–22 (citing specific awards and decrying damages for psychic injury, mental distress, and bystander distress); Sugarman, "Doing Away with Tort Law," 594; O'Connell, "A 'Neo-No-Fault' Contract," 899–900.

48. Huber, *Liability,* 120; Priest, "Insurance Crisis," 1547, 1553; O'Connell, "Proposal to Abolish Defendants' Payment of Pain and Suffering," 341.

49. Victor E. Schwartz and Russell W. Driver, "Warnings in the Workplace: The Need for a Synthesis of Law and Communication Theory," *University of Cincinnati Law Review* 52 (1983): 40; Victor E. Schwartz and Mark A. Behrens, "Punitive Damages Reform: State Legislatures Can and Should Meet the Challenge Issued by the Supreme Court of the United States in Haslip," *American University Law Review* 42 (1993): 1375–76; idem, "The American Law Institute's Reporters' Study on Enterprise Responsibility for Personal Injury: A Timely Call for Punitive Damages Reform," *San Diego Law Review* 30 (1993): 263; Victor E. Schwartz and Liberty Mahshigian, "Offensive Collateral Estoppel: It Will Not Work in Product Liability," *New York Law School Review* 31 (1986): 583.

50. O'Connell, *The Blame Game,* 127; Priest, "Insurance Crisis," 1556, 1560; Huber, *Liability,* 189: "[A]s society adjusts to the legal regime that promotes division, everyone loses but the lawyers. We are all in the soup together. Only the lawyers are here to dine."

51. Huber, *Liability,* 9, 150–52, 194, 225; Priest, "Insurance Crisis," 1556.

52. Huber, *Liability,* 115–132 (pain and suffering), 63–65 (nuisance), 145–46,

150, 193 (collateral source); Priest, "Modern Tort Law," 15; O'Connell, "Proposal to Abolish Defendants' Payment of Pain and Suffering."

53. Huber, *Liability*, 12, 136; Priest, "Insurance Crisis," 1552–53, 1557, 1569–70; Priest, "Modern Tort Law," 14–16.

54. Patricia M. Danzon, "Tort Reform and the Role of Government in Private Insurance Markets," *Journal of Legal Studies* 13 (1984): 524; Huber, *Liability*, 12, 136; Priest, "Insurance Crisis," 1557–58.

55. Huber, *Liability*, 167–69; George Priest, "Puzzles of the Torts Crisis," *Ohio State Law Journal* 48 (1987): 500; Priest, "Insurance Crisis," 1557–58; Victor E. Schwartz and Liberty Mahshigian, "A Permanent Solution for Product Liability Crises," *Denver University Law Review* 64 (1988): 686.

56. Priest, "Puzzles of the Torts Crisis," 500; idem, "Insurance Crisis," 1557; idem, "Modern Tort Law," 17–18.

57. Huber, *Liability*, 136 (unpredictably expanding liability means insurers cannot be sure whose conduct they are insuring), 191–92 (calling for stability in liability); Priest, "Insurance Crisis," 1534–39, 1557–58, 1562–63; Schwartz and Mahshigian, "Permanent Solution for Product Liability Crises," 686.

58. Kenneth S. Abraham, *Distributing Risk: Insurance, Legal Theory, and Public Policy* (New Haven: Yale University Press, 1986) , 46–47; Huber, *Liability*, 13, 133–52.

59. Huber, *Liability*, 133–152.

60. Huber, *Liability*, 10, 110, 45–61; Priest, "Insurance Crisis," 1544, 1563, 1584. See, generally, Deborah Hensler, "Trends in Tort Litigation: The Story Behind the Statistics," *Ohio State Law Journal* 48 (1987): 478.

61. Kenneth S. Abraham, "Making Sense of the Liability Insurance Crisis," *Ohio State Law Journal* 48 (1987): 406; Schwartz and Mahshigian, "Permanent Solution for Product Liability Crises," 687; Sugarman, "Doing Away with Tort Law," 566.

62. Huber, *Liability*, 85–97; Priest, "Insurance Crisis," 1583. See, generally, Richard A. Epstein, "The Legal and Insurance Dynamics of Mass Tort Litigation," *Journal of Legal Studies* 13 (1984): 475.

63. For a discussion of "socio-legal" risks, see Danzon, "Tort Reform and the Role of Government," 536; Priest, "Insurance Crisis," 1544; idem, "Puzzles of the Torts Crisis," 499.

64. Abraham, "Making Sense of the Liability Insurance Crisis," 399, 404; Priest, "Insurance Crisis," 1584; Schwartz and Mahshigian, "Permanent Solution for Product Liability Crises," 686.

65. Abraham, "Making Sense of the Liability Insurance Crisis," 402; Huber, *Liability*, 138–49; Priest, "Insurance Crisis," 1570–82.

66. Priest, "Insurance Crisis," 1544, 1563, 1584; idem, "Puzzles of the Torts Crisis," 499.

67. Priest, "Insurance Crisis," 1565–66, 1580. For a similar observation, see Epstein, "Products Liability as an Insurance Market," 648.

68. Kenneth S. Abraham, "Efficiency and Fairness in Insurance Risk Classification," *Virginia Law Review* 71 (1985): 408; Huber, *Liability*, 134–37; Priest, "Insur-

ance Crisis," 1560–63. For a description of adverse selection, see Robert E. Keeton and Alan I. Widiss, *Insurance Law* (St. Paul, Minn.: West Publishing Co., 1988), 14.

69. For further discussion on the nature of risk classification, see Abraham, *Distributing Risk;* Leonard R. Freifelder, *A Decision Theoretic Approach to Insurance Ratemaking,* (Philadelphia: University of Pennsylvania, 1976), 224.

70. Abraham, *Distributing Risk,* 64; Abraham, "Efficiency and Fairness," 408; Epstein, "Products Liability as an Insurance Market," 650; Priest, "Insurance Crisis," 1540.

71. Common risk-classification practices include automobile insurers' using risk classifications such as age and marital status to determine rates, as well as fire insurers' using risk classifications such as a building's size and its materials to determine rates. Regina Austin, "Insurance Classification Controversy," *University of Pennsylvania Law Review* 131 (1983): 517, 538–42. Epstein, "Products Liability as an Insurance Market," 652.

72. Epstein, "Products Liability as an Insurance Market," 650; Huber, *Liability,* 16, 136; Priest, "Insurance Crisis," 1566.

73. Huber, *Liability,* 138–42; Priest, "Insurance Crisis," 1560–63, 1564–65, 1570–82; Priest, "Modern Tort Law," 17.

74. Priest, "Modern Tort Law," 13; idem, "Insurance Crisis," 1560–63, 1570–82. For examples of "consumer moral hazard," see Sugarman, "Doing Away with Tort Law," 584–85 (citing the demoralization of defendant machine manufacturers whose workers have been injured because machines' safety features have been removed, often by the very workers who were injured). See also Richard A. Posner, "Can Lawyers Solve the Problems of the Tort System?" *California Law Review* 73 (1985): 747–48 (asserting that a strict liability approach toward auto manufacturers is insensitive to the possibility that adding substantial liability costs to the costs of doing business may actually impede manufacturers' safety efforts, and that individuals can be efficient accident preventers).

75. Epstein, "Products Liability as an Insurance Market," 653; Mark V. Pauly, "The Economics of Moral Hazard," *American Economics Review* 58 (1968): 531, 535; Priest, "Insurance Crisis," 1547; Steven Shavell, "On Moral Hazard and Insurance," *Quarterly Journal of Economics* 93 (1979): 541.

76. Abraham, *Distributing Risk,* 64; Priest, "Insurance Crisis," 1548.

77. Abraham, "Efficiency and Fairness," 445–46.

78. Epstein, "Products Liability as an Insurance Market," 667; Priest, "Insurance Crisis," 1547–53.

79. Priest, "Modern Tort Law," 16 (since third-party insurance has no deductibles or coinsurance to affect consumer behavior, premiums will be higher than for the same coverage through first-party plans that do contain such behavioral incentives); idem, "Satisfying the Multiple Goals of Tort Law," *Valparaiso University Law Review* 22 (1988): 643 (noting that "[w]ith respect to accident control, modern tort law seems largely ineffective").

80. Priest, "Insurance Crisis," 1547–48.

81. See Sugarman, "Doing Away with Tort Law," 583. Sugarman explains that tort law can discourage safety improvements in the face of pending liability. In product liability cases, the defendant's safety improvements are admissible in many jurisdictions as proof of the feasibility of an alternative design, and according to Sugarman such proof is probably sufficient for a plaintiff's verdict. Because defendants fear that the introduction of new safety improvements might suggest that such measures could have been taken prior to the accident, they are deterred by the threat of liability from introducing them. See also Priest, "A Theory of Consumer Product Warranty," 1347–51.

82. Huber, *Liability,* 13 (arguing that the bank president and the janitor each pay the same added "insurance premium" on products). Priest, "Insurance Crisis," 1546, 1557, 1559–60, 1565–66, 1585–86; idem, "Modern Tort Law," 17.

83. Huber, *Liability,* 13, 151–52; Priest, "Insurance Crisis," 1586.

84. Holmes, *The Common Law,* 82.

85. This argument is particularly strong among proponents of product liability reform who support a broadly based return to negligence principles in that area of law. See, e.g., James A. Henderson and Aaron D. Twerski, "Doctrinal Collapse in Products Liability: The Empty Shell of Failure to Warn," *New York University Law Review* 65 (1990): 265 (product liability based on failure to warn deters technological innovation); Victor Schwartz, "The Post-Sale Duty to Warn: Two Unfortunate Forks in the Road to a Reasonable Doctrine," *New York University Law Review* 58 (1983): 892, 899, 901; John Wade, "On the Effect on Product Liability of Knowledge Not Available Prior to Marketing the Product," *New York University Law Review* 58 (1983): 734, 755. For similar arguments regarding the technological chilling effects from product liability based on product design, see James A. Henderson, "Manufacturer's Liability for Defective Product Design: A Proposed Statutory Reform," *North Carolina Law Review* 56 (1978): 625; idem, "Renewed Judicial Controversy over Defective Product Design: Toward the Preservation of an Emerging Consensus," *Minnesota Law Review* 63 (1979): 733; John Wade, "On Product 'Design Defects' and Their Actionability," *Vanderbilt Law Review* 33 (1980): 551.

86. See James A. Henderson, "Product Liability and the Passage of Time: The Imprisonment of Corporate Rationality," *New York University Law Review* 58 (1983): 765; Henderson and Twerski, "Doctrinal Collapse," 265; Priest, "Modern Tort Law," 13.

87. Huber, *Liability.*

CHAPTER FOUR

1. The "decision tree" is a concept derived from business decision making. As the term is used here, it connotes a decisional flow chart designed to map the steps involved in the analysis of complex situations in which various alternative strategies are advanced. Jonathon Green, *Dictionary of Jargon* (London: Routledge & Kegan Paul, 1987), 160. See Howard Raiffa, *Decision Analysis: Introductory Lectures on*

Choices Under Uncertainty (Reading, Mass.: Addison-Wesley, 1968), 10–38. For an example of its use in legal analysis, see David Kaye, "Probability Theory Meets Res Ipsa Loquitor," *Michigan Law Review* 77 (1979): 1456, 1469.

2. Leon Green, "Tort Law, Public Law in Disguise," *Texas Law Review* 38 (1959): 2. Green argues that outside interests such as society at large or "groups who are identified with the interest of social order . . . are a party to every lawsuit." Furthermore, those "public" interests may be so important as to outweigh traditional private-party concerns.

3. For a discussion of the inherent tension between this "corrective justice" view of tort law and the insurance rationale, see Ernest J. Weinrib, "The Insurance Justification and Private Law," *Journal of Legal Studies* 14 (1985): 681.

4. As is discussed more fully in Part III, during the decade of the 1980s considerable legislative activity was directed toward restructuring some aspects of tort law through statutory intervention. Kenneth S. Abraham, "What Is a Tort Claim? An Interpretation of Contemporary Tort Reform," *Maryland Law Review* 51 (1992): 172, 180. See also the DOJ Report; *Insuring Our Future,* a report of the Governor's Advisory Commission on Liability Insurance: Cuomo Commission (April 1986). For a discussion on the trend toward legislating tort law and away from traditional common-law development, see Edward Dauer, "Introduction to the Symposium: Some Cautioning Implications of Legislative Tort Reform," *Denver Law Review* 64 (1988): 613.

5. For similar listings of relevant policy goals, see Guido Calabresi, *The Costs of Accidents: A Legal and Economic Analysis* (New Haven: Yale University Press, 1970), 24; Leon Green, "The Duty Problem in Negligence Cases: II," *Columbia Law Review* 29 (1929): 255.

6. This list of goals is surely not exhaustive. For example, Sugarman recognizes a goal of protecting individuals from the unwanted publicity of a tort suit. Stephen D. Sugarman, "Doing Away with Tort Law," *California Law Review* 73 (1985): 561.

7. For scholarly debate on how damage awards should be assessed, see James F. Blumstein, Randall R. Boubjerg, and Frank A. Sloan, "Beyond Tort Reform: Developing Better Tools for Assessing Damages for Personal Injury," *Yale Journal on Regulation* 8 (1991): 171; Dorsey D. Ellis Jr., "Fairness and Efficiency in the Law of Punitive Damages," *Southern California Law Review* 56 (1982): 1; David G. Owen, "Deterrence and Desert in Tort: A Comment," *California Law Review* 73 (1985): 665; idem, "Civil Punishment and the Public Good," *Southern California Law Review* 56 (1982): 103; Cornelius Peck, "Compensation for Pain: A Reappraisal in Light of New Medical Evidence," *Michigan Law Review* 72 (1974): 1355; George Priest, "Insurability and Punitive Damages," *Alabama Law Review* 40 (1989): 1009; William L. Prosser, *Handbook of the Law of Torts*, 4th ed. (St. Paul, Minn.: West Publishing Co., 1971), 9, § 2; Harold See, "Punitive Damages: Introduction and Synopsis," *Alabama Law Review* 40 (1989): 687.

8. For a discussion on social dislocation and the desire to avoid it by spreading the burden of loss on many instead of one, see Calabresi, *The Costs of Accidents,*

391. See also George Priest, "Puzzles of the Torts Crisis," *Ohio State Law Journal* 48 (1987): 497, 501.

9. Proponents of various kinds of socially mandated public insurance systems include Richard Abel, "A Socialist Approach to Risk," *Maryland Law Review* 41 (1982): 695; Marc A. Franklin, "Replacing the Negligence Lottery: Compensation and Selective Reimbursement," *Virginia Law Review* 53 (1967): 774; Sugarman, "Doing Away with Tort Law," 642.

10. Calabresi, *The Costs of Accidents,* 144–50.

11. Oliver Wendell Holmes Jr., *The Common Law,* ed. Mark DeWolfe Howe (Cambridge: Harvard University Press, 1963), 77–78.

12. For discussions identifying some of these factors, see Guido Calabresi, "Some Thoughts on Risk Distribution and the Law of Torts," *Yale Law Journal* 70 (1961): 499; Albert Ehrenzweig, *Negligence Without Fault,* (Berkeley and Los Angeles: University of California Press, 1951), 63–65; Fowler Harper and Fleming James Jr., *The Law of Torts* (Boston: Little, Brown, 1956), 2, §§ 13.1–13.7, 26.1–26.5; Fleming James Jr., "Accident Liability Reconsidered: The Impact of Insurance," *Yale Law Journal* 57 (1948): 551, 557–58, 566–68; Robert E. Keeton, "Conditional Fault in the Law of Torts," *Harvard Law Review* 72 (1959): 401.

13. Kenneth S. Abraham, *Distributing Risk: Insurance, Legal Theory, and Public Policy* (New Haven: Yale University Press, 1986) , 64; Richard Epstein, "Products Liability as an Insurance Market," *Journal of Legal Studies* 14 (1985): 648; George Priest, "The Current Insurance Crisis and Modern Tort Law," *Yale Law Journal* 96 (1987): 1543.

14. Abraham, *Distributing Risk,* 2, 66–68; Epstein, "Products Liability as an Insurance Market," 650; Priest, "Insurance Crisis," 1540, 1547–49.

15. Robert Rabin, "Indeterminate Risk and Tort Reform: Comments on Calabresi and Klevorick," *Journal of Legal Studies* 14 (1985): 633, 640 (arguing for "disaggregation" of tort system). Scholars treating particular accidents differently include Kenneth S. Abraham, "Individual Action and Collective Responsibility: The Dilemma of Mass Tort Reform," *Virginia Law Review* 73 (1987): 845; Jeffrey O'Connell and Robert H. Joost, "Giving Motorists a Choice Between Fault and No-Fault," *Virginia Law Review* 72 (1986): 61. For a discussion and criticism of the trend by tort scholars toward unifying standards and principles, see G. Edward White, *Tort Law in America: An Intellectual History* (New York: Oxford University Press, 1980), 211–43.

CHAPTER FIVE

1. See Morton J. Horwitz, *The Transformation of American Law, 1780–1860* (Cambridge: Harvard University Press, 1979), 227–37.

2. For a summary of the roots of modern liability insurance, see Mary Coate McNeely, "Illegality as a Factor in Insurance," *Columbia Law Review* 41 (1941): 26, 28. Lengthier descriptions appear in Sylvester C. Dunham, "Accident Insurance: Historical Sketch," in *The Business of Insurance II,* ed. Howard P. Dunham (New

York: Ronald Press Co., 1912), 3, and in John H. Magee and Oscar N. Serbein, *Property and Liability Insurance,* 4th ed. (Homewood, Ill.: R. D. Irwin, 1967), ch. 2.

3. The insurance-law concept of insurable interest "requires that there be some significant relationship between the insured and the person, the object, or the activity that is the subject of an insurance transaction." Robert E. Keeton and Alan I. Widiss, *Insurance Law* (St. Paul, Minn.: West Publishing Co., 1988), 135.

4. See Fleming James Jr., "Accident Liability Reconsidered: The Impact of Insurance," *Yale Law Journal* 57 (1948): 549, 551; McNeely, "Illegality as a Factor in Insurance," 28.

5. For a brief sketch of the development of marine insurance, see Keeton and Widiss, *Insurance Law,* 19–20.

6. See Edwin Patterson, "Insurable Interests of Bailees," *Journal of American Insurance,* November 1927, 20, and December 1927, 21.

7. McNeely, "Illegality as a Factor in Insurance," 27. See Eastern R.R. v. Relief Fire Ins. Co., 98 Mass. 420 (1868). McNeely concludes that "[w]hile none of these [developments] was a direct root of modern liability insurance, collectively they pointed the way for the modern forms." Ibid., 27–28.

8. Waters v. The Merchants' Louisville Insurance Co., 11 Pet. 222 (36 U.S. 213) (1837).

9. 36 U.S. at 221.

10. Phoenix Insurance Co. v. Erie & Western Transportation Co., 117 U.S. 312 (1886).

11. Ibid. at 312, 324–35 (1886).

12. California Insurance Co. v. Union Compress Co., 133 U.S. 387, 414–15 (1890).

13. For cases following the Supreme Court's lead, see, e.g., Trenton Passenger Ry. Co. v. Guarantors Liability Indem. Co., 37 A. 609 (N.J. 1897); Casualty Ins. Co.'s Case, 82 Md. 535, 576–82 (1896); Kansas City, Memphis & Birmingham R. Co. v. Southern Railway News Co., 52 S.W. 205 (Mo. 1899). But see the contrary opinion of Judge Woodson in Breeden v. Frankfort Marine, Accident & Plate Glass Ins. Co., 119 S.W. 576, 578–89 (Mo. 1909), which argues strenuously that liability insurance against negligence should be contrary to public policy because of its tendency to promote careless behavior. He argues in part that

> [t]he very foundation upon which this class of insurance rests is built upon sand, and will not support the important structure which the business interests of the country are attempting to erect upon it. The very corner stone thereof and all of its accompanying parts are essentially an act of negligence, necessarily resulting in the death or the infliction of some personal injury upon the passenger, confessedly and invariably committed by the negligent act of the party who claims the right to make the contract and collect the indemnity provided for therein. . . .
>
> And if such policies of insurance are valid, then the insured must come into court and stultify himself by stating in his petition that he had disre-

> garded the duties he owed to the public and to his passengers or employes, and as a result thereof he had negligently injured or killed him. . . . Should a court of justice uphold such a policy of insurance and assist the self-confessed wrongdoer, who has wrongfully killed or injured his fellow man, to collect the policy, and thereby enable him to escape the penalties incident to his own wrong? I think not, for it is axiomatic that courts will not assist a person to take advantage of his own wrong.

Judge Woodson's position was not accepted by the full court upon rehearing in banc. But the fact that this argument was still current in the first decade of the twentieth century suggests that judicial suspicion of insurance covering negligence died hard.

14. The need for insurance in such situations was particularly acute because most courts were unwilling to release railroads from liability for personal injury or death caused by their own negligence. They could, however, contract with third parties to insure their own assets against such losses. Thus, in Kansas City, Memphis & Birmingham R. Co. v. Southern Railway News Co., the Supreme Court of Missouri held that a contract between a railroad and a newspaper company that indemnified the carrier from liability for injuries or losses sustained by the news service was valid despite a clause releasing liability for negligence of the railroad staff. In the case cited, a newsboy was killed on a train while selling books and papers for Southern Railway News Company. The boy's family received $5,000 from the railroad, which in turn sued Southern Railway News to recover that loss. The court allowed the suit, both because the consideration given by Southern Railways News was "valuable" and because "a mere contract of insurance is nothing more nor less than a contract of indemnity against loss, as is this with the defendant, and the principles governing must be the same in each, and as nothing can be predicated of the contract in this case which could interfere with or affect the liability of the carrier to the person injured, there is nothing in it to . . . render it obnoxious to public policy." Kansas City, Memphis & Birmingham R. Co. v. Southern Railway News Co., 52 S.W. 205, 209 (Mo. 1899).

15. Connecticut General Statutes, sec. 3735, enacted in 1881, provided for liability of railroads for losses occasioned by fires caused by their engines. After stating that "such company shall be held responsible in damages to the extent of such injury to the person so injured," the statute provided that "[e]ach such company shall have an insurable interest in the property for which it may be so held responsible in damages, and may procure insurance thereon in its own behalf." Although the statute did not explicitly describe it as such, this was effectively liability insurance. The statute was upheld against constitutional attack in Grissell v. Housatonic R. Co., 9 A. 137 (Conn. 1886).

16. McNeely, "Illegality as a Factor in Liability Insurance," 28.

17. See, e.g., the Breeden case, discussed in *supra* note 13.

18. See, e.g., Hartford Fire Ins. Co. v. R.R., 175 U.S. 91 (1899); Wager v. Providence Ins. Co., 150 U.S. 99 (1893); Boston & A. R. Co. v. Mercantile Trust & Deposit Co., 34 A. 778 (Md. 1896); Trenton Passenger Ry. Co. v. Guarantors' Liability Indem. Co., 37 A. 609 (N.J. 1897); Finley v. U.S. Cas. Co., 83 S.W. 2

(Tenn. 1904); Sanders v. Frankfort Marine, Accident & Plate Glass Ins. Co., 57 A. 655 (N.H. 1904); Connolly v. Bolster, 72 N.E. 981 (Mass. 1905).

19. As late as 1948, Fleming James Jr. commented, "Legally, liability insurance was at first (and still largely is) regarded as an altogether irrelevant fact in the consideration of tort liability. It was a private contract of indemnity between the defendant and an outsider, by which the latter undertook to protect the insured from loss on account of his individual legal liability. As to the injured person it was . . . none of his business." James, "Accident Liability Reconsidered," 551.

20. See, e.g., James Stewart & Co. v. Newby, 266 Fed. 287, 295 (4th Cir. 1920) ("The only purpose for which such evidence is presented is to prejudice the jury, and the poison is of such character that, once being injected into the mind, it is difficult of eradication"). This view still prevails. See Collins v. Davis, 366 S.E.2d 769, 770 (Ga. Ct. App. 1988), involving an attempt by the defendant to show plaintiff's coverage, to which the court responded that "evidence of insurance coverage is so prejudicial by nature that it should not be admitted unless it is clearly relevant and unless its relevance outweighs its prejudice." For a discussion and criticism of this time-honored rule, see Leon Green, "Blindfolding the Jury," *Texas Law Review* 3 (1954): 167.

21. For an example of this reasoning, see Flanner v. St Joseph Home for Blind Sisters, 42 S.E.2d 225, 226 (N.C. 1947), where the court stated, "That defendant had the forethought to protect itself against [liability] as the law imposes for [plaintiff's] injuries does not serve to enlarge or extend that liability." The case involved a procedural issue of discovery, but the court's statement is broad enough to encompass any consideration of insurance in setting the terms of liability.

22. A good modern exponent of this distinction between permissible use of insurance considerations at the policy level and impermissible use of them to decide individual cases appears in the opinion of the Connecticut Supreme Court in Dzenutis v. Dzenutis, 512 A.2d 130 (Conn. 1986). The case abolished parent-child immunity in circumstances where the child's injury resulted from parental business activities occurring away from the family home. The decision rested in substantial measure on the court's judgment that the prevalence of liability insurance in business contexts undermined the traditional objections to parental liability to children. Nevertheless, the court refused to make the possession of such insurance the determinant of liability in individual cases. The court drew the distinction between the two different uses of insurance in the following terms:

> Although we are persuaded that the likely availability of insurance coverage in particular situations . . . is pertinent in deciding whether parent-child immunity is applicable, we disagree with the trial court's view that the presence of insurance should be the touchstone of viability of an action by a child against a parent and that recovery should be limited to the insurance policy. . . . [W]e reject . . . the claim that the outcome of a case should depend upon whether the defendant has insurance. We continue to believe that different rules of law should not be fashioned for the insured and the uninsured. . . .

We conclude, nevertheless, that because of the general prevalence of liability insurance in the business activity setting, it is appropriate for us to recognize that in most instances family harmony will not be jeopardized by allowing suits between parents and children arising out of business activities conducted away from the home, as in the case before us. (Dzenutis, 512 A.2d at 135)

23. For examples of this attitude, see Coleman v. United States Railroad Admin., 199 P. 489 (Colo. 1921) (even though the employee's nonnegligent injury is "regrettable," the railroad employer is not an "insurer" of the employee's safety); Escambia County Electric Light & P. Co. v. Sutherland, 55 So. 83 (Fla. 1911) (the electric company is not an "insurer to its patrons against all danger" in the use of electrical equipment installed by the company on the premises; the jury instruction that invited the jury to conclude the contrary was a reversible error); Takacs v. Detroit United Ry., 207 N.W. 907, 910 (Mich. 1926) (where accident was due to the "intervening tort" of another passenger; holding the railroad liable "would make the carrier an absolute insurer of the injured passenger, a liability which the law of negligence does not impose"); Emmons v. City of Virginia, 188 N.W. 561, 563 (Minn. 1922) (holding the city immune from liability for injury to a child in a public park because "[t]o impose liability is practically to make municipalities insurers against defects in public parks and in the appliances therein provided for public enjoyment, for we know how prone juries are to brush aside the questions of contributory negligence and unavoidable accidents and find in favor of the injured where a defendant has means at command"); Cash v. Sonken-Calamba Co. 17 S.W.2d 927 (Mo. 1929) (holding a worker injured in a rail yard to be contributorily negligent for his own injury, because failure to do so, in court's view, would transgress the established principle that the owner of the yard is not the "insurer" of the premises' safety to those who enter upon it); Zitman v. Glueck Box Co., 276 S.W. 23 (Mo. 1925) (holding that in directing work, an employer "is not an insurer of the safety of his employees" and thus is not required to use the safest possible methods, only those that are "reasonably safe"); Negus v. Becker, 38 N.E. 290 (N.Y. 1894) (rejecting a claim for strict liability against the defendant for construction of a defective party wall; court refuses to accept the notion that one who constructs a party wall is "insurer" of its safety); Perret v. George, 133 A. 228 (Pa. 1926) (rejecting liability of a streetcar operator for injury caused when a traveler, upon alighting from the streetcar, fell into a hole in the street: "To hold, under such circumstances, that the duty of stopping at a safe place to alight embraced the obligation to avoid any defect in the highway, between the car and the curb, would cause the company to be liable as an insurer of the safety of a pedestrian in coming from or going to a car").

24. For an early and especially candid expression of this viewpoint, see Ryan v. New York Central R. Co., 35 N.Y. 210 (1866). There the court effectively advocated what we would now call a first-party insurance system, where each individual would be obliged to insure him- or herself against negligent infliction of injury by others.

25. See, generally, John Fleming, "The Collateral Source Rule and Loss Allocation in Tort Law," *California Law Review* 54 (1966): 1478; James Branton, "The Collateral Source Rule," *St. Mary's Law Journal* 18 (1987): 883.

26. See, e.g., Healy v. Rennert, 173 N.E.2d 777 (N.Y. 1960); Conley v. Foster, 335 S.W.2d 904 (Ky. 1960); Hudson v. Lazarus, 217 F.2d 344 (D.C. Cir. 1954); Harding v. Town of Townshend, 43 Vt. 536 (1871). Cf. Richard C. Maxwell, "The Collateral Source Rule in the American Law of Damages," *Minnesota Law Review* 46 (1962): 669.

27. The system of workers' compensation had its origins in German politics. In order to dilute the progressive movement of the reformists in Germany, Otto von Bismarck instituted social insurance reforms, the most famous of which was workers' compensation. Jeffrey O'Connell, "Alternatives to the Tort System for Personal Injury," *San Diego Law Review* 23 (1986): 17, 21.

28. New York's first effort appeared in Chapter 674 of the laws of 1910—"An Act to amend the labor law, in relation to workmen's compensation in certain dangerous employments." Article 14-a of Chapter 674 amended the former labor law and inserted several sections concerning "Workmen's Compensation in Certain Dangerous Employments." Section 217 explained the provisions concerning employer liability: "Basis of Liability: If . . . personal injury by accident arising out of and in the course of the employment . . . is caused to any workman employed therein . . . or the injury caused thereby is in whole or part contributed to by (a) A necessary risk or danger of the employment or one inherent in the nature thereof; or (b) Failure of employer . . . to exercise due care, or to comply with any laws affecting such employment; then such employer shall, subject as hereinafter mentioned, be liable to pay compensation."

29. The idea of workers' compensation struck a generally enthusiastic response among scholars and practitioners, several of whom participated in the drafting process. For a range of views, see Francis Bohlen, "A Problem in the Drafting of Workmen's Compensation Acts," *Harvard Law Review* 25 (1912): 328, 401, 517; P. Tecumseh Sherman, "The Jurisprudence of the Workmen's Compensation Laws," *University of Pennsylvania Law Review* 63 (1915): 823; Eugene Wambaugh, "Workmen's Compensation Acts," *Harvard Law Review* 25 (1911): 129; F. P. Walton, "Workmen's Compensation and the Theory of Professional Risk," *Columbia Law Review* 11 (1911): 36.

30. For discussions of the development of workers' compensation and its relation to tort law, see Richard Epstein, "The Historical Origins and Economic Structure of the Workers' Compensation Act," *Georgia Law Review* 16 (1982): 775; Lawrence Friedman, "The Nature and Origins of Workmen's Compensation," in *A History of American Law*, 2d ed. (New York: Simon & Schuster, 1985), ch. 14, 206; Wex S. Malone, "Damage Suits and the Contagious Principle of Workmen's Compensation," *Louisiana Law Review* 12 (1952): 231; Jeremiah Smith, "Sequel to Workmen's Compensation Acts," *Harvard Law Review* 27 (1914): 235; Arthur Larson, "The Welfare State and Workmen's Compensation," *NACCA Law Journal* 5 (1950): 18.

31. Arthur Larson, "The Nature and Origins of Workmen's Compensation," *Cornell Law Quarterly* 37 (1952): 206–7, 217.

32. Columbia University Council for Research in the Social Sciences, *Report of the Committee to Study Compensation for Automobile Accidents* (New York: Columbia University, 1932). See also Young B. Smith, Austin J. Lilly, and Noel T. Dowling, "Compensation for Automobile Accidents: A Symposium," *Columbia Law Review* 32 (1932): 785.

33. For a retrospective on the Columbia plan and the abortive efforts it spawned, see Fleming James Jr., "The Columbia Study of Compensation: An Unanswered Challenge," *Columbia Law Review* 59 (1959).

34. For a description and discussion upholding the constitutionality of the Massachusetts law, see *Opinion of the Justices,* 147 N.E. 681 (Mass. 1925).

35. For discussion of financial responsibility laws, see Joseph H. Braun, "The Financial Responsibility Law," *Law and Contemporary Problems* 3 (1936): 505; N. P. Feinsinger, "Operation of Financial Responsibility Laws," *Law and Contemporary Problems* 3 (1936): 519; Robbins B. Stoeckel, "Administrative Problems of Financial Responsibility Laws," *Law and Contemporary Problems* 3 (1936): 531; Ross D. Netherton, "Highway Safety Under Different Types of Liability Legislation," *Ohio State Law Journal* 15 (1954): 110; Arthur I. Vorys, "A Short Survey of Laws Designed to Exclude the Financially Irresponsible Driver from the Highway," *Ohio State Law Journal* 15 (1954): 101.

36. For an example, see Chapter 43 of the Revised Statutes of Illinois, 1874—"An act to provide for the licensing of and against the evils arising from the sale of intoxicating liquors"—which dealt entirely with regulating dram shops. Section 9 allowed suits for damages:

> Every husband, wife, child, parent, guardian, employer or other person, who shall be injured in person or property, or means of support, by any intoxicated person, or in consequence of the intoxication, habitual or otherwise, of any person, shall have a right of action in his or her own name, severally or jointly, against any person or persons who shall, by selling or giving intoxicating liquors, have caused the intoxication, in whole or in part, of such person or persons; and any person owning, renting, leasing or permitting the occupation of any building or premises, and having knowledge that intoxicating liquors are to be sold therein, or who . . . shall knowingly permit therein the sale of any intoxicating liquors that have caused, in whole or in part, the intoxication of any person, shall be liable . . . with the person or persons selling or giving intoxicating liquors aforesaid, for all damages sustained. (Hurd Illinois Revised Statutes 1874, 439–40)

37. Ives v. South Buffalo Railway Co., 94 N.E. 431 (N.Y. 1911).

38. New York Central Ry. v. White, 243 U.S. 188 (1916).

39. E.g., Powers v. Massachusetts Homeopathic Hospital, 109 F. 294 (1st Cir. 1901), *cert. denied,* 183 U.S. 695 (1901); Parks v. Northwestern University, 218 Ill. 381 (1905); McDonald v. Massachusetts General Hospital, 120 Mass. 432 (1876);

Perry v. House of Refuge, 63 Md. 20 (1885); Vermillion v. Woman's College of Due West, 88 S.E. 649 (S.C. 1916). See Carl Zollman, "Liability of Charitable Institutions," *Michigan Law Review* 19 (1921): 395; Lester Feezer, "The Tort Liability of Charities," *Pennsylvania Law Review* 77 (1928): 191.

40. The leading case is President and Directors of Georgetown College v. Hughes, 130 F.2d 810 (D.C. Cir. 1942) (Rutledge, J.), which is discussed in more detail in Chapter Six; see also Henry W. Putnam Memorial Hospital v. Allen, 34 F.2d 927 (2d Cir. 1929). Cases withdrawing immunity to the extent of liability insurance include O'Connor v. Boulder Colorado Sanitarium Assn., 96 P.2d 835 (Colo. 1939); Morehouse College v. Russell, 135 S.E.2d 432 (Ga. 1964); and McLeod v. St. Thomas Hospital, 95 S.W.2d 917 (Tenn. 1936). For statutory treatment, see N.C. Gen. Stat. 1–539.9; R.I.G.L. 9-1-26 (1956) (hospitals). Recognizing that "[t]he great majority of jurisdictions . . . have forthrightly abolished the immunity," the Restatement (Second) of Torts, Section 895E, takes the position that "[o]ne engaged in a charitable, educational, religious or benevolent enterprise or activity is not for that reason immune from tort liability." For an early article advocating abolition of charitable immunity on insurance grounds, see Comment, "Tort Responsibility of Charitable Corporations," *Yale Law Journal* 34 (1925): 316.

41. E.g., Dunlap v. Dunlap, 150 A. 905 (N.H. 1930) (abolishing intrafamily immunity because of insurance); Rozell v. Rozell, 22 N.E.2d 254 (N.Y. 1939) (same); Worrell v. Worrell, 4 S.E.2d 343 (Va. 1939) (same); Molitor v. Kaneland Community Unit District No. 302, 163 N.E.2d 89 (Ill. 1959) (abolishing governmental immunity, in part because of the ability of governmental agencies to protect public fisc by purchasing liability insurance); Thomas v. Broadlands Community Consol. School Dist., 109 N.E.2d 636 (Ill. App. 1952) (same). Judicial abolition of governmental immunity often provoked legislative responses that either delayed the abrogation of immunity or restored it in part. For a discussion of such developments in California, see Arvo Van Alstyne, "Governmental Tort Liability: Judicial Lawmaking in a Statutory Milieu," *Stanford Law Review* 15 (1963): 163.

42. Keeton and Widiss list eighteen discrete areas in which federal or state governments, or sometimes both, provide or sponsor insurance to compensate various forms of loss: (1) social security benefits; (2) unemployment insurance; (3) workers' compensation insurance; (4) motor vehicle accident funds; (5) crop insurance; (6) bank deposit insurance; (7) bank guaranty funds; (8) public-property insurance; (9) public-official bonding funds; (10) animal damage funds; (11) title insurance; (12) housing mortgage insurance; (13) veterans' life insurance; (14) postal insurance; (15) war risk insurance; (16) nuclear hazards insurance; (17) inner-city property insurance; (18) flood insurance. They note that "[t]he possibility of a governmental subsidy is inherent in every program that involves governmental participation in the business of insuring, whether as insurer or as reinsurer." Keeton and Widiss, *Insurance Law,* 972.

43. For development of a similar thesis with respect to English law, see W. G. Friedmann, "Social Insurance and the Principle of Tort Liability," *Harvard Law Review* 63 (1949): 241.

44. Escola v. Coca-Cola Bottling Co., 150 P.2d 436 (Cal. 1944) (Traynor, J.,

concurring). For sympathetic discussions of Traynor's pathbreaking work in *Escola*, see Harry Kalven, "Torts: The Quest for Appropriate Standards," *California Law Review* 53 (1965): 189; G. Edward White, "Rationality and Intuition in the Process of Judging: Roger Traynor," in *The American Judicial Tradition*, expanded ed. (New York: Oxford University Press, 1988), ch. 13, esp. 297–300. For criticism, see Richard Epstein, *Modern Products Liability Law: A Legal Revolution* (Westport, Conn.: Quorum Books, 1980), 36–48.

45. "Even if there is no negligence . . . public policy demands that responsibility be fixed wherever it will most effectively reduce the hazards to life and health inherent in defective products that reach the market. It is evident that the manufacturer can anticipate some hazards and guard against the recurrence of others, as the public cannot. . . . It is to the public interest to discourage the marketing of products having defects that are a menace to the public. If such products nevertheless find their way into the market, it is to the public interest to place the responsibility for whatever injury they may cause upon the manufacturer, who, even if he is not negligent in the manufacture of the product, is responsible for its reaching the market." 150 P.2d at 440–41.

46. Ibid. at 441.

47. "An injured person . . . is not ordinarily in a position to refute [manufacturer's evidence of due care] or identify the cause of the defect, for he can hardly be familiar with the manufacturing process as the manufacturer himself is." Ibid.

48. "As handicrafts have been replaced by mass production with its great markets and transportation facilities, the close relationship between the producer and consumer of a product has been altered. Manufacturing processes, frequently valuable secrets, are ordinarily either inaccessible to or beyond the ken of the general public. The consumer no longer has means or skill enough to investigate for himself the soundness of a product, even when it is not contained in a sealed package, and his erstwhile vigilance has been lulled by the steady efforts of manufacturers to build up confidence by advertising and marketing devices such as trademarks. . . . Consumers no longer approach products warily but accept them on faith . . . The manufacturer's obligation to the consumer must keep pace with the changing relationship between them." Ibid. at 443.

49. Ibid. at 440–41.

50. Ibid. at 444.

51. The California Supreme Court adopted Traynor's *Escola* rationale in another Traynor opinion, this time for the majority, in *Greenman v. Yuba Power Products, Inc.*, 377 P.2d 897 (Cal. 1963). Other states quickly followed suit: e.g., Kassab v. Central Soya, 246 A.2d 848, 854 n.6 (Pa. 1968) (citing *Escola*'s risk-distribution rationale as support for overruling the requirement of privity of contract between manufacturer and consumer); Webb v. Zern, 220 A.2d 853, 854 (Pa. 1966) (adopted the strict liability principle of Section 402A of the Restatement (Second) of Torts as "the law of Pennsylvania"); McKisson v. Sales Affiliates, Inc., 416 S.W.2d 787, 789 n.2 (Texas 1967) (citing *Escola*, allowing recovery for defective permanent-wave solution); Codling v. Paglia, 298 N.E.2d 622 (N.Y. 1973) (adopted strict product liability through application of Section 402A to an automobile manufacturer

whose defects resulted in an automobile crash and subsequent injuries to a bystander); Suvada v. White, 210 N.E.2d 182 (Ill. 1965) (adopted *Escola* rationale of risk distribution through *Greenman* and Section 402A to hold a manufacturer liable for damages to property as well as bodily harm); Rossingol v. Danbury School of Aeronautics et al., 227 A.2d 418 (Conn. 1967) (strict product liability adopted through Section 402A and applied to the manufacturers and distributors of a defective valve mechanism that resulted in an air crash and subsequent damage to an aircraft). For contemporary discussion of these developments, see John Wade, "Strict Tort Liability of Manufacturers, *Southwestern Law Journal* 19 (1965); W. Page Keeton, "Products Liability: The Nature and Extent of Strict Liability," *University of Illinois Law Forum* 1964 (1964): 693; W. Page Keeton, "Product Liability: Some Observations About Allocation of Risks," *Michigan Law Review* 64 (1966): 1329. For a catalogue of cases from the 1960s and 1970s adopting strict product liability, see Diane Carter Maleson, "Negligence Is Dead but It Rules Us from the Grave: A Proposal to Limit Defendants' Responsibility in Strict Product Liability Actions Without Resort to Proximate Cause," *Temple Law Quarterly* 51 (1978): 1, 38–40.

Even though strict product liability proved to be an immensely popular idea, not every court that adopted it was equally enamored of the insurance rationale. California's next-door neighbor Oregon was a notable holdout. In *Wights v. Staff Jennings,* 405 P.2d 624 (Or. 1965), the court discussed at length the implications of the insurance rationale (the court used the popular term "enterprise liability") for tort law. It expressed reservations about its use, principally because the court saw no basis for containing the principle to cases involving defective products:

> The rationale of risk spreading and compensating the victim has no special relevancy to cases involving injuries resulting from the use of defective goods. The reasoning would seem to apply not only in cases involving personal injuries arising from the *sale* of defective goods, but equally to any case where an injury results from the risk creating conduct of the seller in any stage of the production and distribution of goods. Thus a manufacturer would be strictly liable even in the absence of fault for an injury to a person struck by one of the manufacturer's trucks being used in transporting his goods to market. It seems to us that the enterprise liability rationale employed in the Escola case proves too much and that if adopted would compel us to apply the principle of strict liability in all future cases where the loss could be distributed. (405 P.2d at 628 [footnote omitted])

Nevertheless, the court concluded that "strict liability may be imposed upon the seller in appropriate circumstances through the application of established tort principles directly or by analogy." Ibid. at 629 (footnote omitted). The court referred, for example, to the traditional principle of strict liability for ultrahazardous activity, a principle it found relevant to the case at bar, which involved injuries from the explosion of an engine on a motorboat. Subsequent Oregon cases, though they have expanded product liability well beyond traditional ultrahazardous activities, have continued to reflect suspicion toward the insurance rationale. See, e.g., Phillips v. Kimwood Machine Co., 525 P.2d 1033 (Or. 1974) (strict product liability for defective design in a sanding machine; the court, noting that insurance rationale has never been embraced in Oregon, rejected the defendant's attempt to escape liability on ground that plaintiff was the superior cost spreader).

52. See William L. Prosser, "The Assault on the Citadel (Strict Liability to the Consumer)," *Yale Law Journal* 69 (1960): 1099; idem, "The Fall of the Citadel (Strict Liability to the Consumer)," *Minnesota Law Review* 50 (1966): 635. Prosser's use of this metaphor is borrowed from Cardozo's statement that "the assault upon the citadel of privity is proceeding in these days apace." Ibid., n. 1 (quoting Ultramares v. Touche, 174 N.E. 441, 445 [N.Y. 1931]).

53. E.g., Greenman v. Yuba Power Products, Inc., 377 P.2d 897 (Cal. 1962); Brandenburger v. Toyota Motor Sales, 513 P.2d 268 (Mont. 1973); Dippel v. Sciano, 153 N.W.2d 55 (Wis. 1967); Ogle v. Caterpillar Tractor Co., 716 P.2d 334 (Wyo. 1983). But see Helene Curtis Industries, Inc. v. Pruitt, 385 F.2d 841 (5th Cir. 1968) (declining to use the insurance rationale to extend strict product liability of the manufacturer to the consumer in circumstances where the manufacturer's product was not intended for consumer purchase); Wights v. Staff Jennings, Inc., 405 P.2d 624 (Or. 1965) (adopting strict product liability in tort, but specifically refusing to accept the insurance rationale as the basis for it).

54. E.g., Jordan v. Sunnyslope Appliance Propane & Plumbing Supplies Co., 135 Ariz. 309 (Ariz. App. 1983) (applying strict product liability to sellers of used goods); Vandermark v. Ford Motor Co., 391 P.2d 168 (Cal. 1964) (extending strict product liability to an automobile retailer); Price v. Shell Oil Co., 466 P.2d 722 (Cal. 1970) (extending strict product liability to bailors and lessors of personal property); Turner v. International Harvester Corp., 336 A.2d 62 (N.J. 1975) (applying strict product liability to a seller of used goods); Nath v. National Equipment Leasing Corp., 422 A.2d 868 (Pa. 1981) (equipment-leasing corporation subject to strict product liability, even though it was a "finance-lessor" and not technically a "seller"). But see La Rosa v. Superior Court, 176 Cal. Rptr. 224 (Cal. App. 1981) (refusing to extend strict product liability to a seller of used goods, in part because court found risk-distribution justification unpersuasive in used-goods market); Tauber-Arons Auctioneers Co. v. Superior Court for County of Los Angeles, 161 Cal. Rptr. 789 (Cal. App. 1980) (refusing to extend strict product liability to an auctioneer of used goods); Tillman v. Vance Equip. Co., 596 P.2d 1299 (Or. 1979) (refusing to apply strict product liability to a seller of used goods, because the risk-distribution rationale is subordinate to consumer expectations and inducement of safety; since those cannot be met by imposing strict liability on the used-goods market, risk distribution alone is inadequate to justify such a change).

55. E.g., Santor v. A & M Karagheusian, Inc., 207 A.2d 305 (N.J. 1965) (allowing a strict product liability action for economic loss); Thompson v. Nebraska Mobile Homes Corp., 647 P.2d 334 (Mont. 1982) (same). But see Seely v. White Motor Co., 403 P.2d 145 (Cal. 1965) (Traynor, J.) (limiting the purchaser to recovery under warranty for economic loss); East River Steamship Corp. v. Transamerica Delaval, 476 U.S. 858 (1986) (adopting *Seely* rule and rejecting *Santor* approach in product liability cases under federal admiralty jurisdiction).

56. E.g., Reliance Insurance Co. v. Al E. & C., Ltd., 539 F.2d 1101 (7th Cir.

1976) (extending strict product liability to include injuries to bailees); Williams v. National Trailer Convoy, Inc., 549 F. Supp. 305 (D. Colo. 1982) (extending strict product liability under Colorado law to include injuries to bystanders); Howes v. Hansen, 56 Wis.2d 247 (1972) (bystander liability). But see Cornelius v. Bay Motors, Inc., 258 Ore. 564 (1971) (O'Conner, J., concurring) (objecting to majority's willingness to assume bystander liability, in part on grounds that Oregon courts had never embraced a risk-distribution rationale for strict product liability).

57. In this context, numerous courts have turned to a multifactor analysis for design defects advanced independently in the 1970s by John Wade and W. Page Keeton and now often referred to as the Wade-Keeton approach. Wade included, as one factor, "the feasibility, on the part of the manufacturer, of spreading the loss by setting the price of the product or carrying liability insurance." John Wade, "On the Nature of Strict Tort Liability for Products," *Mississippi Law Journal* 44 (1973): 825, 837–38. See also W. Page Keeton, "Manufacturer's Liability: The Meaning of 'Defect' in the Manufacture and Design of Products," *Syracuse Law Review* 20 (1969): 559; idem, "Product Liability and the Meaning of Defect," *St. Mary's Law Journal* 5 (1973): 30; idem, "Products Liability: Design Hazards and the Meaning of Defect, *Cumberland Law Review* 10 (1979): 293; John Wade, "On Product 'Design Defects' and Their Actionability," *Vanderbilt Law Review* 33 (1980): 551. For cases following the Wade-Keeton approach and thus incorporating insurance considerations into their analysis, see, e.g., Ortho Pharmaceutical Corp. v. Heath, 722 P.2d 410 (Colo. 1986); Cepeda v. Cumberland Engineering Corp., 386 A.2d 816 (N.J. 1978); Johnson v. Clark Equip. Co., 547 P.2d 132 (Or. 1976). For further discussion and critique of the Wade-Keeton approach, see Aaron D. Twerski, "Seizing the Middle Ground Between Rules and Standards in Design Defect Litigation," *New York University Law Review* 57 (1982): 521. But see Prentis v. Yale Mfg. Co, 765 N.W.2d 176 (Mich. 1984) (applying the negligence standard to design defect issues and concluding that a 402A formulation of product liability fails to disclose a complete embrace of the risk-distribution rationale).

58. E.g., Shepard v. Superior Court, 142 Cal. Rptr. 612 (Cal. App. 1977) (allowing recovery for emotional trauma suffered as a result of witnessing a family member's death caused by a defectively designed automobile).

59. E.g., Ortho Pharmaceutical Corp. v. Chapman, 388 N.E.2d 541 (Ind. App. 1979) (treating prescription pharmaceuticals as "unavoidably unsafe" products, exempt under 402A's Comment k from full strict liability, despite the argument of a dissenting judge favoring strict liability for pharmaceuticals on risk-distribution grounds).

60. E.g., Suter v. San Angelo Foundry & Machine Co., 406 A.2d 140 (N.J. 1979) (rejecting the comparative negligence defense in product liability actions involving design defect, based in part on manufacturer's risk-distribution capacity). But see Winston v. International Harvester Corp., 791 F.2d 430 (5th Cir. 1986) (applying comparative negligence in a product liability suit involving injuries from a defective tractor that had been operated at an unsafe speed, reasoning that safety considerations outweighed risk distribution in favoring a comparative negligence standard); Lewis v. Timco, Inc., 716 F.2d 1425 5th Cir. 1983) (using preference for

safety over risk distribution to adopt a comparative negligence defense in product liability actions under federal maritime jurisdiction).

61. E.g., McKay v. Rockwell International Corp., 704 F.2d 444 (9th Cir. 1983), *cert. denied,* 464 U.S. 1043 (1984) (finding the cost-spreading rationale inapplicable to government contracting because contractors are prohibited by law from passing increases in insurance costs on to the federal government); *in re* "Agent Orange" Product Liability Litigation, 506 F. Supp. 762 (E.D. N.Y. 1980), *cert. denied,* 465 U.S. 1067 (1984) (risk distribution is undesirable in the field of government military contracting because it will drive up the price of defense spending, putting pressure on the government to waive its sovereign immunity), *reversed on other grounds,* 635 F.2d at 987 (2d Cir. 1980), *cert. denied,* 454 U.S. 1128 (1981). See also Boyle v. United Technologies Corp., 487 U.S. 500 (1988) (affirming government contractor defense as a matter of federal common law in cases where the government sets specifications for products, based on information about their safety; the court reasoned that distribution of risk to the government is inconsistent with principles of federal sovereign immunity).

62. E.g., Beshada v. Johns-Manville Products Corp., 447 A.2d 539 (N.J. 1982). The decision of the New Jersey Supreme Court in *Beshada* relied in part on risk-distribution considerations to hold that knowledge of a product danger must be imputed to a manufacturer in cases under Section 402A where the alleged product defect involved a failure to warn. The effect of this ruling was to preclude the manufacturer from raising in defense the so-called state-of-the-art evidence, which would show that in light of existing technology the danger was "unknowable" at the time the product was manufactured. *Beshada* is discussed in greater detail in the Chapter Six. For a thorough discussion of the case and the controversy surrounding it, see Ellen Wertheimer, "Unknowable Dangers and the Death of Strict Products Liability: The Empire Strikes Back," *University of Cincinnati Law Review* 60 (1992): 1183.

63. E.g., Martin v. Harrington & Richardson, Inc., 743 F.2d 1200 (7th Cir. 1984) (Cudahy, J., concurring) (using insurance considerations to argue for recognizing a gun manufacturer as engaging in ultrahazardous activity, although concurring with the majority in view that applicable Illinois law exempted gun manufacturers from strict liability).

64. E.g., Becker v. Interstate Properties, 569 F.2d 1203 (3d Cir. 1977), *cert. denied,* 436 U.S. 906 (1978) (duty of a property developer for defects in a subcontractor's work); Smith v. Arbaugh's Restaurant, Inc. 469 F.2d 97 (D.C. Cir. 1972), *cert. denied,* 412 U.S. 939 (1973) (general duty of care of the owners and the occupiers of land, without regard to status of the victim); Hall v. E.I. du Pont de Nemours & Co., 345 F. Supp. 353 (E.D. N.Y. 1972 (adopting the theory of strict "enterprise" liability, where all participants in a single industry are jointly liable, in a case involving the ultrahazardous activity of manufacturing blasting caps); Alaska v. Abbott, 498 P.2d 712 (Alaska 1972) (finding duty of care under state statutes regarding highway maintenance); Becker v. IRM Corp., 698 P.2d 116 (Cal. 1985) (adopting strict liability of landlords to tenants in cases involving injury from latent defects); Bigbee v. Pacific Tel. & Tel. Co., 665 P.2d 947 (Cal. 1983) (telephone company owes to patrons duty of care with respect to dangerous location of a tele-

phone booth); Tarasoff v. Regents of University of California, 551 P.2d 334 (Cal. 1976) (duty of a psychologist to warn a third party endangered by a patient's violent tendencies); Rowland v. Christian, 443 P.2d 561 (Cal. 1968) (general duty of care of landowners and occupiers—discussed in Chapter Six); Archer v. Sybert, 213 Cal. Rptr. 486 (Cal. App. 1985) (liability of a car owner for torts of a car thief when the car owner left the keys in the ignition); Schipper v. Levitt & Sons, Inc., 207 A.2d 314 (N.J. 1985) (mass housing vendor owes duty of care to ultimate occupants); Mariorenzi v. Joseph DiPonte, Inc., 333 A.2d 127 (R.I. 1975) (general duty of care of landowners and occupiers).

65. E.g., Dzenutis v. Dzenutis, 512 A.2d 130 (Conn. 1986) (eliminating parental immunity in a business setting); Rousey v. Rousey, 499 A.2d 1199 (D.C. App. 1985) (eliminating parental immunity); Curtis v. Cobb County, 333 S.E.2d 595 (Ga. 1985) (per curiam) (under state statute, sovereign immunity waived to the extent of purchase of liability insurance); Eule v. Eule Motor Sales, 170 A.2d 241 (N.J. 1961) (spousal immunity inapplicable in action by wife against business partnership in which husband was a principal); Collopy v. Newark Eye and Ear Infirmary, 141 A.2d 276 (N.J. 1958) (eliminating charitable immunity); Surnack v. Surnack, 282 A.2d 66 (N.J. Super. 1971) (eliminating spousal immunity, at least in circumstances where spouse is insured); Hack v. Hack, 495 Pa. 300 (1981) (eliminating spousal immunity); Friend v. Cove Methodist Church, Inc., 396 P.2d 546 (Wash. 1964) (eliminating charitable immunity). Cf. Overcash v. Statesville City Bd. of Education, 348 S.E.2d 524 (N.C. App. 1986) (applying statute limiting charity liability to the amount of its liability insurance coverage).

66. E.g., United States v. Romitti, 363 F.2d 662 (9th Cir. 1966) (extending the scope of an employer's vicarious liability under the Federal Tort Claims Act to include liability for an employee's negligent driving in traveling under the employer's direction from one work site to another); Bryan v. Kitamura, 529 F. Supp. 394 (D. Hawaii 1982) (upholding a state statute imposing vicarious liability on parents for torts of their minor children); Beeck v. Tucson General Hospital, 500 P.2d 1153 (Ariz. App. 1972) (hospital vicariously liable for the negligence of an X-ray technician); Hinman v. Westinghouse Elec. Co., 471 P.2d 988, (Cal. 1970) (explaining vicarious liability of employers for negligence of employees as based upon employers' ability to distribute risks); Soldano v. O'Daniels, 190 Cal. Rptr. 310 (Cal. App. 1983) (tavern owner vicariously liable for bartender's negligent failure to permit a patron to use the tavern's telephone to summon aid during a fight); Strait v. Hale Construction Co., 103 Cal. Rptr. 487 (Cal. App. 1972) (under "borrowed servant" doctrine, both the employer and the borrower of a borrowed servant may be held liable for that servant's negligence); Bleeda v. Hickman-Williams & Co. 205 N.W.2d 85 (Mich. Ct. App. 1972) (supplier of coke vicariously liable under law of nuisance for damage done by a coke-screening operation run by processor according to supplier's specifications).

67. Steinhauser v. Hertz Corp., 421 F.2d 1169 (2d Cir. 1970) (liberalizing application of the proximate-cause doctrine in a case involving suit for mental injury allegedly precipitated by an automobile accident); Sindell v. Abbott Laboratories, 607 P.2d 924 (Cal. 1980) (adopting market share liability for a class action against

manufacturers of DES) (discussed in Chapter Six); Haft v. Lone Palm Hotel, 478 P.2d 465 (Cal. 1970) (absolving the defendant of specific proof of causation in a case involving the motel owner's breach of a statute setting standards for safe operation of hotel and motel swimming pools); Payton v. Abbott Labs, 437 N.E.2d 171 (Mass. 1982) (market share liability for DES). But see Starling v. Seaboard Coast Line Railroad Co., 533 F. Supp. 183 (S.D. Ga. 1982) (rejecting market share liability for asbestos-related injuries); Vigiolto v. Johns-Manville Corp. 643 F. Supp. 1454 (W.D. Pa. 1986) (same).

68. E.g., Kirby v. Larson,. 256 N.W.2d 400 (Mich. 1977) (adopting comparative negligence).

69. See, generally, Michael Dore, *Law of Toxic Torts* (New York: Clark Boardman, 1987), vol. 3; Michael D. Green, "When Toxic Worlds Collide: Regulatory and Common Law Prescriptions for Risk Communication," *Harvard Environmental Law Review* 13 (1989): 209.

70. Cyr v. B. Offen & Co., 501 F.2d 1145 (1st Cir. 1975) (liability of successor corporation for injuries due to product defect) (New Hampshire law); Ray v. Alad Corp., 19 Cal. 3d 22, 560 P.2d 3, 136 Cal. Rptr. 574 (same); Turner v. Bituminous Cas. Co., 244 N.W.2d 873 (Mich. 1976) (same); Ramirez v. Amsted Industries, Inc., 86 N.J. 332, 431 A.2d 811 (1981) (same).

71. E.g., Putney v. Gibson, 289 N.W.2d 837 (Mich. Ct. App. 1979) (per curiam) (denying the defendant, under the Dram Shop Act, a right of contribution against an intoxicated driver), *reversed on other grounds,* 324 N.W.2d 729 (Mich. 1982); Keckonen v. Robles, 705 P.2d 945 (Ariz. 1985) (distinguishing between dram shop liability and social host liability on the basis of a commercial vendor's access to insurance). But see Chartrand v. Coos Bay Tavern, Inc., 696 P.2d 513 (Or. 1985) (noting that concerns over the cost of liability insurance had led the legislature to repeal the Dram Shop Act and replace it with a new statute extending more-limited liability); Garcia v. Hargrove, 46 Wis. 2d 724 (1970) (refusing to establish common-law liability of tavern owners for negligent acts of intoxicated patrons despite tavern owners' presumed ability to purchase insurance).

72. E.g., Brown v. Merlo, 506 P.2d 212 (Cal. 1973) (holding the California automobile guest statute, which immunized drivers from liability to guest passengers, unconstitutional; the court concluded that discrimination against guests was irrational in view of fact that drivers' liability would be covered by insurance, so that immunity was not needed). For a detailed discussion of cases in this category, see Richard C. Turkington, "Constitutional Limitations on Tort Reform: Have the State Courts Placed Insurmountable Obstacles in the Path of Legislative Responses to the Perceived Liability Insurance Crisis?" *Villanova Law Review* 32 (1987): 1299.

73. E.g., Roy v. Star Chopper Co., 584 F.2d 1124 (1st Cir. 1978), *cert. denied,* 440 U.S. 916 (1979) (choice of law involving product liability); *in re* Air Crash Disaster at Washington, D.C., 559 F. Supp. 333 (D.C. Cir. 1983) (choice of law involving product liability in mass tort case); Kopp v. Rechtzigel, 141 N.W.2d 526 (Minn. 1966) (choice of law involving guest statute); Miller v. Miller, 237 N.E.2d 877 (N.Y. 1968) (choice of law in wrongful death action); Zelinger v. State Sand & Gravel Co., 156 N.W.2d 466 (Wis. 1968) (choice of law regarding rights of contri-

bution); Labree v. Major, 306 A.2d 808 (R.I. 1973) (choice of law involving guest statute); Conklin v. Horner, 157 N.W.2d 579 (Wis. 1968) (choice of law involving guest statute).

74. By 1988, forty-one state legislatures had passed tort reform measures of some kind or other. These were the direct result of liability insurance policy rates for many businesses being raised precipitously or of the policies themselves being canceled; at the same time, insurer and industry lobbying groups mounted an intense campaign in state legislatures in support of a variety of reform measures. The most common reforms included caps on damages, especially for noneconomic loss; total or partial abrogation of the collateral source rule; modifications of joint tortfeasor liability; changes in statutes of limitation; and creation of qualified tort immunities for certain actors. For a thorough discussion of the tort law "crisis," see Elliot Blake, "Comment: Rumors of Crisis: Considering the Insurance Crises and Tort Reform in an Information Vacuum," *Emory Law Journal* 37 (1988): 401.

75. The term "band-aid response" was used by Kenneth Vinson to describe such measures as "limiting joint and several liability, modifying the collateral source rule, capping pain and suffering damages and attorneys' fees, and reducing the time within which damage claims may be filed in court." He stated that such acts are "inadequate to deal with the real problem [behind tort reform]." Kenneth Vinson, "Constitutional Stumbling Blocks to Legislative Tort Reform," *Florida State University Law Review* 15 (1987): 31, 37–38.

76. For example, in 1984 the Florida legislature contemplated and then backed away from an initiative to limit pain and suffering damages to $100,000. Stephen D. Sugarman, "Doing Away with Tort Law," *California Law Review* 73 (1985): 617. See, generally, Vinson, "Constitutional Stumbling Blocks to Legislative Tort Reform," 35.

CHAPTER SIX

1. President and Directors of Georgetown College v. Hughes, 130 F.2d 810 (D.C. Cir. 1942).
2. Rowland v. Christian, 443 P.2d 561 (Cal. 1968).
3. Reyes v. Wyeth Laboratories, 498 F.2d 1264 (5th Cir. 1974), *cert. denied,* 419 U.S. 1096 (1974).
4. Sindell v. Abbott Laboratories, 26 Cal.3d 588, 607 P.2d 924, 163 Cal. Rptr. 132 (1980), *cert. denied,* 449 U.S. 912 (1980).
5. Beshada v. Johns-Manville Products Corp., 90 N.J. 191, 447 A.2d 539 (1982).
6. Anderson v. Owens-Corning Fiberglas Corp., 810 P.2d 549 (Cal. 1991).
7. 130 F.2d at 823–24.
8. Ibid. at 824.
9. Ibid.
10. Ibid. at 825, 827.
11. Ibid. at 828.

12. 443 P.2d at 564.
13. Ibid.
14. Ibid. at 567.
15. Ibid. at 567–68.
16. Ibid. at 569.
17. Tarasoff v. Regents of University of California, 551 P.2d 334 (Cal. 1976) (psychologist owes duty to a third party to warn her of a patient's violent intentions; the court adopts and applies *Rowland* factors to justify imposition of duty).
18. Section 402A was promulgated by the American Law Institute (ALI), which is responsible for developing the Restatement of Torts, in the mid-1960s. The ALI recently has embarked on the project of creating a Third Restatement concentrating on product liability. Although the project is still in the drafting stages, it is evident from the early Council Drafts that product liability will be wholly restructured and that much of the strict liability flavor of Section 402A, as well as its reliance on insurance considerations, will be eliminated.
19. Helene Curtis Industries, Inc. v. Pruitt, 385 F.2d 841 (5th Cir. 1967), *cert. denied,* 391 U.S. 913 (1968).
20. Helen Curtis Industries, Inc., 385 F.2d at 862, quoted in Reyes, 498 F.2d at 1294 (emphasis added).
21. Reyes, 498 F.2d at 1294 (footnote omitted).
22. This may not be strictly true. Judge Wisdom did note that another form of vaccine was available, the Salk vaccine, which used a killed virus and thus did not present the same risk. The chief advantage of Reyes' vaccine, the Sabin vaccine, was that it could be administered orally rather than through a series of relatively painful injections.
23. 607 P.2d 937 (Cal. 1980).
24. Ibid.
25. Ibid. at 936
26. Ibid. (citations omitted).
27. Ibid. at 941 (Richardson, J., dissenting).
28. For a general account of the asbestos catastrophe, see Paul Brodeur, *Outrageous Misconduct: The Asbestos Industry on Trial* (New York: Pantheon Books, 1985).
29. Beshada, 447 A.2d at 546.
30. Ibid. at 547.
31. Ibid., quoting W. Page Keeton, "Products Liability: Inadequacy of Information," *Texas Law Review* 48 (1970): 398, 408.
32. Beshada, 447 A.2d at 548.
33. Ibid.
34. Ibid. at 549.
35. For a thorough discussion of the issues raised by *Beshada* and judicial reactions to them, see Ellen Wertheimer, "Unknowable Dangers and the Death of Strict Products Liability: The Empire Strikes Back," *University of Cincinnati Law Review* 60 (1992): 1183.

36. Feldman v. Lederle Laboratories, 479 A.2d 374 (N.J. 1984), *cert. denied,* 112 S.Ct. 3037 (1992).

37. For a discussion of the impact of *Anderson* on California product liability law, see Wertheimer, "Unknowable Dangers and the Death of Strict Products Liability," 1249–61.

38. Brown v. Superior Court, 751 P.2d 470 (Cal. 1988).

39. Anderson, 810 P.2d at 556 (summarizing *Brown*).

40. "The possibility that the cost of insurance and of defending against lawsuits will diminish the availability and increase the price of pharmaceuticals is far from theoretical. Defendants cite a host of examples of products which have greatly increased in price or have been withdrawn or withheld from the market because of the fear that their producers would be held liable for large judgments." Brown, 751 P.2d at 479. The court went on to discuss several specific instances where this had occurred.

41. 810 P.2d at 559 (footnote omitted).

42. Ibid. at n. 14, quoting John Wade, "On the Effect in Product Liability of Knowledge Unavailable Prior to Marketing," *New York University Law Review* 58 (1983): 734, 755.

43. Ibid. at 560–61 (Broussard, J., concurring); ibid. at 561–63 (Mosk, J., concurring and dissenting).

44. Wertheimer, "Unknowable Dangers and the Death of Strict Products Liability," 1260–61.

45. William L. Prosser, "The Assault on the Citadel (Strict Liability to the Consumer)," *Yale Law Journal* 69 (1960): 1121–22.

CHAPTER SEVEN

1. See, e.g., the prominent reliance on safety in the *Georgetown, Rowland,* and *Sindell* cases discussed in the previous chapter.

2. Oliver Wendell Holmes Jr., *The Common Law,* ed. Mark DeWolfe Howe (Cambridge: Harvard University Press, 1963), 77–79. See Chapter One. For an astute assessment of the choice between privately and publicly structured insurance arrangements, see W. G. Friedmann, "Social Insurance and Principles of Tort Liability," *Harvard Law Review* 63 (1949): 241.

CHAPTER EIGHT

1. *The Compact Edition of the Oxford English Dictionary* (Glasgow: Oxford University Press, 1971), 605.

2. Peter Huber's work provides an example of the grim vision of insurance and tort law in *Liability: The Legal Revolution and Its Consequences* (New York: Basic Books, 1988) . For other scholars using somewhat less alarmist language, see Victor Schwartz, "Tort Law Reform: Strict Liability and the Collateral Source Rule Do Not

Mix," *Vanderbilt Law Review* 39 (1986): 569; Richard Epstein, "The Unintended Revolution in Product Liability Law," *Cardozo Law Review* 10 (1989): 2193.

3. Stephen D. Sugarman, "Taking Advantage of the Torts Crisis," *Ohio State Law Journal* 48 (1987): 333; George Priest, "The Current Insurance Crisis and Modern Tort Law," *Yale Law Journal* 96 (1987): 1589; W. Kip Viscusi, "The Determinants of the Disposition of Product Liability Claims and Compensation for Bodily Injury," *Journal of Legal Studies* 15 (1986): 321; Jeffrey O'Connell and C. B. Kelly, *The Blame Game: Injuries, Insurance, and Injustice* (Lexington, Mass.: Lexington Books, 1987), 85, 110.

4. Robert Rabin, "Some Reflections on the Process of Tort Reform," *San Diego Law Review* 25 (1988): 13; Kenneth S. Abraham, "Making Sense of the Liability Insurance Crisis," *Ohio State Law Journal* 48 (1987): 399; Neil K. Komesar, "Injuries and Institutions: Tort Reform, Tort Theory, and Beyond," *New York University Law Review* 65 (1990): 23.

5. For a variety of conclusions regarding the upsurge in liability rates during the 1980s, see, e.g., the DOJ Report 35–42, 45–52 (arguing that the insurance crisis has resulted from the frequency of tort claims and has increased the size of damage recoveries in successful tort cases); Governor's Advisory Commission on Liability Insurance: Insuring Our Future (1986): 15 (arguing that the crisis was a result of the insurance-cycle theory, which provides that when interests rates rise, premiums go down); Stephanie Goldberg, "Manufacturers Take Cover," *Journal of the American Bar Association,* July 1, 1986, 52, 55 (the common view provides that the insurance crisis has been caused by explicit price fixing by commercial-casualty insurers); American Law Institute Reporters' Study, *Enterprise Responsibility for Personal Injury* (Philadelphia: American Law Institute, 1991) (henceforth cited as ALI Study), 1:75–76 (gives three causes underlying the crisis). See, generally, Scott E. Harrington, "Prices and Profits in the Liability Insurance Market," in *Liability: Perspectives and Policy,* ed. Robert E. Litan and Clifford Winston (Washington, D.C.: Brookings Institution, 1988), 42, 77–82.

6. Priest, "Insurance Crisis," 1540. See also Kenneth S. Abraham, *Distributing Risk: Insurance, Legal Theory, and Public Policy* (New Haven: Yale University Press, 1986) , 46.

7. DOJ Report, 35 (describing the "explosive growth" in damage awards); Jeffrey O'Connell, "A Proposal to Abolish Defendants' Payment for Pain and Suffering in Return for Payment of Claimants' Attorneys' Fees," *University of Illinois Law Review* 2 (1981): 333; Huber, *Liability,* 10.

8. E.g., Marc S. Galanter, "The Day After the Litigation Explosion," *Maryland Law Review* 46 (1986): 3; idem, "Reading the Landscape of Disputes: What We Know and Don't Know (and Think We Know) About Our Allegedly Contentious Society," *UCLA Law Review* 31 (1983): 4; David J. Nye and Donald G. Gifford, "The Myth of a Liability Insurance Explosion: An Empirical Rebuttal," *Vanderbilt Law Review* 41 (1988): 909; National Center for State Courts and Conference of State Court Administrators, *State Court Caseload Statistics: The State of the Art* (Denver: National Center for State Courts, 1978), ch. 2; Insurance Services Offices,

1985: A Critical Year: A Study of the Property/Casualty Insurance Industry (New York: Insurance Services Offices, 1985).

9. ALI Study, 1:22.

10. See, generally, Leonard R. Freifelder, *A Decision Theoretic Approach to Insurance Ratemaking,* (Philadelphia: University of Pennsylvania, 1976); Abraham, *Distributing Risk*, 64.

11. Abraham argues that the most plausible explanation for the size and suddenness of the premium increases is the decline in the insurance industry's confidence to predict future liability. Thus, an additional premium is assessed to cover the "unpredictable risk." Abraham, "Making Sense of the Liability Crisis," 405. See also Galanter, "The Day After the Litigation Explosion," 3; Robert Rabin, "Some Reflections on the Process of Tort Reform," 28–37; Dominic Vetri, "The Integration of Tort Law Reforms and Liability Ratemaking in the New Age," *Oregon Law Review* 66 (1987): 277.

12. Galanter, "The Day After the Litigation Explosion," 21–25; Rabin, "Some Reflections on the Process of Tort Reform," 31; Abraham, "Making Sense of the Liability Crisis," 404.

13. For further discussion on the monopolistic, price-fixing theories, see Priest, "Insurance Crisis," 1527 (criticizing theory); Ralph Nader, "The Corporate Drive to Restrict Their Victims' Rights," *Gonzaga Law Review* 22 (1986): 15; Goldberg, "Manufacturers Take Cover," 52, 55 (reporting that Jay Angoff of the National Insurance Consumer Organization argues that the insurance companies uniformly hiked rates and justified such action based on a crisis in the courts).

14. See, generally, Priest, "Insurance Crisis," 1522; Abraham, "Making Sense of the Liability Insurance Crisis," 402. Proponents of tort reform use these facts to support the argument that widespread implementation of the insurance rationale is destructive. See the DOJ Report, 51 (insurance rate increases and selective withdrawals are due to increases in tort frequency and the size of damage recovery). See also Basil L. Bradley, "Why Tort Reform Was Needed in Washington," *Gonzaga Law Review* 22 (1986): 3. Opponents of tort reform use these facts to support the argument that the insurers' mismanagement led to the so-called "crisis." David J. Moskal and Peter H. Berge, "Tort 'Reform': Minnesota Does Not Need Legislation That Makes Victims Pay for the Negligence of Others," *William Mitchell Law Review* 13 (1987): 347, 355; Nader, "Corporate Drive," 15.

15. For an example of this view, see Sean F. Mooney, "The Liability Crisis: A Perspective," *Villanova Law Review* 32 (1987): 1235.

16. Bradley, "Tort Reform," 12 n. 18; Michael J. Saks, "Comment on Galanter: If There Be a Crisis, How Shall We Know It?" *Maryland Law Review* 46 (1986): 63, 70. Cf. Michael Cooper, "Trends in Liability Awards: Have Juries Run Wild?" (Consumer Federation of America, May 1986, mimeo).

17. Typical industries subject to long-tail liability include asbestos manufacturers, chemical manufacturers, and pharmaceutical manufacturers. Priest, "Insurance Crisis," 1583; Abraham, "Making Sense of the Liability Insurance Crisis," 407; Richard Epstein, "The Legal and Insurance Dynamics of Mass Tort Litigation," *Journal of Legal Studies* 13 (1984): 475.

18. Risky activity included the services of directors and officers; the work of nurse midwives; operation of day-care centers, bars, and restaurants; and the practice of obstetrics in certain settings. Abraham, "Making Sense of the Liability Insurance Crisis," 404; George Priest, "Puzzles of the Torts Crisis," *Ohio State Law Journal* 48 (1987): 497; Sugarman, "Taking Advantage of the Torts Crisis," 333; DOJ Report, 6–13.

19. Thus, for example, it has been asserted that vaccines and pharmaceuticals have been withdrawn from the market despite prior FDA approval, because of the severity of contemporary tort liability. Priest, "Insurance Crisis," 1567; Louis Lasagna, "The Chilling Effect of Product Liability on New Drug Development," in *The Liability Maze: The Impact of Liability Law on Safety and Innovation* ed. Peter Huber and Robert Litan (Washington, D.C.: Brookings Institute, 1991), 334. See also "Sorry Your Policy Is Cancelled," *Time,* March 24, 1986, 18.

20. Insurance Information Institute, "Working Toward a Fairer Civil Justice System" (Insurance Information Institute, New York, 1987, pamphlet), 8 (discussing the need to destroy the myth of insurance companies as "deep pockets" and the injustice of allowing an insolvent wrongdoer to evade completely the consequences of his or her fault); DOJ Report, 33–34; Bruce Chapman and Michael J. Trebilcock, "Punitive Damages: Divergence in Search of a Rationale," *Alabama Law Review* 40 (1989): 741, 777.

21. Moskal and Berge argue that even during the insurance "crisis," insurance companies' main concern was profit from investments. However, since they artificially lowered premiums during the late 1970s and early 1980s to compete for premium dollars, they were unable to manage a drastic drop in interest rates during and after the 1982 recession. Thus, they created the myth of the insurance crisis, blaming their mismanagement on the civil litigation system. Moskal and Berge, "Tort 'Reform,'" 355. See also, Francis X. Belloti, John Van DeKamp, Lucy Thornburg, Jim Mottox, Charlie Brown, and Bronson Lafollette, *An Analysis of the Causes of the Current Crisis of the Unavailability and Unaffordability of Liability Insurance* (Report prepared for the National Association of Attorneys General, May 1986) (arguing that the recent insurance crisis emanated from price cutting by insurance companies rather than from any increase in tort litigation).

22. Moskal and Berge, "Tort 'Reform,'" 355; Nader, "Corporate Drive," 15; *Towards a Jurisprudence of Injury: The Continuing Creation of a System of Substantive Justice in American Tort Law,* (Chicago: American Bar Association, 1984), 11–43.

23. Moskal and Berge, "Tort 'Reform,'" 354; Nader, "Corporate Drive," 15; Jerry J. Phillips, "Tort Reform and the Insurance Crisis in the Second Half of 1986," *Gonzaga Law Review* 22 (1986): 277; idem, "Comments on the Report of the Governor's Commission on Tort and Liability Insurance Reform," *Tennessee Law Review* 53 (1986): 679; Priest, "Insurance Crisis," 1527 (raises this theory along with others, ultimately concluding that this is only a limited explanation).

24. The McCarran-Ferguson Act, 15 U.S.C. §1012 (1982), immunizes the insurance industry from most federal antitrust laws prohibiting monopolistic business practices. This is done to the extent that the business of insurance is regulated by the

states. Since premium rates are state regulated, insurers are legally permitted to collude on pricing. State regulators, of course, could step into the void by prohibiting rate increases that are in their opinion exorbitant. In the late 1980s a few intrepid state insurance commissioners did precisely that. But state regulators would be unlikely to prohibit premium increases if insurers could point to external factors that were driving costs up. Hence, from the trial-lawyer viewpoint, the claim of escalating liability became a convenient means of persuading state regulators to allow huge premium increases that otherwise would have generated suspicion and might have been denied.

25. Consumer advocate Ralph Nader calls for federal regulation and state disclosure laws for the insurance industry. Nader, "Corporate Drive"; idem, "The Assault on Injured Victims' Rights," *Denver Law Review* 64 (1988): 625.

26. A reinsurer is essentially an insurer of insurance companies. For reasons that remain in dispute, during the early to mid 1980s reinsurers suddenly cut back on the amount of American liability insurance they were willing to underwrite. ALI Study, 1:75.

27. ALI Study, 1:70–71; DOJ Report, 17; Mark Peterson, *The Civil Jury: Trends in Trials and Verdicts in California and Cook County, IL* (Santa Monica, Calif.: Rand Corp., 1987), 16–20; Moskal and Berge, "Tort 'Reform,'" 355.

28. For example, during the thirty years from 1958 to 1988, net premiums for comprehensive general liability insurance increased from $784 million to roughly $20 billion. ALI Study, 1:70–71. Of course, those numbers are probably at least partly misleading because they represent insurers' success at marketing their product to many enterprises that thirty years ago might not have insured at all or might have insured in much lower amounts. They also partly reflect the massive proliferation of business activity itself that occurred during the same period.

It is worth noting that increased premiums have allowed insurers to enjoy continued profitability. Between 1975 and 1984, for example, the General Accounting Office reported that property/casualty insurers had net gains of $75.2 billion. See the statement of Johnny C. Finch, senior associate director, General Government Division, Profitability of the Property/Casualty Insurance Industry, hearings before the Subcommittee on Oversight of the House Commission on Ways and Means, 99th Cong., 2d Sess. (April 28, 1986). According to Ralph Nader, "The property/casualty insurance industry, using its own accounting definitions," calculated "that net profit for the first half of 1986 totaled $5.7 billion, up from $930 million a year earlier." Nader, "Corporate Drive," 18 n. 15 (citing Karen Slater, "Property and Liability Insurers Report Strong Profits Signalling Easing of Crisis," *Wall Street Journal*, August 28, 1986, sec. 1 at 4, col. 2). Apparently the "crisis" of the early 1980s was one the insurance industry itself was able fairly comfortably to survive.

29. See *supra* note 18 for examples of insurance unavailability in some industries.

30. The number of lawyers has been rising much faster than the general population during the postwar period. In 1951 there was one lawyer for every 695 Americans. By 1980 there was one for every 418 Americans. By one estimate, the ratio in 1995 may be one lawyer for every 279 Americans. Robert J. Samuelson, "Comments

on Galanter: The Litigation Explosion: The Wrong Question," *Maryland Law Review* 46 (1986): 78.

31. Samuelson describes the rise in lawyers as follows: "The more conflict that can be converted into legal action, the more lawyers prosper. Contingent fee plaintiffs' attorneys have a clear interest in identifying and suing wealthy defendants. Attorneys who respond to these strong incentives are not venal, but their collective behavior may pervert the civil justice system." Samuelson, "Comments on Galanter," 78.

32. In Bates v. State Bar of Arizona, 433 U.S. 350 (1977), the Supreme Court held that attorney advertising is "commercial speech" protected under the First Amendment. The Court held that state legal ethics rules prohibiting attorney advertising are unconstitutional. One result of this ruling has been a proliferation of attorney advertising, including radio and television advertising, even billboard advertising. Advertisements for personal injury clients are among the most common.

33. For a discussion of the role of the contingent fee in American law, see Frederick Benjamin Mackinnon, *Contingent Fees for Legal Services* (Chicago: Adline Publications, 1964).

34. See Edward D. Ohlbaum, "Basic Instinct: Case Theory and Courtroom Performance," *Temple Law Review* 66 (1993): 1–6; Ronald L. Carlson, "Competency and Professionalism in Modern Litigation Training: The Role of the Law Schools," *Georgia Law Review* 23 (1989): 689, 692; Edward J. Imwinkelreid, "The Educational Philosophy of Trial Practice Course: Reweaving the Seamless Web," *Georgia Law Review* 23 (1989): 663, 666. For a discussion on the growth and diversity of the contemporary bar, legal education, and legal thought, see Kermit Hall, *The Magic Mirror* (Oxford: Oxford Press, 1989), 288–91; John Guinther, *The Jury in America* (New York: Roscoe Pound Foundation, 1988), 133.

35. The American Trial Lawyers Association upgraded the performance of the plaintiffs' lawyers by developing networks of colleagues specialized in various areas of the law. Guinther, *The Jury in America,* 135.

36. E.g., Warren E. Burger, "Remarks on Trial Advocacy: A Proposition," *Washburn Law Journal* 7 (1967): 15, 16. Not only has Chief Justice Burger questioned the adequacy of lawyers' basic skills, he has suggested that lawyer incompetence may be contributing to unnecessary litigation. Idem, "Isn't There a Better Way?" *ABA Journal* 68 (1982): 274. (In the midst of the litigation explosion, Burger questions whether lawyers are fulfilling their traditional and historical obligation of being healers of human conflict.) See also Kevin C. McMunigal, "The Costs of Settlement: The Impact of Scarcity of Adjudication on Litigating Lawyers," *UCLA Law Review* 37 (1990): 833.

37. The quantitative evidence suggests a gradual rise in the number of civil and criminal cases filed in state trial courts. The increase has been steeper in federal courts. Between 1960 and 1980 the number of cases filed in the federal courts of appeals almost quintupled, and during the same period filings in the Supreme Court more than doubled. Of course, most of these cases had nothing to do with tort law. Galanter, "Reading the Landscape of Disputes," 4, 38; Hall, *Magic Mirror,* 288.

38. For a state-by-state survey of the adoption of the Federal Rules, see John B.

Oakley and Arthur F. Coon, "The Federal Rules in State Courts: A Survey of State Court Systems of Civil Procedure," *Washington Law Review* 61 (1986): 1367 (concluding that the Federal Rules have been completely adopted in twenty-three states and dominate the procedural systems of a substantial majority of the other states).

39. For a discussion on the relation of class actions and mass disaster cases, see Roger H. Transgrud, "Joinder Alternatives in Mass Tort Litigation," *Cornell Law Review* 70 (1985): 779; Paul D. Rheingold, "Mass Disaster, Litigation, and the Use of Plaintiffs' Groups," *Litigation* 3 (Spring 1977): 18; Note, "Class Actions and Mass Toxic Torts," *Columbia Environmental Law Journal* 8 (1982): 269.

40. The use of expert witnesses to render authoritative opinions on issues in dispute has increased dramatically. Fleming James Jr. and Geoffrey Hazard, *Civil Procedure* (Boston: Little, Brown, 1977), 202; Comment, "Cross Examination of Expert Witnesses: Dispelling the Aura of Reliability," *Miami Law Review* 42 (1988): 1073. For a trenchant critique, see Peter Huber, *Galileo's Revenge* (New York: Basic Books, 1991). For a response to Huber, see Kenneth J. Chesebro, "Galileo's Retort: Peter Huber's Junk Scholarship," *American University Law Review* 42 (1993): esp. 1642, 1696–705.

41. Peter Shuck, "The Role of Judges in Setting Complex Cases: The Agent Orange Example," *University of Chicago Law Review* 53 (1986): 337; Thomas Lambros, "The Judge's Role in Fostering Voluntary Settlements," *Villanova Law Review* 29 (1984): 1363. For a discussion advancing an absolutist approach against settlement, see Owen Fiss, "Against Settlement," *Yale Law Journal* 93 (1984): 1073.

42. For an argument opposing this practice, see Fiss, "Against Settlement," 1078.

43. For example, the DOJ Report states, relying upon Jury Verdict Research statistics, that between 1975 and 1985 the average malpractice jury verdict increased from $220,018 to $1,017,716 and the average product liability jury verdict increased from $393,580 to 1,850,452. DOJ Report, 35–36. For a classic study of the group dynamics of juries, see Harry Kalven Jr. and Hans Zeisel, *The American Jury* (Chicago: Chicago University Press, 1971).

44. For discussions disputing the popular view that juries are reflexively proplaintiff, see Cooper, "Trends in Liability Awards," iv; Guinther, *The Jury in America*, 171; Moskal and Berge, "Tort 'Reform,'" 351.

45. Patricia M. Danzon, *Medical Malpractice Theory, Evidence, and Public Policy* (Cambridge: Harvard University Press, 1985), 58–65. For discussions on the issue of tort reform in the field of medical malpractice, where advances in medical technology have had a particularly pronounced effect, see Frank M. McClellan, *Medical Malpractice: Law, Tactics, and Ethics* (Philadelphia: Temple University Press, 1994), 77–98; Paul C. Weiler, *Medical Malpractice on Trial* (Cambridge: Harvard University Press, 1991), 85–88, 104.

46. Danzon, *Medical Malpractice*, 146–49; Mark Grady, "Why Are People Negligent? Technology, Nondurable Precautions, and the Medical Malpractice Explosion," *Northwestern Law Review* 82 (1988): 293, 296; Mark A. Hall, "The Defensive Effect of Medical Malpractice Policies in Malpractice Litigation," *Law and Contemporary Problems* 54 (spring 1991): 119.

47. Medical costs are a large part of awards, averaging about 25 percent of total

awards in the 1970s. Overall, between 1975 and 1984, health-care cost increased by 23 percent more than inflation. Hospital costs increased almost 56 percent more than inflation. Cooper, "Trends in Liability Awards," ii.

48. Between 1975 and 1984, real income grew 17 percent, life expectancy increased 3 percent, and elderly income grew by 10 percent compared with the national average. Cooper, "Trends in Liability Awards," ii; Abraham, "Making Sense of the Liability Crisis," 404.

49. The most publicized disasters include diseases and injuries from Agent Orange exposure, Bendectin, DES, Dalkon Shield, and asbestos. See, generally, Kenneth S. Abraham, "Individual Action and Collective Responsibility: The Dilemma of Mass Tort Reform," *Virginia Law Review* 73 (1987): 845; Richard Epstein, "The Legal and Insurance Dynamics of Mass Tort Litigation," 475, 477; Guinther, *The Jury in America,* 177.

50. For an extensive account of the asbestos disaster, see Paul Brodeur, *Outrageous Misconduct: The Asbestos Industry on Trial* (New York: Pantheon Books, 1985).

51. See Thomas E. Willging, *Trends in Asbestos Litigation* (Washington, D.C.: Federal Judicial Center, 1987).

52. As of 1984, claimants received more than $236 million. Lawyers, however, earned $164 million, and the defendants incurred more than $600 million in expenses. See James S Kakalik, Patricia A. Ebner, William L. Flestiner, and Michael G. Shanley, "Costs of Asbestos Litigation" (Rand Corp., Santa Monica, Calif., 1983, pamphlet), 5; Stephen D. Sugarman, "Doing Away with Tort Law," *California Law Review* 73 (1985): 600–601.

53. For example, Johns-Manville went into bankruptcy as a result of asbestos claims, even though its net worth at the time was more than $1 billion. See Edwin Chen, "Asbestos Litigation Is a Growth Industry," *Atlantic Monthly,* July 1984, 24; Sugarman, "Doing Away with Tort Law," 600–601.

54. The breadth of insurer exposure on asbestos claims was established in the early 1980s, when several courts rejected insurer attempts to establish a restrictive definition of a covered "occurrence" under liability insurance policies that had been issued to asbestos manufacturers. Depending on what definition minimized their risk, some insurers argued that an "occurrence" should be "triggered" by initial exposure to asbestos particles, whereas others argued that it should be triggered by manifestation of symptoms of disease. Beginning with *Keene Corp. v. Insurance Co. of North America,* 667 F.2d 1034 (D.C. Cir. 1981), *cert. denied,* 455 U.S. 1007 (1982), several courts adopted broad definitions of "occurrence" that used a "triple-trigger" approach and extended coverage under all policies in effect from initial exposure to asbestos particles, through the latency period of subclinical injury to lung tissues, and ending with the manifestation of symptoms of disease. This effectively "stacked" coverage for most lawsuits under multiple liability insurance policies that manufacturers had purchased over a period of several successive years.

55. For discussions of the problem that a very long latency period poses in predicting costs in toxic fields, see Abraham, *Distributing Risk,* 47; Epstein, "The Legal and Insurance Dynamics of Mass Tort Litigation," 505.

56. In particular, during the 1980s the savings and loan industry suffered a major financial disaster, with many savings and loans going under as a result of poor return on investments. The disaster required massive federal intervention through a variety of agencies, most prominently the Resolution Trust Corporation, which was created for the purpose, as well as through expenditure of many billions to bail out troubled financial institutions. See Lawrence J. White, "The S&L Debacle," *Fordham Law Review* 59 (1991): S-57.

CHAPTER NINE

1. DOJ Report, 59–71; George Priest, "The Current Insurance Crisis and Modern Tort Law," *Yale Law Journal* 96 (1987): 1565–66.

2. See, generally, Lawrence Friedman, *Total Justice* (New York: Russell Sage Foundation, 1985), 5, 57–63, 147–52.

3. For a listing of various government-sponsored (and -subsidized) insurance programs, see Robert E. Keeton and Alan I. Widiss, *Insurance Law* (St. Paul, Minn.: West Publishing Co., 1988), 972.

4. Priest, "Insurance Crisis," 1545–47; idem, "A Theory of Consumer Product Warranty," *Yale Law Journal* 90 (1981): 1350.

5. To offer another personal example, I have used an electric razor nearly every day since I was a teenager. Only recently I learned that the electromagnetic field in the razor may be a potential source of cancer. Cf. Paul Brodeur, *Currents of Death* (New York: Simon & Schuster, 1989).

6. See Guido Calabresi, *The Costs of Accidents: A Legal and Economic Analysis* (New Haven: Yale University Press, 1970), 56–58.

7. Robert E. Keeton and Jeffrey O'Connell, *Basic Protection for the Traffic Victim* (Boston: Little, Brown, 1965) , 69–71, 228–29; Stephen D. Sugarman, "Doing Away with Tort Law," *California Law Review* 73 (1985): 596 (as a result of our "fabulously expensive" tort system, less than half of liability insurance costs go to paying benefits to plaintiffs).

8. Jeffrey O'Connell, "Balanced Proposals for Products Liability Reform," *Ohio State Law Journal* 48 (1987): 322 (arguing the advantage of speedy compensation as a virtue of the author's "neo-no-fault" proposal for products).

9. For contemporary debate on the desirability of automobile no-fault insurance, see Richard Epstein, "Automobile No-Fault Plans: A Second Look at First Principles," *Creighton Law Review* 13 (1980): 769; William M. Landes, "Insurance, Liability, and Accidents: A Theoretical and Empirical Investigation of No-Fault Accidents," *Journal of Law and Economics* 25 (1982): 49; Jeffrey O'Connell and Saul Levmore, "A Reply to Landes: A Faulty Study of No-Fault's Effects on Fault," *Missouri Law Review* 48 (1983): 649; Symposium, *University of San Diego Law Review* 26 (1989): 977.

10. For a summary and qualifiedly favorable appraisal of automobile no-fault insurance, see Keeton and Widiss, *Insurance Law,* 410–25.

11. See Jeffrey O'Connell, "A Draft Bill to Allow Choice Between No-Fault and Fault-Based Auto Insurance," *Harvard Journal on Legislation* 27 (1990): 143.

12. Many of the no-fault plans set an injury "threshold" below which an action for tort compensation was prohibited, but above which such an action might proceed. See, e.g., Gillman v. Gillman, 319 So.2d 165 (Fla. 1975) ("permanent disfigurement" threshold); Elliott v. Simon, 371 A.2d 836 (N.J. Super. 1977) (medical expense threshold), *reversed on other grounds,* 385 A.2d 249 (N.J. 1978).

13. Keeton and Widiss, *Insurance Law,* 424.

14. Echoing the rationale for workers' compensation, first-party proponents often attempt to justify this on the ground that reduced compensation is a necessary trade-off for speedier and more certain compensation. See O'Connell, "Balanced Proposals for Product Liability Reform," 321 ("The key to both workers' compensation and auto no-fault reforms, unlike those being proposed by insurers and product sellers, is balance: it is easier for the injured party to be paid but he or she is paid less"). This argument, however, assumes comprehensive coverage in which only the amounts of compensation, not the types of protection, are reduced. The danger in a piecemeal approach is that some victims will be deprived of any meaningful protection.

15. Priest, "Insurance Crisis," 1547.

16. For an excellent discussion the failure of first-party insurance to classify according to risk, see Jon D. Hanson and Kyle D. Logue, "The First-Party Insurance Externality: An Economic Justification for Enterprise Liability," *Cornell Law Review* 76 (1990): 129, 141–59.

17. Ibid., 145–51, 164–68.

18. Ibid., 146 ("first-party insurers make little or no effort to segregate insureds according to consumption choices").

19. Ibid., 138–39.

20. Of course, they would still be motivated toward safety by their desire to avoid personal injury. But if that interest is sufficient to alleviate concerns about consumer moral hazard under a first-party insurance approach, it is equally so under third-party liability supported by the insurance rationale.

21. Mark C. Rahdert, "Reasonable Expectations Reconsidered," *Connecticut Law Review* 18 (1986): 323, 329, 337.

22. Guido Calabresi, "Fault, Accidents, and the Wonderful World of Blum and Kalven, *Yale Law Journal* 75 (1965): 216; Guido Calabresi, "Views and Overviews," *Illinois Law Forum* (1967): 600, 611. See Calabresi, *The Costs of Accidents,* 144–45.

23. Stephen D. Sugarman, *Doing Away with Personal Injury Law* (New York: Quorum Books, 1989), ch. 7.

24. For a discussion and elaboration of the distinction between specific and general deterrence approaches to accident costs, see Calabresi, *The Costs of Accidents,* 68–129.

25. See Kenneth S. Abraham, "Making Sense of the Liability Insurance Crisis," *Ohio State Law Journal* 48 (1987): 405–9.

26. For example, the estimated value of valid claims against the asbestos industry

exceeds the combined financial resources of all asbestos producers and their insurers. This has resulted in bankruptcies from liability for asbestos-related disease. W. Kip Viscusi, "Structuring an Effective Occupational Disease Policy: Victim Compensation and Risk Regulation," *Yale Law Journal of Regulation* 2 (1984): 53.

27. Of course, as the discussion in Part II reveals, it would be erroneous to assume that courts and/or legislatures have implemented anything like a full, thoroughgoing "best-insurer" standard for liability.

28. United States v. Carroll Towing Co., 159 F.2d 169 (2d Cir. 1947). See Chapter 3, note 8.

29. Sometimes commentators use the term "self-insurance" to describe any situation in which an actor chooses to forgo liability insurance protection. This is not appropriate in the context of adverse selection, since the adverse selection argument is cast in terms of the likelihood that good risks will pursue an alternative (more efficient) form of cost spreading, not that they will forsake cost spreading altogether. Here, I am using the term "self-insurance" more narrowly, to describe situations in which an actor takes on for itself the functions an insurer ordinarily would perform. Thus, a self-insurer would attempt to make actuarial predictions of its risk, and it would charge itself "premiums" sufficient to create a monetary-loss reserve adequate to pay projected losses as they accrue. A self-insurer would accordingly spread its losses over time, and it would figure the cost of its program of self-insurance as a factor in determining the price of its products or activities, thus spreading the cost to consumers. The chief difference between such a program of self-insurance and a commercially available insurance policy is that the self-insurer would not be able to spread any portion of its losses to other participants in an insurance pool. Its "pool" would be a pool of one.

30. Whether the costs of insurance for medical practitioners were truly prohibitive—in the sense that they would have made continuing in practice economically infeasible—or were just so costly that they would have deprived the practitioner of his or her desired level of income is a seriously debatable question.

31. Risk classification is a method of competing for protection dollars by classifying potential insurance purchasers into groups according to their probability of loss and the potential magnitude of losses if they occur. By classifying, an insurer can offer low-risk individuals lower prices by placing insureds with similar expected losses into the same class, so that each may be charged the same rate. For an in-depth discussion of the conflict between risk classification and risk spreading, see Kenneth S. Abraham, "Efficiency and Fairness in Insurance Risk Classification," *Virginia Law Review* 71 (1985): 407–8.

32. Priest, "Insurance Crisis," 1544.

33. There is no evidence that adverse selection from insurance pools played any role in the asbestos disaster. To the contrary, as noted in the previous chapter, insurers failed to identify asbestos manufacture as a highly risky activity until it was too late.

34. See *supra* Chapter Three, pages 48–49.

35. With respect to consumers, there is some evidence the introduction of new safety elements on products can dull consumer vigilance. For example, consumers

may be less likely to keep pharmaceuticals away from children if they know that the bottles in which they come have child-resistant caps. W. Kip Viscusi, "Consumer Behavior and the Safety Effects of Product Safety Regulation," *Journal of Law and Economics* 28 (1985). But this is not the same as consumers taking chances with safety because they are confident of compensation through third-party liability if they are injured.

36. Johnson and Johnson, for example, recalled all Tylenol capsules in 1982 and then temporarily withdrew the product in 1986 after six cyanide poisonings, resulting in multimillion-dollar losses. This action was followed by SmithKline Beckman taking similar steps after finding rat poisoning in Contac capsules in 1986. Burroughs Wellcome Co. also recalled Sudafed capsules in 1991 after fatal tampering. "A Tough Corporate Decision" (editorial), *Los Angeles Times,* February 20, 1986, part 2, col. 4; "Rat Poison in Capsules: Three Products Withdrawn," *Chicago Tribune,* March 26, 1986, p. 1, zone c; Michael Hiltzik, "Tylenol Scare Cited as J & J Loss," *Los Angeles Times,* April 25, 1986, part 4, p. 2; Philip J. Hilts, "Cyanide in a Drug Kills Two and Forces a National Recall," *New York Times,* March 4, 1991, sec. A, p. 1. Pharmaceutical firms have since alleviated product-tampering dangers by developing tamper-resistant packaging.

37. Saul Levmore, "Self-Assessed Valuation Systems for Tort and Other Law," *Virginia Law Review,* 68 (1982): 771, 818; Hanson and Logue, "The First-Party Insurance Externality," 187.

38. In contingent-fee personal injury cases, a referring attorney often receives one-third of the total fee. See Geoffrey Hazard, *Ethics in the Practice of Law* (New Haven: Yale University Press, 1978), 98–99. See also Lester Brickman, "Attorney-Client Fee Arbitration: A Dissenting View," *Utah Law Review* (1990): 277.

39. In the early 1950s Louis Jaffe made this suggestion in an influential article on damages. It has often been repeated since. Jaffe, "Damages for Personal Injury: The Impact of Insurance," *Law and Contemporary Problems* 18 (1953): 219, 234–35.

40. Abraham, "Risk Classification," 449.

41. See Kenneth S. Abraham, *Distributing Risk: Insurance, Legal Theory, and Public Policy* (New Haven: Yale University Press, 1986), 64; Leonard R. Freifelder, *A Decision Theoretic Approach to Insurance Ratemaking* (Philadelphia: University of Pennsylvania, 1976) , 94; C. Arthur Williams and Richard M. Heins, *Risk Management and Insurance,* 6th ed. (New York: McGraw-Hill, 1989), 361–65, 645–46.

42. The General Accounting Office report on product liability actions in five states reported that defendants who paid their attorneys on an hourly basis paid fees ranging from $1,500 to $400,000 with an average of $41,000. U.S. General Accounting Office, *Product Liability: Verdicts and Case Resolution in Five States,* Report to the chairman of the House Subcommittee on Commerce, Consumer Protection, and Competitiveness of the House Committee on Energy and Commerce, Committee Print, 25, 53 (Washington, D.C., September 1989).

43. See *supra* Chapter Three, pages 49–50.

44. For assumption (2), see Peter Huber, *Liability: The Legal Revolution and Its Consequences* (New York: Basic Books, 1988), 13–14, 159; George Priest, "Prod-

ucts Liability Law and the Accident Rate," in *Liability: Perspectives and Policy,* ed. Robert E. Litan and Clifford Winston (Washington, D.C.: Brookings Institution, 1988), 1550–51; idem, "Insurance Crisis," 1558–60. For assumption (3), see ibid., 1566. Assumption (3) is a central feature of the insurance rationale. See Escola v. Coca-Cola Bottling Co., 150 P.2d 436, 441 (Cal. 1944) (Traynor, J., concurring) (stating that "the cost of an injury and the loss of time or health may be an overwhelming misfortune to the person injured, and a needless one, for the risk of injury can be insured by the manufacturer and distributed among the public as a cost of doing business").

45. For a discussion of product substitution, see Lawrence Anthony Sullivan, *Handbook of the Law of Antitrust* (St. Paul, Minn.: West Publishing Co., 1977), 51; William H. Page, "The Scope of Liability for Antitrust Violations," *Stanford Law Review* 37 (1985): 1445, 1465.

46. "There is no reason to believe that for a given injury, low income consumers would receive lower nonpecuniary-loss damage awards than high income consumers." Steven P. Crowley and Jon D. Hanson, "What Liability Crisis? An Alternative Explanation for Recent Events in Products Liability," *Yale Law Journal on Regulation* 1, no. 8 (1991): 34.

47. Clarence Morris, *Morris on Torts,* 2d ed. (Philadelphia: Foundation Press, 1980), 232; Guido Calabresi, "Some Thoughts on Risk Distribution and the Law of Torts," *Yale Law Journal* 70 (1961): 527; Charles O. Gregory, "From Trespass to Negligence to Strict Liability," *Virginia Law Review* 17 (1990): 361–65.

48. Priest, "Insurance Crisis," 1565, 1585–86; idem, "Puzzles of the Torts Crisis," *Ohio State Law Journal* 48 (1987): 502. Cf. Richard Epstein, "The Unintended Revolution in Product Liability Law," *Cardozo Law Review* 10 (1980): 2214.

49. A tax is regressive if lower-income individuals pay a larger proportion of their income in taxes than those with higher incomes. Under a progressive tax system, those with higher incomes bear a greater proportion of the tax burden. A progressive tax system is based on the idea that tax rates should correlate with one's ability to pay. Edgar K. Browning and Jacqueline M. Browning, *Public Finance and the Price System* (New York: Macmillan, 1979).

50. See *supra* Chapter Three, page 50.

51. See *supra* Chapter One, pages 12–16.

52. Pharmaceutical firms demanded immunity from liability as a condition for the production of the vaccine because they were unable to obtain private liability insurance. See Peter Huber, "Safety and the Second Best: The Hazards of Public Risk Management in the Courts," *Columbia Law Review* 85 (1985): 287 n. 49. See also John A. Siciliano, "Corporate Behavior and the Social Efficiency of Tort Law," *Michigan Law Review* 85 (1987): 1820, 1852 n. 111.

53. *The National Swine Flu Immunization Program of* 1976 Pub. L. No. 94–380, 90 Stat. 1113, 42 U.S.C. §247b (1976) (authorizing claims against the government for liability of swine flu vaccine manufacturers). See also Sparks v. Wyeth Laboratories, Inc., 431 F.Supp. 411, 414–16 (W.D. Okla. 1977) (interpreting the Swine Flu Immunization Program legislation and finding the defendant immune from suit). The

federal government has since developed a program of no-fault social insurance that provides for compensation to individuals injured under a variety of vaccination programs. See *National Childhood Vaccine Act of 1986*, 42 U.S.C. §300aa 1–34.

54. For an example of such a case, see Overton v. United States, 619 F.2d 1299 (8th Cir. 1980).

55. See John Wade, "On Product 'Design Defects' and Their Actionability," *Vanderbilt Law Review* 33 (1980): 551; idem, "On the Nature of Strict Tort Liability for Products," *Mississippi law Journal* 44 (1973): 825; idem, "Strict Tort Liability of Manufacturers, *Southwestern Law Journal* 19 (1965): 17.

56. For a background on the development of Section 402A and a proposed revision of it, see James Henderson Jr. and Aaron D. Twerski, "A Proposed Revision of Section 402A of the Restatement (Second) of Torts," *Cornell Law Review* 77 (1992): 1512; for a discussion roughly contemporaneous with the adoption of 402A, see William L. Prosser, "The Fall of the Citadel (Strict Liability to the Consumer)," *Minnesota Law Review* 50 (1966): 791; for a discussion concerning the limits that Section 402A places on liability for "unavoidably unsafe products" in comment k, see Joseph A. Page, "Generic Product Risks: The Case Against Comment K and for Strict Tort Liability," *New York University Law Review* 58 (1983): 853.

57. See *supra* Chapter Two, pages 30–31.

58. Fleming James Jr., "Accident Liability Reconsidered: The Impact of Insurance," *Yale Law Journal* 57 (1948): 549 (encouraging social insurance as a basis for administering loss to protect the victim from risk of financial ruin); idem, "Accidental Liability: Some Wartime Developments," *Yale Law Journal* 55 (1946): 365; Lester Feezer, "Capacity to Bear Loss as a Factor in the Decision of Certain Types of Tort Cases," *University of Pennsylvania Law Review* 78 (1930): 805. See, generally, Calabresi, *The Costs of Accidents*, 39.

59. If the Clinton administration's proposals for national health insurance are adopted, the gaps in personal health insurance coverage discussed here may well be eliminated. See Sheryl T. Dasco and Juanita Petty-Hankins, "Practical Aspects of Managed Care from the Standpoints of Providers and Consumers," in *ALI-ABA Course of Study: Qualified Plans, PCs, and Welfare Benefits* (Philadelphia: American Law Institute, 1994), 271; Timothy Stotzfus and Sandra J. Tannenbaum, "Selling Cost Containment," *American Journal of Law and Medicine* 19 (1993): 95. Such a development would further limit the strength of the access-to-insurance theme. The proposals for national health insurance do not, however, address the additional costs that victims of injury would suffer in lost future earnings, nor do they deal with compensation for pain and suffering.

60. See *supra* Chapter Two, pages 31–32.

61. See *supra* Chapter Two, page 32.

62. See *supra* Chapter Two, page 34.

63. Much of the recent complexity of workers' compensation has occurred at its boundaries, where plaintiffs dissatisfied with the often meager compensation available under workers' compensation statutes seek an escape from the system and a chance to sue someone other than the employer. Complications have also resulted

from both employer and employee attempts to exempt certain kinds of workplace injury from statutory coverage, and from disputes about whether certain kinds of injury are in fact work related. These phenomena, by challenging the original simple structure of workers' compensation, tend to reinforce the assertion in the text that legal doctrines that generate uncertainty by introducing complexity also tend to aggravate transfer costs.

64. See *supra* Chapter Two, pages 32–33.

65. For extensive discussion of these issues, see, e.g., John Prather Brown, "Toward an Economic Theory of Liability," *Journal of Legal Studies* 2 (1973): 323; Guido Calabresi and Jon Hirschoff, "Toward a Test for Strict Liability in Torts," *Yale Law Journal* 81 (1972); Mark Grady, "A New Positive Economic Theory of Negligence," *Yale Law Journal* 92 (1983): 799; William Landes and Richard A. Posner, *The Economic Structure of Tort Law* (Cambridge: Harvard University Press, 1987) , ch. 3; Richard A. Posner, "Strict Liability: A Comment," *Journal of Legal Studies* 2 (1973): 205; idem, *Economic Analysis of Law*, 4th ed. (Boston: Little, Brown, 1992), ch. 6; Steven Shavell, "Strict Liability Versus Negligence," *Journal of Legal Studies* 9 (1980): 1; idem, *Economic Analysis of Accident Law* (Cambridge: Harvard University Press, 1987), 26–46.

66. See Calabresi, *The Costs of Accidents*, 150–52.

67. For a thoughtful discussion of this issue, in the context of product liability, see Steven P. Croley and Jon D. Hanson, "Rescuing the Revolution: The Revived Case for Enterprise Liability," *Michigan Law Review* 91 (1993): 683.

68. Consumers can exert some influence over manufacture or design through their ability to choose from among competing products the ones that are better made and more safely designed. This capacity for control, however, is limited by consumers' probable lack of information on the safety aspects of many products; their inability (perhaps even disinclination) to compare safety records of potential substitutes; their inability to incorporate safety information into cost comparisons between competing products; and their scant knowledge of design alternatives that, while technologically feasible, have not been registered in the market.

69. Calabresi and Hirschoff, "Toward a Test for Strict Liability in Torts," 1060–61: "[T]he strict liability test would simply require a decision as to whether the injurer or the victim was in the better position both to judge whether avoidance costs would exceed foreseeable accident costs and to act on that judgment. The issue becomes not *whether* avoidance is worth it, but which of the parties is relatively more likely to find out whether avoidance is worth it."

70. See Croley and Hanson, "Rescuing the Revolution," 770–87.

71. See *supra* Chapter Two, pages 33–34.

72. See *supra* Chapter Two, page 34.

73. See *supra* Chapter Two, pages 34–35.

74. Guido Calabresi, "The Decision for Accidents: An Approach to Non-Fault Allocation of Costs," *Harvard Law Review* 78 (1965): 716–17.

75. Ibid., 715.

CHAPTER TEN

1. Escola v. Coca-Cola Bottling Co., 150 P.2d 436, 441 (1944) (Traynor, J., concurring).

2. Oliver Wendell Holmes Jr., *The Common Law,* ed. Mark DeWolfe Howe (Cambridge: Harvard University Press, 1963), 69.

3. For a discussion of the doctrine of subrogation as applied to insurance, see Robert E. Keeton and Alan I. Widiss, *Insurance Law* (St. Paul, Minn.: West Publishing Co., 1988), 219–52. The doctrine is rooted in principles of equity. In its traditional application, it allows an insurer who has paid for a covered loss to step into the shoes of the insured and sue a third party who was legally responsible for the loss, to recover the amount of the payout. For example, a health insurer who paid for doctor bills for an insured who was injured by another's negligence would have the option of suing the negligent actor (in the insured's name) to recoup the payments to the doctor. A decision on the role of collateral sources in determining damages for tort liability necessarily entails some judgment about subrogation. My suggestion here is that in cases where collateral sources of compensation exist, the equitable doctrine of subrogation could be adapted by courts to fashion a judgment about which source should bear what portion of the damages, based in part on an assessment of which source—the plaintiff's first-party insurance or the defendant's third-party insurance—would do a more effective job of spreading the loss.

4. Leon Green, "Tort Law, Public Law in Disguise," *Texas Law Review* 38 (1959): 1, 257.

INDEX